THE DAY WILL COME

The Day Will Come

Michael H. Brown

CHARIS

Servant Publications
Ann Arbor, Michigan

Charis Books is an imprint of Servant Publications especially designed to serve Roman Catholics.

Unless otherwise noted, Scripture references have been taken from the *New American Bible*, © 1970 by the Confraternity of Christian Doctrine, Washington, D.C. 20017 and are used by permission of copyright owner. All rights reserved.

Verses marked RSV are from the Revised Standard Version of the Bible, copyrighted 1946, 1952, 1971 by the Division of Christian Education of the National Council of Churches of Christ in the USA. Used by permission.

Published by Servant Publications
P.O. Box 8617
Ann Arbor, Michigan 48107

Cover design: Paul Higdon

96 97 98 99 00 10 9 8 7 6 5 4

Printed in the United States of America
ISBN 0-89283-944-9

Library of Congress Cataloging-in-Publication Data

Brown, Michael Harold.
    The day will come / Michael H. Brown.
        p.   cm.
    Includes bibliographical references and index.
    ISBN 0-89283-944
    1. Mary, Blessed Virgin, Saint—Apparitions and miracles—History—20th century. 2. Miracles—History—20th century.   3. Visions—History—20th century.   4. Private revelations—History—20th century.   5. Second Advent.   6. Judgment Day.   7. Catholic Church—Doctrines.   I. Title.
BT650.B738   1996
231.7'3—dc20   96-13414
                                                                              CIP

CONTENTS

To the great St. Joseph,
who listened to his dreams.

On that day, a great trumpet shall blow, and the lost in the land of Assyria and the outcast in the land of Egypt shall come and worship the Lord on the holy mountain, in Jerusalem.

Isaiah 27:13

O N E

~

Unanswered Questions

M ANY OF YOU KNOW ABOUT THE PHENOMENA and the rest of you have at least heard of them. They're everywhere, from news magazines to the afternoon talk shows. There are locutionists who claim to hear an inner "voice." There are visions. There are apparitions, nearly countless apparitions, of the Blessed Virgin. In some instances saints are seen, and there are even folks who claim to have encountered Jesus.

There are phenomena—occurrences of holy mysticism—in every state and now nearly every diocese. You've heard about weeping statues or the bleeding crucifix or oil that flows from religious artwork. You've heard about cures, conversions, and other "unsolved mysteries." According to a recent Gallup survey, so extensive are the reports that 79 percent of Americans now believe in miracles. There are visions from tiny Malibu to deepest Africa.

The situation burst upon the scene several years ago, and although it has roots way back in the early 1800s, much of the supernatural activity connects with that place known as Medjugorje. There, in 1981, an entity who identified herself as Mary, mother of Christ, began appearing to six astounded youngsters. Like the woman of Revelation, she came in a white veil with a crown of twelve stars. She warned of sin. She warned of ethnic tensions. She said that darkness engulfs the earth and that important events loom in the future. She gave messages that have reached the eyes of the pope as well as leaders like Reagan and Gorbachev. So powerful is the experience that an estimated ten to twenty million have ventured to Medjugorje, many doing so despite the war in Bosnia-Hercegovina, where the village is located. And so intense is the experience that there are now similar claims—supernatural claims—in hundreds of other places.

It's an eruption in the true sense of the word, and it continues to dazzle us with its voltage. There are thousands who see phenomena in the sky or who flock to the latest locutionist. There are visions of Padre Pio and St.

> *In the end, we all want to know what heaven is like and how to get there.*

Joseph. There are angels. There are devils. There are dramatic and often dire prophecies.

And there are questions, the gripping and endless questions: What in the world is going on? How much is real? How much should we take with a grain of salt? What does it all mean? When did it start? *Where* did it start? What led up to Medjugorje? What will now follow it? Are we on the verge of major events? Will there be yet greater wonders?

The questions range from the sublime to the apocalyptic. Is there a new world order? Could we be approaching the Second Coming? What about the "three days of darkness"? How do the events of today relate to Sacred Scripture?

We also want answers to the more mundane questions. We want to know how all the phenomena correlate with current events. We want to know if it's true that one apparition of the Blessed Mother predicted the holocaust in Rwanda more than a dozen years before it actually happened.

And then, most importantly, there are the personal questions, the questions that affect us most directly: How can we benefit from the legitimate mysticism? How do we deepen our spirituality? What are the best defenses against evil? What are the hidden powers behind Mass, Confession, and the Blessed Sacrament?

What evidence is there that Christ is really present?

What effect does the occult have on us? How do we deliver and protect our families in this era of such spiritual darkness?

So intriguing are the questions that I've decided to put them into book form. I get them from church audiences and from television producers as I travel the country. I get them every day in the mailbox. Which cases do you think are most authentic? Where do you think the Virgin Mary is really appearing? How can we benefit from the legitimate messages?

What do the visionaries say about prayer and spiritual warfare?

This book is one huge question-and-answer period. Many of the questions are ones I ask myself. I've formulated them in an attempt to understand more fully the current spiritual episode. An episode is an upsurge of activity, and a supernatural episode is one that involves the spiritual. There have been a number of episodes since the time of Christ—during the Classical period and the Middle Ages—but none more powerful or revealing than that which we now encounter.

> *We must always be cautious. We must always strive for discernment. But we must also make sure that our worldliness, our "rationality," doesn't strangle legitimate blessings.*

What are the visions of heaven and hell like? How do they compare with reports of "near-death" experiences? What about controversies surrounding the mystical revelations of Garabandal and the *Poem of the Man-God*? Do all the phenomena tie into the end of our millennium? What do you see happening around the year 2000? What's the latest from the credible sites of apparition?

I get questions about fasting. I get questions about the Rosary. I get questions about the most effective devotions.

In the end, we all want to know what heaven is like and how to get there.

I certainly don't pretend to know all the answers. I'm but an evangelistic journalist. I rely on the many priests, nuns, ministers, mystics, theologians, bishops, exorcists, and seers whom I have met in speaking in more than 140 towns and cities. Many of the questions have come after those speeches, during the Q-and-A. In answering them I rely on Church tradition and the literature of mystical theology.

Above all, I rely on the New Testament.

My prayer is that, in dealing with the many questions that follow, I answer with candor and balance. My prayer is for the Holy Spirit. I do not write for any one school of thought, nor, I hope, do I let anyone else's presumptions engineer my responses. This is a personal book. This is between you and me. And while I'm a conservative Catholic, with a special and unabashed devotion to Our Blessed Mother, I hope to provide useful information to my Protestant and Jewish friends.

I used to be a secular author. I used to be a worldly journalist. But things changed and now my focus is mysticism. Now my focus is not this world but what comes after it. I plan on taking you behind the scenes of the famous phenomena. I don't pretend to speak for the Church, and I'm well aware that there are plenty of gray areas when it comes to spirituality. We must always be cautious. We must always strive for discernment. But we must also make sure that our worldliness, our "rationality," doesn't strangle legitimate blessings. As John Paul II says, "Christian mysticism in every age up to our own—including the mysticism of marvelous men of action like Vincent de Paul, John Bosco, Maximilian Kolbe—has built up and continues to build up Christianity in its most essential elements."

Here then is an attempt at getting to the bottom of the current supernatural eruption. Here is an attempt at answering questions I haven't previously tried answering. Here is an attempt at inspiring love and peace through the authentic mysticism, which means through the Holy Spirit.

For in the end it is only the Spirit who can answer our questions.

TWO

~

VISIONS EVERYWHERE

You mention the Book of Revelation. You mention the millennium. Does that mean we're in the Latter Days or End Times?

I get that question at every stop. By the end of this book we'll have thoroughly explored the matter. What I'll report for now is that we're in special times. We're in a transition period. We're at the end of one era and the beginning of another.

What do you mean by "special"? What do you mean by the "end of an era"?

Special means unique. Special means unusual. It's an exciting moment, a stage in human history when God is intervening. He's showing us that He exists. He's opening portholes. Portholes of prophecy. Portholes to the supernatural. He's doing so through the Virgin Mary. For some reason, for reasons we'll examine, He wants us to pay more attention to our spiritual state and to do so right now, with a degree of urgency.

And the "end of an era"?

An era is a major passage, a volume, of history. There was the era of the early Christians, there was the era of the Middle Ages, and now there's our own Modern Era. It's ending and according to Jesus, when an era is ending there are "signs of the times" (Mt 16:3). There are wars, plagues, and tremors. There's famine and persecution. There are false prophets, against which we must always be on guard (seeMatthew 24:6-11). There are also "great signs," authentic wonders, which is what I mean by "supernatural episodes" (Lk 21:11).

Let me tell you, the signs are every place I go. I mean everywhere.

Such as?

Apparitions and locutions. Communication with holy spirits. Prophecy that comes from an external source.

I'll give you a couple of examples. A short while ago, just days before writing this, I was speaking in Providence, Rhode Island. I was at a fund-raiser for refugees in Bosnia. Before my talk I agreed to do an autograph session at a local Christian bookstore. It was early afternoon, and I don't think I was there more than a few minutes before someone plopped four sheets of paper on the store counter next to me. Typed on the pages were messages that came from a prayer group in nearby Connecticut. It so happens that some statues there have been shedding tears and that a man, the son of the prayer group leader, is claiming to see apparitions of the Blessed Virgin. He says that she appears to him in a visual way and also speaks, in effect dictating messages and advice for the prayer group. The messages are about spiritual development and the state of the world. The prayer group logs them and prays for guidance.

That was the first phenomenon—the first *alleged* phenomenon—I was made aware of. Weeping statues and an apparition. I had passed the place a short time before.

It's no small thing when you're praying and suddenly tears flow from a statue and someone claims to see a supernatural figure, an ethereal image. It's not really fleeting, not your standard "ghost." Most people who claim these things say they can make out detail, such as skin tone, facial features, and the color of Mary's clothes.

From the bookstore I went to a radio station and then back to my hotel. I rested a bit and headed up to the ballroom for the fund-raiser. As soon as I got to the head table I was approached by a woman—a normal, apparently level-headed woman—who couldn't wait to tell me about a miracle or "manifestation" *she* witnessed recently while on pilgrimage. It was at a place called Betania (which just happens to translate as "Bethany") in Venezuela. I pay particular attention to claims from Betania because it has been officially accepted by the Church.

The woman claimed she glanced toward a grotto of the Virgin Mary and saw an image, the figure of Jesus, above the grotto. He was smaller than life size but looked like a living being. He wasn't transparent. She couldn't see the trees through Him. He was there with long hair, a beard, and a brown tunic. She looked away and then looked back to make sure she wasn't seeing things. An image of Jesus in the rain forest! He was there as she watched with her eyes open. Maybe a minute. Maybe two minutes. She claimed the Lord had shown Himself in distinct fashion as she and others prayed, and she was still excited, very animated about it. A holy form among the trees near a small water-fall. She said the image was so clear that afterward she went up to the spot expecting to find a statue, but of course found nothing that could explain what she'd seen a few moments before.

Later, there was yet a third report of apparitions. This time it involved a site in Massachusetts that's just forty-five minutes from Providence. So many people were going there that the group which owns the land decided to close the site to

> *I thought there was a lot going on in the early 1990s, when I first started to investigate this stuff, but there is currently as many or more reported phenomena than ever.*

the public. They were planning to build a religious community, and the bishop was investigating. Hundreds say they've seen miraculous signs there, including the sun acting in a peculiar fashion and columns of inexplicable light.

As at other sites in the United States, people claim to hear voices, and they have taken photos that reveal unusual lights or clouds. A rock found at another site has an erosion pattern that seems to harbor the image of Jesus. There have also been apparitions of the Virgin Mary. (A vision is more an interior image, in the mind's eye; an apparition is seen with the physical eyes.)

Now, I'm not endorsing such claims. I can't possibly verify every testimony. I've heard hundreds, and there are many that seem like exaggerations or even the work of false prophets. I'm only reporting the occurrances that were reported to me in less than six hours' time. It was impressive. In that short time I was given information about an apparition associated with a prayer group in Connecticut, I was directed to a second site of alleged miracles in nearby Massachusetts, and I was told about a purported manifestation—not quite a full-bodied apparition, but a manifestation or image of Jesus—on a hillside in Venezuela.

That's what I encountered on just one occassion.

I hear similar accounts on an absolutely constant basis. It's unusual when I *don't* hear them. I thought there was a lot going on several years ago, in the early 1990s, when I first started to investigate this stuff, but there is currently as many or more phenomena—more reported phenomena—than ever. Every time I give a speech, someone comes up to me and claims to be receiving locutions—hearing an interior, heavenly voice—or seeing apparitions. That, or they tell me about a friend who's having these experiences. They show me "miraculous" photos or rosaries that have changed color. They tell me about miraculous healings, the lame walking, or cancer going into spontaneous remission. Although I thought it would peak several years ago, and although in some ways things have settled down a bit, the episode has continued its expansion. There are more reports of miracles than ever.

Can you give an estimate? How many are having visions? How many are reporting voices?

I can't come up with a figure because there's no central registry. But in the first chapter I said there are thousands of claims, and I meant it.

Let's take the example of what are called "inner locutions." That's the hearing of an internal voice, as opposed to hearing with the ears. We'll be discussing locutions in more depth, and you'll see why we must be very, very careful with such stuff. But let me tell you, the prevalence of these claims is stunning. Just mind-boggling. It's unusual to visit a diocese or even a single church, a single parish, *without* someone coming up and telling me that they're "hearing" a voice which they usually take to be that of Mary. Other times it's an angel or even the Lord.

Of all the current mysticism, locutions are most frequently reported. And although the Church doesn't have any kind of comprehensive data, let's be conservative and say locutions are occurring in 10 percent of the Catholic parishes.

That would tally to nearly 2,000 cases in America, since there are about 19,400 Catholic churches. And it's a conservative estimate. Often there's more than one purported locutionist—a person who hears a spiritual voice—in a single prayer group. These are folks who write down prophetic messages, or at least what they think are heavenly messages. Protestants would call them "words of knowledge."

How many do you think are real?

A fraction are purely spiritual experiences, without involvement of the subconscious. But even a fraction means something.

Then there are the apparitions. Let's stop a moment and make sure we appreciate what's meant by "apparition": seeing something supernatural with the physical eyes. Eyes open! That's quite a claim. It's one thing to see something in your mind, quite another to see something ocularly.

We think of such events as rare, and they were—until recently. Now they're everywhere. I remember visiting Denver during the autumn of 1992 and, though I was there for less than twenty-four hours, I met five different people who claimed to be seeing apparitions of the Blessed Mother. Five apparitionists in one city! I had lunch with one and attended Mass with another.

Right off the top of my head I can name eighteen states where apparitions, usually of the Virgin Mary, are claimed to be occurring. I wouldn't be shocked if the actual number is double that. The same is true with other nations. Take Canada. I've met three people in Ontario who claim to be receiving high-level apparitions, and there are several others about whom I've heard or read. I went to the home of one fourteen-year-old girl who says she's been visited by Mary since 1992. She's Filipino, and in her house are a number of statues that exude oil. One statue is Our Blessed Mother with the Immaculate Heart. I watched and videotaped as oil dripped from two fingers on the left hand of that statue. I saw oil exuding from every part of it. Right there in front of me. So much emanates that they put a pan underneath to collect the oil. I estimated the drippings were half an inch deep. There was also oil coming out of a statue of the young Jesus. They say healings occur with the oil and that it also flows from statues brought by strangers or priests to the home.

I'm not sure what to think of every such claim, but after a while it's hard to discount them all. I know about trickery. I've brought in magicians to look at paranormal phenomena. I've dealt with my share of scientists. I've interviewed a man who is probably the most well-known skeptic in America, whose mission is debunking anything supernatural. I understand their questions, biases, and concerns. But these emanations have been known to occur not only when people are watching but also as a statue is being searched for hidden tubes. Some statues have even been x-rayed by skeptics who have gone so far as to claim that if there are no hidden tubes, then the perpetrators must be using a squirt gun!

After a while such skepticism can become very hollow. After a while we realize that those who are overly skeptical simply lack faith. When witnesses can actually watch the tears forming, and when this goes on for several hours—not to mention days or weeks or months—in front of many people, with tests showing that they are real human tears, or that it's real human blood, or that it's olive oil, it tends to argue against normal explanations.

Some say the tears are tears of joy for the converted and tears of sorrow for those who remain in darkness. As for the oil, it's been analyzed as olive oil, and we know what the olive branch symbolizes. Peace. We need to put peace in our hearts. Oil is a sign of spiritual healing and nourishment.

Does this supernatural activity also portend some kind of crisis or upheaval? Is there something apocalyptic coming?

There are often major events at the end of an age, and that's why God intervenes. That's why He shows Himself. That's why, in my opinion, He allows phenomena. He never leaves us alone. He's preparing us. He does this as He always has, through prophets and through legitimate wonders.

The greater the era, the greater will be the holy phenomena and the greater will be the transformation. There have been supernatural episodes since time began, starting with God speaking to Adam and Eve in the Garden.

There was similar communication in the time of Abraham, and then of course the tremendous wonders during the time of Moses. Out of the thirty-nine pages in the Book of Exodus, more than thirty—75 percent—contain supernatural locutions.

They consume entire chapters.

The term "signs and wonders" is first used way back in Exodus 7:3, just before the plagues hit Egypt.

Mysticism announces change, and miracles, which are a form of mysticism, often parallel the end of an era. They forewarn us. They give us direction. They prepare for renewal and direct us from danger.

That's not to say that prophecy is perfect. To the contrary, prophets are often wrong when they get too specific, when they try to predict every little detail, or when they predict specific dates.

But as it says in 1 Corinthians 14:4, prophecy "builds up the Church" and gives us a sense or forewarning of historical movement. The overwhelming theme of modern prophecy is that we're facing the change of a period or an age or an era.

Isn't that enough to make us a little squeamish? Doesn't the mention of plagues or war cause folks to get apprehensive?

That's the last thing we should be. We should be excited and expectant and prepared—spiritually prepared, not at all fearful. To be frank, I think some people greatly overestimate the fear factor. Most people don't get frightened so easily. They're more expectant than scared. They can sense that our era is changing. They can sense transformation. This is a glorious and challenging time and I believe we should welcome change. We really do need it.

Why does God bother with hints? Why does He tell us what He plans on doing?

It's a part of His ineffable mercy. It's to ready us for the improvements as well as the birth pangs. God speaks before He moves His finger. He considers prophets to be His valued servants. They're the forerunners of change. As it says in Amos 3:7, "Surely the Lord God does nothing, unless He reveals His secret to His servants the prophets."

THREE

~

THE FIRST SECRET

Why don't these things happen to non-Catholics, to Protestants?

They do. I get regular correspondence from a Protestant deacon in Alabama who claims to be receiving not just locutions but apparitions of the Virgin. What makes his case doubly interesting is that he was an aerospace engineer who once worked as a division chief with the highest security clearance at an Army missile command site. He's a scientist. His church is non-denominational, the type that roundly disclaims apparitions.

Protestants also encounter the phenomena with statues, and when that happens it's interesting because Protestants are especially wary of the way Catholics venerate statues. I remember a talk in 1992 at an Episcopalian church in Greenville, South Carolina. After the speech I was signing books and greeting members of the audience when suddenly I noticed a group of people oohing and aahing. They were congregating around a statue of Our Lady of Fatima. They were staring at it and pointing, excited and awed. A hush fell on the church and they dropped to their knees. Protestants kneeling in front of a statue!

I went over to see what was causing such a reaction and they told me the statue was forming tears. They said there was moisture in the eyes. The statue was weeping.

It did look like the corneas were glistening but I couldn't tell for sure. I wondered if, instead, it might be paint that was extra glossy.

I tried to touch one of the eyes and place a tissue against the plaster to see if it would absorb liquid from the eyes, but these good Protestants stopped me. They didn't want my little examination to destroy the atmosphere. They also didn't want me poking my finger in the Virgin's eyes!

I also remember speaking at the University of Arizona when one of the students, a Jewish fellow from New York, told me about a widely reported miracle at a local church called St. Demetrios, which is Greek Orthodox. A bleeding icon. I decided to meet with the priest, Fr. Anthony Moschonas, who showed me a small icon of the Crucified Christ on the cover of his liturgical Bible. It was a decorative icon that had been exuding blood. It started during solemn services on Holy Thursday in 1989, he said. Drops of the substance had formed at the wound in Christ's side. The priest told us he noticed it when, in the midst of the services, he suddenly had difficulty lifting the Bible. It was inexplicably weighty, too heavy to lift! After a procession, he returned to the altar to continue services. "As I stood in front of the holy altar," he wrote to his bishop, "my eyes focused on the Holy Gospel's icon of the Crucifixion. With great astonishment, I saw blood on the holy body of Our Lord.... The blood was on the holy icon of Christ on the right side of His body at the place where He was pierced. Blood also appeared on the left side of His chest."

That's what made him take a closer look, and that's when Fr. Moschonas noticed the oozing blood. I saw it for myself—he'd placed it in a special glass display—and found the priest to be low-key and credible. More recently newsmen have reported a bleeding statue in Civitavecchia, Italy. It's the Madonna of Medjugorje, a fifteen-inch statue at St. Agostino Church, and the substance has been identified as male blood.

That's what you mean by a supernatural episode?

The statues are but a small part. The main phenomena are the apparitions and locutions.

And those have a precedent? They've happened throughout history?

There are certain types of phenomena at certain times and eras. They vary in magnitude. The greatest episode was two thousand years ago and involved the miracles of Our Savior. It was the end of the Old Covenant and the beginning of the new one. It was the beginning of the Christian Era. And as usual, that great change was accompanied by a truly major and awesome glimpse of the supernatural.

When we think back, Jesus of Nazareth was a walking miracle. He was a walking episode. He prophesied. He commanded the wind. He levitated over the Sea of Galilee, or at any rate walked across the water to calm His disciples. He radiated light. Like Adam and Abraham and Moses, He spoke to the Father. He healed the sick and cast out evil spirits. He raised the

dead. He multiplied the loaves and created wine from water. The very earth
quaked and the dead rose when He was
crucified.

Those are major miracles, the greatest
on record, which only makes sense since
Jesus is the Son of God. Most impressive
is how after His death the disciples witnessed Jesus as a full-bodied or "corporeal" apparition.

For forty days the Apostles were privy
to visitations from the risen Savior. They
could touch Him, embrace Him, eat
with Him—facts which many today find
hard to believe, just as they find it hard
to believe in statues that exude oil. When

> *Jesus of Nazareth was a walking miracle, a walking episode. He prophesied. He commanded the wind. He levitated over the Sea of Galilee,... He healed the sick and cast out evil spirits. He raised the dead.... Most impressive is how after His death the disciples witnessed Jesus as a full-bodied or "corporeal" apparition.*

the forty days were over the Apostles watched Christ "lift up before their
eyes in a cloud which took Him from their sight" (Acts 1:9). And it didn't
stop there. Certain phenomena continued with His followers after
Pentecost.

On the day of Pentecost a strong, driving wind was heard and tongues
of fire appeared and rested on the Apostles. Suddenly, filled with the Holy
Spirit, they were able to speak in foreign tongues and make bold proclamations, sort of like the bold proclamations we hear in current prophecies.
Afterwards, according to Acts 2:43, "a reverent fear overtook them all, for
many wonders and signs were performed by the Apostles." They began cel-
ebrating the mystical breaking of bread, which we today know as the
Eucharist. They cured cripples and encountered angels, just as we today
record remarkable healings. Like Christ they cast out demons and experienced visions. They recorded strange events in nature, such as the earthquake that struck and rumbled through the earth as Silas and Paul were
praying and singing hymns in prison. The phenomena continued right
through St. Paul's experiences and on to the incredible visions of John in
Revelation. The episode actually began a couple of hundred years before

> *Much of the Old Testament includes heavenly locutions. "The Lord said" or "God spoke." We see that all over the Bible…. if the Lord can turn a rod into a snake, or rain down manna,… He can certainly cause oil or tears to exude from a holy statue.*

Christ with the Jewish apocalyptic literature and continued for at least fifty years after His birth. Nothing in history was more momentous.

And we're seeing that now?

I would never compare anything to the days of Our Savior. That episode stands alone. But there have been plenty of lesser episodes. The current one began about two hundred years ago and continues to gather momentum. It's already one of the longer episodes, but we won't know its real significance until it is accomplished. As you'll see, it goes far beyond statues.

And you believe there are biblical precedents?

There are interactions with God throughout the Bible, starting, as I said, with Adam. Much of the Old Testament includes heavenly locutions. "The Lord said" or "God spoke." We see that all over the Bible. As for physical phenomena, if the Lord can turn a rod into a snake, or rain down manna, or manifest His power in the Ark of the Covenant, He can certainly cause oil or tears to exude from a holy statue.

When it comes to the issue of apparitions, when it comes to a precedent for that type of phenomena, the most relevant passage may be Matthew 17:1-9, when Christ brought Peter, James, and John up a high mount, possibly Tabor, and was transfigured before them.

Jesus' face shone and His clothes became as white as light, similar to descriptions we hear of angels. He was in a transcendental state. He was between earth and heaven. And He was experiencing apparitions of Moses and Elijah and talking with them. They were also seen by the dumbstruck disciples.

Elijah and Moses appeared to Jesus and His disciples in the form of what we call "sensible exterior visions," or apparitions. Whereas a vision is usually in the mind's eye, an apparition is a living, moving, and usually a talking spirit.

While the apparitions were in progress, while Jesus conversed with Elijah and Moses, a bright cloud passed overhead. Out of it came an auditory, or auricular, locution. They heard it with their ears: "This is My beloved Son, in Whom I am well pleased. Hear Him!" It was directed at the disciples.

Jesus told them not to mention the incident. They weren't to tell the others. They were to keep what they saw and heard confidential. It was the first secret attached to an apparition. But as we'll see, it wasn't the last.

FOUR

~

ORIGIN OF THE PHENOMENA

So there are many places where these apparitions are said to occur?
Dozens.

And hundreds of visionaries?
Hundreds. It was fashionable for a while to say that three hundred cases are under investigation, but really no one has a firm number.

These are folks who claim they actually can see a heavenly being?
Yes. Mostly the Blessed Virgin.

And then the locutionists?
People hearing her voice, as well as the countless peripheral phenomena. At many places people are seeing the sun act in a strange way, whirling and changing colors, or pulsating. They see the sun send out unusual rays. And they see crosses, doves, or other images formed by the light. It's a phenomenon more common than weeping statues. The sun seems to jump around the sky and radiate an aura of pink or violet, but unlike any sunset. The auras are huge and these are what shift in color. It's similar to what was reported in 1917 when there were famous apparitions of the Blessed Virgin Mary at Fatima, Portugal.

Most of you know about that. Fatima is one of the most well-known apparitions of the Virgin. And it involved inexplicable movements of the sun. On October 13, 1917, more than fifty thousand saw the solar orb move in such a way that they thought it was going to crash to the earth.

Apparitions of Jesus, Mary, and Joseph were seen in concurrence with the sun movements.

Once so rare—occurring only at places like Fatima—sun miracles are now seen in many nations, from Africa to the Philippines.

And such phenomena have deep roots. They span the past two centuries. It's not only in our decade that prophets have come out of the woodwork. While the sun miracles are relatively recent, the general mystical eruption, the episode itself, had its origin two hundred years ago. It began with a flurry of prophets—many of them doomsayers—during the French Revolution.

In that atmosphere, amid the turbulence of modernism, there was an upsurge of nuns, monks, and laymen who prophesied against the Revolution and predicted wars and persecutions because of mankind's new godlessness.

They saw disasters of every sort. War. Food shortages. Attacks on the Church. Some of the calamities were realized in the upheavals of the 1800s, which saw continued revolutions in places like France, the world wars in our own century, and then the persecutions engineered by Communists. There were even popes prophesying. There were popes warning that mankind was embarking upon a strange and dangerous new course. They warned that modernism, materialism, and rationalism were being taken to an extreme. In heading down the road of godlessness—in elevating intellect above spirit, in idolizing the human mind instead of God—we were on the quick slope of chastisement. They warned that it was not just a sociological issue but one that involved spiritual forces.

Back then, like today, the prophets were unabashedly apocalyptical. We won't know until the events occur (or don't occur) whether they were authentic. We know only that at the turn of the nineteenth century, as social upheaval continued, there were loads of forewarnings. There were mystics in Italy. There were nuns prophesying in France. There were prophets in Germany. Most were concerned not just with the rise of evil but with a whole array of chastisements that would *accompany* such evil—some of which were fulfilled during horrors like those spawned by World War II.

More than anything, they foresaw a *spiritual* chastisement. There were mystics like Anna-Katarina Emmerich and Jeanne le Royer, famous seers and nuns who saw swarms of spirits ascending out of the pit, a real onslaught of darkness. They saw demons everywhere, obscuring the light of goodness. Another mystic, Elizabeth Canori-Mora, explained that it was precisely because of mankind's impiety, because of the attempt at dethroning God, because of the intellectual artifices and heresies—the era of modernism, which began after the Middle Ages and hit full stride with the

French Revolution—that Our Lord gave permission for infernal spirits to rise from the bowels of the earth. "Countless legions of demons shall overrun the earth—the instrument of divine justice—and causing terrible calamities and disasters," said this mystic, who died in 1825. "They shall attack everything. They shall injure individual persons and entire families"—which has proven to be only too true.

Canori-Mora's prophecy was repeated six decades later by Pope Leo XIII, who according to legend had a vision of Satan being granted a century to test the Church.

Many prophets not only foretold wars and persecution that indeed arrived but also foresaw special trials for Russia. One seer named Br. Louis Rocco correctly predicted that Russia would experience a "bloody revolution."

Sr. Jeanne le Royer focused on Western Europe, which, as she continued to emphasize, would suffer because of what was spawned by the French Revolution. "The storm began in France, and France shall be the first theatre of its ravages after having been its cradle," she said sometime before 1800. "Armies will come into frightful collisions and will fill the earth with murder and carnage. These internal and foreign wars will cause enormous sacrifices, scandals, and infinite evils, because of the incursions that will be made into the Church."

But, added Sr. Emmerich in 1820, "I saw also that help was coming when distress had reached its peak. I saw again the Blessed Virgin ascend on the Church and spread her mantle [over it]."

So you can trace current prophecies to the movements spawned by secular philosophy?

The French Revolution was more than a political revolution. It was a moral revolution. I can't repeat this enough. It brought to a peak the resurrection of Aristotle's ideas, which meant explaining everything "rationally" with only physical, this-worldly answers. When we do that, when we discount our spiritual purpose and with it the supernatural, we're committing the entirely dangerous act of discounting God. The straying from God opened the doorway of evil and set the stage for our current moral breakdown.

> *The French Revolution was more than a political revolution. It was [also] a moral revolution.... It was too instantaneous and pervasive, too well orchestrated, to be solely of human origin.*

And you believe it was satanic, not just human foible?

It was too instantaneous and pervasive, too well orchestrated, to be solely of human origin. Mystics provided astonishingly similar prophecies of a special period in which evil would run rampant—an evil that was born with modernism, got its wings during the French Revolution, and then burst upon the scene in a big way by the end of the 1800s.

This was in line with locutions received by some mystics in which the Lord explained that His Beloved Mother had been given a special role of intercession against the devil. She was a mother coming to the aid of her children. It was what St. Louis de Montfort said when he predicted that during latter times "the power of Mary over all devils will be particularly outstanding."

Knowing firsthand her maternal talent, Christ had given His beloved mother an important new role as intercessor.

And indeed, in 1830, the Virgin arrived in a big way. She had been appearing for centuries to innumerable seers. She'd appeared to dozens of saints, starting way back in the first century. She'd appeared to monks and shepherds beyond number. She appeared to a widow in England and to St. Nicholas during the Council of Nicaea. She had come in images and visions and as a sign in the clouds.

But never like what has occurred in the current episode.

Nothing like what started in 1830.

It was in 1830 that a nun who is now canonized, St. Catherine Labouré, encountered Our Blessed Mother in a chapel late at night in Paris. Mary gave her messages about the coming turbulence in France and asked Catherine to have a medal struck showing the Virgin radiating grace from her downstretched palms. *"The times are evil,"* said Our Blessed Mother. *"Misfortunes will fall upon France. The throne will be overthrown. The entire world will be overcome by evils of all kinds. But come to the foot of this altar.*

There graces will be poured on all those who ask for them with confidence and fervor. They will be poured out on the great and the humble."

You've seen this apparition depicted on medals or in statues showing Mary stepping on the head of the serpent (as promised in Genesis 3:14-15 when God told the devil he would "put enmity between you and the woman").

That was how Catherine saw Mary, as a special aid against Lucifer, and as a messenger. It was the beginning of the Age of Mary.

Many would call your belief in demons superstitious.

Excuse me for saying this, but that would be spiritual blindness. There are many demons and angels. Countless numbers. But we can sense them only with spiritual eyesight.

Demons *want* you to doubt their existence. They work best in the dark.

Didn't the apparition in Paris include a "secret"?

Yes, a confidential message was given to St. Catherine, a secret that went to the grave with her. This would become a trait of the Holy Mother's: She would give seers insight into the future and then instruct them not to publicly discuss it, just as Jesus didn't want those two disciples talking about the apparition on Tabor.

Why would Mary give someone a secret?

In part I think Our Blessed Mother began giving secrets so that mystics could pray with special fervor about certain events—so they could realize the danger and convey a sense of gravity—but without panicking people.

Also, secrets involve events that God can change and Mary may keep them secret, between her and the seer, precisely because they may change.

What's the difference between a mystic and a visionary or seer?

They're often the same, but whereas a visionary only experiences apparitions, visions, or locutions, a mystic's phenomena may go beyond that and include other gifts like healing and the ability to "read" souls.

Since 1830 seers reporting apparitions of the Blessed Mother, along with secrets, have greatly proliferated. Sightings of Mary, especially those

> *"Nature is asking for vengeance.... The earth will be struck by calamities of all kinds.... The seasons will be altered...."*

officially recognized by the Church, surged with unprecedented force. There were more apparitions approved after 1830 than in all the previous centuries.

And, taking up the earlier cry, these modern apparitions repeated the warnings of people like le Royer and Emmerich, warnings about the future. I think especially of La Salette, France, where Mary appeared to two unsophisticated youngsters, warning that mankind was risking all kinds of grave consequences because of its straying from the Lord. She summarized the previous prophecies with reputed statements like:

God will strike in an unprecedented way. Woe to inhabitants of the earth! God will exhaust His wrath upon them, and no one will be able to escape so many afflictions together.... God will allow the old serpent to cause divisions among those who reign in every society and in every family.... Justice will be trampled underfoot and only homicides, hate, jealousy, lies, and dissension will be seen without love for country or family.... Physical and moral agonies will be suffered. God will abandon mankind to itself.... Churches will be locked up or desecrated.... A great number of priests and members of religious orders will break away from the true religion.... There will be bloody wars and famines, plagues and infectious diseases.... Lucifer, together with a large number of demons, will be unloosed from hell.... They will put an end to faith little by little....

A general war will follow which will be appalling. For a time God will cease to remember France and Italy because the Gospel of Jesus Christ has been forgotten. All the civil governments will have one and the same plan, which will be to abolish and do away with every religious principle, to make way for materialism, atheism, occultism, and vice of all kinds.

Most curiously, Mary was said to have added that *"nature is asking for vengeance.... The earth will be struck by calamities of all kinds.... The seasons will be altered...."*

FIVE

~

A CENTURY OF WARNINGS

*P*enitence, penitence, penitence, said Mary. *Pray for sinners.*

That was the message at Lourdes, and no one in the Church really doubts it. Today Lourdes remains a great site of healing and pilgrimage.

When was that?

September 19, 1846. The message remains in dispute—there are those who think the seer was simply imitating the dire earlier prophecies—but then St. Bernadette had her historic encounters with the Blessed Mother in 1858 at Lourdes, France.

France again?

Yes, Mary was focusing her attention on that nation because, as prophesied, the French were bearing the brunt of chastisement. The eighteenth century was one of terrific turmoil. There was rebellion after rebellion. There were events like the Franco-Prussian War. Germany and its allies invaded France, and at the height of the conflict, on January 17, 1871, Mary appeared to six children in another French town called Pontmain, hovering over a house.

There were stars on her robe, and words supernaturally scrawled in the winter sky. The youngsters actually claimed to see writing: "PRAY, MY CHILDREN. GOD WILL HEAR YOU IN A SHORT TIME. MY SON PERMITS HIMSELF TO BE MOVED" (or *"Mon fils se laisse toucher"*).

At that very time German troops were poised to attack a nearby town called Laval.

The French were on the verge of yet more suffering, but many across the nation had been praying a "national vow" to the Sacred Heart of Jesus. It was later learned that Germany's Supreme Command called off its incursion the night of the apparition.

Within ten days the war ended.

The apparition of Pontmain was approved by the Bishop on February 2,

> *On July 12, 1912, Mary allegedly predicted that the heir to the Catholic empire of Austria-Hungary would be killed. Two years later Archduke Francis Ferdinand was assassinated by a Serb in Sarajevo.*

1875. Thanks to prayer, that conflict was over—but there was more trouble ahead for all of Europe.

There was also much more Marian activity, apparitions at places like Blangy, France, and Knock, Ireland. At Knock the Holy Virgin was seen with St. Joseph and a third figure many thought was John the Evangelist, holding a book they took to be the Apocalypse. That same year, 1879, there was a potato famine, the second major one of the century in Ireland, which caused food shortages.

There were also reports that Mary appeared near the ancient city of Pompeii, as if giving us a clue, since Pompeii had been destroyed by a volcano. By 1900 apparitions and secrets were given to a priest, Fr. (Père) Lamy, in LePailly, France, predicting World War I and World War II if mankind didn't return to God.

I can't tell you how many times that instruction has been repeated: it's the message of John the Baptist, "Reform your lives! The reign of God is at hand" (see Matthew 3:2).

Repent before He comes. Disaster is avoidable.

In Brussels, starting in 1911, a woman named Berthe Petit began claiming to have visions and apparitions. She saw the hearts of Jesus and Mary interweaving and said Our Blessed Mother told her to spread devotion to her Sorrowful Heart. *"It is through* [my Sorrowful and Immaculate Heart] *that graces of mercy, of conversion, and of salvation shall be granted and spread everywhere,"* said the Holy Mother.

On July 12, 1912, Mary allegedly predicted to Berthe that the heir to the Catholic empire of Austria-Hungary would be killed. Indeed, two years later Archduke Francis Ferdinand was assassinated by a Serb in Sarajevo.

That event triggered World War I, which coincided with the remarkable occurrences in Fatima.

At Fatima Our Blessed Mother prophesied the coming of Communism and a greater war if men continued to sin and ignore the Immaculate Heart. The same message was given to Berthe. Soon after World War I she claimed that Our Lord told her, *"It will soon become apparent how unstable peace is when it is arranged without Me.... Trouble and danger will spread to all countries. It is because this peace is none of Mine that wars will blaze up again everywhere.... Humanity is rushing towards a dreadful storm."*

As the Second World War approached, Berthe's messages became all the more strident, expanding upon those many warnings of a century before. One cardinal listened to Berthe and consecrated England to Mary's Sorrowful and Immaculate Heart. Some people believe this consecration saved Britain during World War II.

In Poitiers, France, at a monastery that had been closed during the French Revolution, a Spanish mystic, Sr. Josefa Menendez, is said to have been given a beautiful prayer to Mary by Jesus Himself:

Oh tender and loving mother, most prudent Virgin, Mother of my Redeemer, I come to salute you today with all the love that a child can feel for its mother. Yes, I am indeed your child and because I am so helpless I will take the fervor of the Heart of Your Divine Son. With Him I will salute you as the purest of creatures, for you were framed according to the wishes and desires of the thrice-holy God. Conceived without sin, exempt from all corruption, you were ever faithful to the impulses of grace, and so your soul accumulated such merit that it was raised above all other creatures.

Josefa had many experiences with Mary and was told not to let anyone persuade her that confidence in the Immaculate Heart detracted from her tenderness for Jesus.

She was also given a secret that was transmitted in 1923 to her Mother General.

The main message was love. Mary told her, *"Love! Love! Love!"* The Poitiers apparitions were followed by alleged apparitions in places like Poland, Brazil, and Germany. The seers were men and women and children. (I often say "supposedly" or "alleged" because I'm at a loss to fathom half these cases. I've thrown up my hands any number of times.) Again, many prophecies. Many, many warnings. Whether or not they're copycats, there's a remarkable consistency among just about all of them, a consistency in the urgent warnings and motherly love. In 1932 Our Blessed Mother gave secrets to three seers in Beauraing, Belgium. I have confidence in this case because the site was approved by the Church.

Who approves apparitions? The Vatican?

No, mainly the local bishop. It's in his hands unless Rome takes it from him.

And Fatima was approved?

Oh yes, along with Lourdes and Knock. They have constituted the major aspect of our current episode, and they continued at full throttle throughout our own century. I wrote about this in my book *The Final Hour*. There were apparitions in Italy and Lithuania and at Espis, France, where one of the seers was given a secret message on November 13, 1949. This secret was then transmitted to Monsignor John Montini, who became Pope Paul VI. There were also apparitions in Marienfried, Germany, where Mary warned that *"the Father pronounces a dreadful woe upon all who refuse to obey His Will."* She said *"the star of the infernal regions"* would rage more violently than ever and would cause frightful destruction *"because he knows that his time is short and because he sees that already many have gathered around my sign."*

This theme would also be repeated time and again: that it's the devil's era but that, as spoken in Revelation 12:12, his time is running out.

From 1949 to 1952, secrets were purportedly granted to a group of children in Heroldsbach, Germany. The following year, in Sabana Grande, Puerto Rico, the Virgin allegedly prophesied a day when the vault of heaven would darken with tribulation and asked again, begged again, for repentance.

She promised to give a sign and said there would be many false apparitions that the devil would use to confuse the real messages.

There's no getting around the stark warnings. There's no soft pedaling. True or false, the apparitions were laden with suspenseful prophecies. Some proved to be untrue. Others were at least questionable. I can think of an apparition in Italy where a revelation was given in 1966 saying that if the world didn't change in six or seven years, the earth would shake and the sun would spin with explosions. The moon would be in "mourning." There would be a cosmic disturbance.

Seven years came and went, and so it was an untrue prophecy. Unless, of course, it's something that's still in the future.

There were very strong prophecies coming out of Spain around the same time, while in Hungary a seer warned that families were in disarray and that our refuge would be in "the flame of Mary's love."

Do you know how many apparitions were publicized?

I don't pretend to have an actual tally, but from one compilation I counted at least thirty-one places where secrets were given to visionaries in at least two dozen countries in the course of this century.

Oh, how often did Mary seem to beseech us to seek protection under her mantle, in her Immaculate Heart! Prayer. Sacrifice. The Rosary. She begged folks to pray to her Son. She begged for sacrifice. As many as fourteen apparitions were reported to Catholic officials every year in the late 1940s and early 1950s, and who knows how many went unreported. Since then, they've skyrocketed. I have one list, already outdated, that cites 244 apparitions since the Miraculous Medal. According to another list there were 232 noteworthy apparitions or like wonders between 1928 and 1975 alone.

In Rome a nun was told that if men did not cease offending Christ, divine justice would take the form of an unforeseen fire that would descend upon the entire earth. This sounded almost exactly like a message that was recorded in Akita, Japan, a few years before.

This nun also spoke of Mary as "the Mother of All Peoples," which is precisely how she had identified herself in the apparitions at Betania, Venezuela.

At Betania Our Blessed Mother called for reconciliation between peoples and nations and predicted that a great event, a hopeful event—some form of manifestation of Christ—approached humanity along with a "difficult moment."

> *If the mystics around 1800 were the first rumbling in a mountain, and if smoke began coming out of the volcano in 1830, followed by great sparks and billows in the first half of our own century, since Medjugore there's not just the pouring smoke but now also the flames of lava.*
>
> *The cap has blown off the mountain.*

There were apparitions in Egypt and Nicaragua. Canada. California. You really can't make a list. During the past fifteen years it's been an explosion.

A great evil was rising. A spirit of antichrist. And Mary was warning about it. There would be a reckoning one day, a purification. But also great hope. It was in the secret prophecies, which we'll study. It was said with a consistency that was little short of astounding.

How come we never hear much about these accounts at church? Why aren't they mentioned from the pulpit?

The Church must exercise caution. It is a wise Church with two thousand years of experience. It has been burned before. The Church has seen many mystics fizzle into disappointment, and it knows that even canonized saints can utter false prophecy.

The Church knows there is grace in mysticism. But there is also danger.

Our Church, praise God, is prudent. Many prophecies are false or even demonic. The Church knows that and doesn't want to promote those. In Matthew we're warned that false prophets will come showing signs and wonders so as to deceive, if it were possible, even the elect (24:24).

But there's another reason for the silence about these occurrences, a reason you don't hear much—and it's not quite as admirable. This other reason has to do with the influence of modernism, which denigrates and snickers at the supernatural. Many clergy have fallen into this trap, becoming overly skeptical.

But the phenomena are so numerous as to rise right above that. They are accepted by a great number of lay people and have reignited interest in church. There's so much supernatural activity that it has twice made the front page of *The New York Times* and has been featured on the covers of *Time, Newsweek,* and *U.S. News and World Report.*

It reached yet greater heights when Our Blessed Mother began to appear in 1981 at Medjugorje.

If the mystics around 1800 were the first rumbling in a mountain, and if smoke began coming out of the volcano in 1830, followed by great sparks and billows in the first half of our own century, and then even more smoke—well, since Medjugorje there's not just the pouring smoke but now also the flames of lava.

The cap has blown off the mountain.

Ten years ago a Lutheran friend of mine, Wayne Weible, owned a weekly newspaper in Myrtle Beach, South Carolina. He put out a compilation of his columns about the apparitions in Medjugorje—a kind of handout or supplement. His organization reports that there was such demand for these handouts that in the course of ten years, literally millions of copies were distributed around the world.

There's an explosion of interest because there's a real movement of the Holy Spirit. The extent of the phenomena is unknown even to many of us who are familiar with the situation. We're always groping to understand its size—along with the hidden omens.

SIX

~

HIDDEN OMENS

Where does Medjugorie fit in to the latest episode?

It's a key part, perhaps *the* key part, of the latest episode. But let me say up front, it's a lot more sedate than many of the other apparitions. While dramatic, it's not sensationalistic. The Church has not yet ruled on it, but I accept the Medjugorje appearances.

It started on June 24, 1981, when a peasant girl named Ivanka Ivankovic spotted a light on a hillside and, upon investigating with several friends, found that in that light was the Blessed Virgin.

From then on, Our Lady came every day. It was the beginning of apparitions that continue to this moment, the longest series of major Marian appearances on record. Never before have so many pilgrims been able to visit a site of apparition while the apparitions are in progress. Millions have gone to Medjugorje, and it has become as famous as Lourdes or Fatima.

Did it just happen out of the blue, or did something lead up to Medjugorje?

Really the episode at Medjugorje started long before 1981, and this is where we get into what I call its hidden origins. As far as I can determine, its phenomena go back to 1933, the year villagers in this hardscrabble region of Bosnia-Hercegovina constructed a large cross atop a local mountain. It's made of concrete, perhaps ten meters high, visible for miles. According to one legend, a priest from the area, Fr. Bernardin ("Brno") Smoljan, was called to Rome in 1933 by Pope Pius XI, who had a dream in which he felt inspired to raise a cross "on the highest Golgotha in Hercegovina." It was very unusual, this dream, because the pope wasn't even familiar with the area. Yet that was the heavenly prompt: Build a cross, a prominent cross, in Hercegovina.

Linked with neighboring Bosnia, the territory of Hercegovina is one of the republics that made up Yugoslavia. It is obscure peasant territory, far from the world's major thoroughfares. Poor. Dirt poor. Bound in time-honored poverty. The parish where the cross was to be built consisted of five hamlets on the Brotnjo plateau, and among the five was Medjugorje, which is pronounced *medj-u-goria* and means "between the hills." It's the edge of the Dinarian Alps.

When Fr. Smoljan returned home, according to this legend, parishioners set about building the cross on the local mountain called Sipovac ("Pomegranate Hill"). At 1,760 feet above sea level, Sipovac would allow the cross to be displayed as the pope instructed.

That's one version. Keep in mind that because of the language barrier, as well as the war, it's often hard to corroborate details. Inaccuracies and folklore abound in religious literature, where a premium is put on the spiritual, not the technical. One old Medjugorje priest I reached said he never heard of such a story. More likely, the cross was built as protection, a holy talisman against the violent hailstorms which used to destroy crops in the tobacco fields and vineyards. Still others believe it was done in reparation for the bitter clashes between Croatians and Serbians. Not far from Medjugorje is a large grave that resulted from one such massacre.

Whatever the precise motive, and whether or not the pope had any such vision, the important point is that a highly visible cross made of concrete was erected on Sipovac in 1933 by peasants lugging buckets of material up a rocky and often treacherous goat path. At the very least it was an act of penance to commemorate the nineteen-hundredth anniversary of Christ's Crucifixion. The rise was soon renamed "Krizevac," which means "Cross."

Now, I don't know exactly how many tons of material they lugged up there, but I do know it takes a good forty-five minutes to get to the top of Mount Krizevac *without* carrying burdensome building materials. Can you imagine hauling buckets of sand and water? There are all kinds of stiff inclines and crevices. The path consists of sharp Karst limestone. It's incredible to contemplate the hundreds of times those peasants trudged up and down the mountain. Obviously, it was a very pious area—folks still said the family Rosary—so it wasn't strange that they would begin such an endeavor up a huge hill known previously for its poisonous snakes (*poskoci*) and wild boars.

The cross was built on sort of a stone rostrum, directly overlooking the village of Medjugorje. Located less than twenty miles southeast of Mostar,

Medjugorje is an area that was settled by Croatians, a Slavic people who formed a nation next to Bosnia and who originally hailed from the western Carpathians. As Slavs they are the ethnic cousins of their bitter enemies, the Serbs, who came from the eastern Carpathians. Both groups are Slavs but with a deadly difference: through the centuries Croatians became Roman Catholics, while the Serbs were drawn into the Orthodox Church. They have developed different languages and have an entirely different alphabet. Croatians are loyal to Rome, while the Serbians have long allied themselves with Byzantine or "eastern" culture. It's an area of the world where East truly meets West, the dividing line or cutting edge of both religion and politics. Although Croatians predominate in Medjugorje, overall there are more Serbs than Croatians in Bosnia-Hercegovina. Added to this volatile mix is a third large group of Slavs, who are neither Catholic nor Orthodox. They're Muslims. They converted to Islam when Turks invaded Bosnia during the fifteenth century.

These three groups—Catholics, Orthodox, and Muslims—all settled in Bosnia-Hercegovina, as well as other parts of the former Yugoslavia, and basically glowered at each other.

So Yugoslavia was a group of smaller republics or nations that did not like each other?

Right. And Bosnia-Hercegovina was caught in the middle, heavily populated by Muslims and located between Croatia and Serbia, both of which had sent many of their people into Bosnia-Hercegovina. You had three rival religions in the same small republic. Several hours east of Medjugorje is Sarajevo, the capital of war-torn Bosnia.

Didn't you just say it was Sarajevo that was also involved in starting World War I?

Absolutely, because of Ferdinand's assassination, which caused Austria-Hungary to declare war on the Serbs.

The Serbs were backed by Russia, Britain, and France, while Austria-Hungary was backed by Germany. That was World War I—and there were ten million dead before it was over.

How does that relate to a supernatural episode?

My point is that in a nearly hidden and mystical fashion, this rather obscure region has played a major role in world history. It's every bit as tense and charged as the Middle East.

And along with other parts of former Yugoslavia, it bears striking similarities to Israel. Like Israel, Bosnia consists largely of parched and rock-strewn hillsides, along with a beautiful sea, the Adriatic. The highlands bring to mind the "hill country" that Our Blessed Mother traveled when she visited her kinswoman Elizabeth (see Luke 1:39). Like Israel, Bosnia can trace its history back as far as history goes. It has long served as a cross-roads of the world. Many people don't know that Neanderthals—those primitive men with huge browridges—inhabited Yugoslavia. And there is evidence that these particular Neanderthals indulged in cannibalism. Fossils found at Krapina include charred limb bones and skulls that were broken into thousands of gruesome fragments.

There's something violent in the very fabric of the area, many potent forces. It's land that is equally blessed and cursed, a true spiritual battle-field, some sort of arcane membrane or threshold. If you believe in Medjugorje, which I obviously do, it seems like it was designed from the beginning as a spiritual beacon, a beacon to dissuade us from fratricide. The Franciscans sent some of their first missionaries to Bosnia-Hercegovina (in fact, St. Francis' missionaries are said to have visited the very area of Medjugorje). Bosnia-Hercegovina is also where the Turks were stopped in their advance on Western Europe, when they sought to conquer that continent and quash Christianity once and for all. It's significant territory and it possesses some kind of hidden mystical importance.

Like Israel?

Like Israel. The very geography forms sort of a supernatural amphitheatre.

If this area started World War I, do you believe it could trigger another major conflict?

I do. But for the moment let's stay with the mysticism. My point is that a cross, a very special cross, was erected on the mountain in this vicinity of several peasant hamlets—the Croatian Catholics who dominate this region of Bosnia-Hercegovina claim that this cross put an end to most of the severe and destructive hailstorms which had long plagued their vineyards. There was a real, living faith among these poor people who had to live most of the century under the yoke of Soviet-style Communism, along with the internal ethnic tensions. These were people who suffered like the peasants in the Soviet Union, Yugoslavia's great ally and frequent bene-factor. Yet the Croatians, at least some of the older peasants, maintained their piety and devotions. They kept a strict Lenten fast of bread and water and out of reverence didn't work on feast days like that of John the Baptist.

There was a living faith, a remnant faith, in this part of Bosnia-Hercegovina. As in older, wiser times, the peasants saw God's grace, His approval, in a sprinkle of rain during a parched summer. They took events in nature to be signs of heavenly favor or rebuke. They believed that the Lord speaks through all kinds of natural events, especially the weather. I don't know what to make of it, but in 1937, several years after the cross was erected, a small earthquake shook Medjugorje and damaged the origi-nal church, which was located in the hamlet of Bijakovici. A new church had to be built, and the site chosen was the adjoining hamlet of Medjugorje. It took the next thirty-two years, but in 1969 the new church, a surprisingly large structure seating six hundred, with three naves and two highly distinctive towers, was finally completed. Built at the foot of Mount Krizevac, this church was designed to serve the five hamlets.

Now when a thunderstorm threatened, the peasants rang the bells in those towers and swore that when they did, storm clouds changed direc-tion and unloaded their hail on the highlands surrounding Medjugorje, sparing the village itself.

The size of the church, the fact that such a large church would be built on the spare plain, and its resonant simplicity seemed like a subtle prophecy of the throngs—the thousands and then millions—who would later jour-ney to Medjugorje.

Another omen was the church's name. It was dedicated to St. James the Greater (or "elder"), son of Zebedee, one of the first four apostles. You may remember that James was in a boat on the Sea of Galilee, mending fishing nets with his brother John, when Jesus called to them (see Matthew

4:21-22). He and his family were closely tied not only to the ministry of Jesus but also to the Crucifixion. James was one of those who accompanied Jesus to the Garden of Gethsemane, and James' mother watched with Mary Magdalene as Christ hung on the cross.

So there is a connection, a mystical connection, between James and the Crucifixion?

Yes. And significantly, we see that the church of St. James was located right beneath Cross Mountain. But it goes beyond that, and here is where the plot really thickens. According to Church tradition, the first miracle or manifestation of Our Blessed Mother, the first apparition in recorded history, was on January 2 in 40 A.D., seven years after the Crucifixion. It occurred, legend has it, along the Ebro River in a province of Spain known as Celtiberia, where James, heeding the directive of Christ to evangelize the world (see Mark 16:15), had been preaching to the Spaniards. The Apostle was at a place known as Saragossa (or "Caesar-Augusta") when the apparition occurred. One evening, according to an old manuscript kept at Saragossa, James retreated with seven or eight of his own disciples to a solitary spot in order to rest after a difficult day of evangelization. They had begun to meditate and pray when James was startled by the sound of a heavenly choir. The angels were chanting, *"Ave Maria, gratia plena."*

The story goes that a radiant light appeared and James fell to his knees, enthralled with the sight before him. Descending from the clouds was the Blessed Virgin Mary, empowered by her Son. She was surrounded by two companies of angels and seated on a marble pillar.

There are those who say that the story is of doubtful authority. There is no verifiable date on the manuscript at Saragossa, and we certainly don't find this incident in the Bible. But as it says in John 21:25, "There are still many other things that Jesus did, yet if they were written about in detail, I doubt there would be room enough in the entire world to hold the books to record them." Later a basilica was built to honor Mary at Saragossa and it included a beautiful image of the Virgin holding the Child Jesus, Who was credited with the entire miracle.

Whether it was an apparition or a case of bilocation (there are those who say the Virgin was still alive, in the care of John the Evangelist) I'll leave for others to determine. All we know is that the first mystical appearance of Mary is said to have occurred just a few years after her Son's Crucifixion and involved James the Elder. When the Medjugorje apparitions occurred, it was at the foot of a cross in a church named after James, the first Marian visionary. The very church is named for a seer. And the cross reminds us that James' mother witnessed the Crucifixion. I don't believe such things are coincidental.

Was there anything else that seemed to foretell of Medjugorje?

Up in France, at La Salette, the other mountain where Mary appeared in 1846, is an interesting painting. It's in a small, nearly abandoned chapel along the mountainous road to the site of the apparition. It's a large painting of the two visionaries, Melanie Calvat and Maximin Giraud, in front of a church with two spires. The church in this painting bears an uncanny resemblance to St. James Church in Medjugorje.

While such structures are not exactly rare in Europe, and while it may have been what the local parish there in France looked like, there is a sense, as at Saragossa, that La Salette was a forerunner of the phenomena claimed at Medjugorje. It involved the two peasant children who were pasturing cows when they spotted a large circle of brilliant, vibrant light. It was outshining the sun, and that naturally scared them.

The light gyrated a bit, seeming to turn on itself, and there was what seemed to be an elliptical face within the luminosity. Before they could flee, the light opened and in it Maximin and Melanie saw Our Lady seated. She came toward them along the brook, and as at Saragossa (and later Medjugorje), she was a woman of magnetic love and beauty.

She began to speak those prophetic warnings. She said that if sinfulness remained, the harvest would be ruined. She was especially concerned about those who swore, using the name of her Son in vain, or who labored on Sundays. She warned that if matters continued, there would be a famine. It would be people's own fault for rejecting Christ's protective powers. She warned that wheat would not be good to sow, the grapes would rot, and worms would eat the walnuts. According to one version of the events, there were also prophecies for the entire world. As stated in chapter four, Melanie and Maximin were supposedly told that a great evil was descending upon the world and mankind was turning to humanism, self-indulgence, and rebellion. Civil governments would do away with religious principles, Mary prophesied, and there would be grave problems in the Church, among both the laity and the clergy. Three-fourths of France would lose the faith, and the same would happen elsewhere. There would be scandals among priests, and certain nuns would turn toward occultism. As a result, great chastisements threatened not just the vicinity of La Salette, not just the diocese of Grenoble, but the world. "There are scourges that menace not only France, but Germany and Italy as well. All Europe is culpable and merits chastisements," said Pope Pius IX after reading the secret, which some believe also contained reference to the Anti-Christ and the rising of a great beast, a great evil, at the beginning of the twentieth century. It seemed like a pretty good prediction of Communism, secular humanism, and the world wars that soon ravaged Europe.

While there remains confusion about La Salette, and while old controversies about the prophecies hold us back from an absolutely full preaching of the message, the apparition itself was approved by the local bishop in 1851 and fits within the larger picture of Marian intervention. As elsewhere, the prophecies were originally secret, and as at Medjugorje, Mary chose peasant children to carry a stern message.

Have you seen other similarities?

I've always seen impressive similarities among the major, authentic apparitions, consistencies that could never have been staged. The apparitions are pieced together like a huge, invisible puzzle. The major ones usually occur in remote, "God-forsaken" parts of the world, as if heaven were trying to emphasize that the deepest spirituality is not to be found in the "sophistication" of our urban centers. Often the visionaries are simple shepherd children. At La Salette they were tending cows; at Fatima and Medjugorje, it was sheep. The apparitions often occur on rocky hillsides that resemble the parched and unyielding hills to be found in parts of Israel, especially near Nazareth. The visionaries are mostly poor, humble, and uneducated children whose minds are uncluttered by philosophy and skepticism. Their clear, unquestioning dispositions allow them to report what they witnessed without putting their own "spin" on it. The simplicity breeds credibility.

At Fatima the apparitions were preceded by flashes that resembled lightning, and when the Blessed Mother left, it was with a clap of thunder. As at Lourdes and La Salette, there were sudden weather changes. The Virgin came to Fatima during World War I, which, as stated, began in Sarajevo, connecting it to Medjugorje. At Fatima she had said the war would soon end but a greater one would follow if mankind did not convert. It was an echo of the warning at La Salette seventy years before.

That second war also came, of course—World War II—and at the end of it there was the intriguing series of apparitions right in the belly of the beast, Germany.

I'm speaking of Marienfried, which means "the peace of Mary." It is ironic, because when Mary appeared in Medjugorje four decades later, she called herself the "Queen of Peace." Her main message in Medjugorje, in this land of ethnic hatred, has been peace and reconciliation. She specifically asked for reconciliation between Croats, Serbs, and Muslims, and she did so long before there was an inkling of the current civil war. In Medjugorje, as at Marienfried, she spoke of a period during which Satan—the "star of the infernal regions,"—has been unusually powerful.

I don't know much about the German apparitions, but I do know of one more "coincidence": they ended on June 25, 1946, which would later become Medjugorje's official anniversary. It was the first day Mary spoke *to* the Croatian children. *"Peace, peace,"* she told a seer the following day. *"There must be peace on earth. You must be reconciled with God and with each other."*

SEVEN

~

LITTLE MYSTERIES

What about actual prophecies? Were there specific prophecies about Medjugorje?

According to one published account, Padre Pio predicted that Mary would visit Yugoslavia. It was said that before he died, this fascinating Italian priest told a group of Hercegovinian pilgrims that "the Blessed Virgin will soon be visiting your homeland."

Such rumors can't be readily verified. Many are not credible. But we do know of another prophecy that took the form of a painting, a small and simple painting, which now hangs from the choir loft in St. James.

It was done by an artist named Vlado Falak. He was from Medjugorje and painted it in 1974—seven years before the first apparitions. In the painting Falak portrayed the Blessed Virgin Mary appearing at Medjugorje in a white dress with a blue belt and white veil. She was outside, hovering over Medjugorje, her arms outstretched over the village.

Below is Mount Krizevac and on the left side is a cluster of trees next to the plain, twin-spired church where the apparitions would soon take place.

That's a fairly straightforward prophecy, and God often speaks through art. He also whispers through little mysteries. Two months before Mary first appeared, the children of the Ivankovic family, living down the road from Mount Krizevac in the hamlet of Bijakovici, were preparing to get some firewood with their cart. Sixteen-year-old Vicka (pronounced Vishka), and her brother Franjo, hopped into the cart. When Franjo jumped in, he found two strange rosaries in or next to the toolbox. Two rosaries in that simple little wagon. One of them had a large cross with all fourteen Stations of the Cross. On the cross of the other rosary was a relic.

They looked ancient. No one could explain where the rosaries had come from. Two rosaries, two old relics, as if from nowhere.

The Ivankovic family was in wonder. Vicka's mother went around the village trying to see if the rosaries belonged to anyone, but no one claimed them. The mystery was solved only when Our Blessed Mother appeared and explained that the rosaries were put there as part of her plan, for young Vicka was soon to become one of the six visionaries.

There were also prophecies from charismatics, signs of something big coming. Shortly before the first apparition a priest named Heribert Mühlen was giving a lecture in Zagreb, which is to the north of Medjugorje. Fr. Mühlen was the head of the charismatic movement in Germany. Addressing a number of Croatian priests, and with language reminiscent of Padre Pio, he announced that "God is preparing great things in your homeland, which will greatly influence the destiny of all of Europe."

Another prophecy came in the late spring of 1981. This time the scene was Rome, where there was a congress of charismatics. For those of you who aren't familiar with them, charismatics are Christians who worship in a lively way, singing heartfelt songs, praising the Lord with arms outstretched, and often speaking in tongues. A "charism" is simply a grace such as prophecy or healing.

The charismatic movement swept through Protestant and Catholic circles during the 1970s and 1980s, a small but vibrant aspect of Christianity, a movement of the Holy Spirit. One of the attendees at the Rome congress was a priest named Tomislav Vlasic, who was seeking prayer for the Church in Bosnia-Hercegovina.

While she was praying over Fr. Vlasic, Sr. Briege McKenna had a vision. It was a prescient vision related to Medjugorje. "I saw a white church with twin steeples," she recalled. "Father was sitting in the main celebrant's chair in the sanctuary of this church, and streams of living water were flowing from the altar. Many people were coming and cupping the water in their hands to drink."

Obviously the twin spires belonged to St. James, and the Holy Spirit was represented by the water. Vlasic was also prayed over by a charismatic priest named Emiliano Tardif, who, speaking for the Lord, said, *"Do not be afraid. I am sending you My mother."*

Soon after, Vlasic, who was in Caplinja at the time, found himself transferred to Medjugorje.

By then the apparitions were in progress. They'd begun just weeks after the charismatic conference. It was June 24, 1981. There was a tremendously violent thunderstorm. Lightning seemed to be hitting everywhere.

There was even a fire. It was such an intense storm that one farmer, Pero Vasilj, compared it with the Day of Judgment.

The following afternoon, hours after the storm, Ivanka Ivankovic experienced the first apparition on that hillside called Podbrdo, and soon five others, including Vicka, were also seeing the Virgin, who began to appear on a daily basis—on the hill, at the rectory, in a room opposite the sacristy, and, yes, in the choir loft.

Didn't something like that happen at Fatima? Wasn't there a violent storm there, too?

There was a gargantuan storm across Europe just before the last apparition on October 13, 1917.

And Lourdes?

Before her first apparition Bernadette "heard a great noise like the sound of a storm."

Why would storms be associated with apparitions?

No one knows. Some think it's like a heavenly exclamation point. Others see Satan trying to disrupt things. After all, he fell from heaven like a lightning bolt (see Luke 10:18).

Lightning is associated with supernatural visions. It's associated with prophets like Daniel and Ezekiel. It's a way in which heaven acts and talks. In Job it says the voice of God rumbles like thunder. And we know from Matthew (24:27) that "as the lighting from the east flashes to the west, so will the coming of the Son of Man be." I think the most relevant allusions may be in 1 Samuel, where it says that "the adversaries of the Lord shall be broken to pieces; out of heaven shall He thunder upon them; the Lord shall judge the ends of the earth; and He shall give strength unto His king, and exalt the horn of His anointed" (2:10, KJV).

A thunderstorm is an interesting phenomenon. It can be frightening but it also washes away pollutants, replenishes the underground springs, and nurtures the new growth of trees and vegetables. A thunderstorm refreshes. It renews. It's a purification. During my fourth visit to Medjugorje I encountered a tremendously ferocious thunderstorm. It was as bad as what

> *At the end of the appari- tion Mary said, "Go in the peace of God." She speaks Croation in a perfect local dialect.*

I'd once experienced while visiting Minnesota during tornado season. Even the peasants found the storm unusual. Lightning brightened our room despite the closed shutters, and thunder echoed off Mount Krizevac and the hill where the first apparition occurred.

Ironically, the storm hit right after we'd spoken to Vicka about her "secrets"—the confidential messages she has been given, the messages that have been given to all six Medjugorje seers, messages that have to do, we're told, with a coming purification. I will have much more to say about that in the following chapters.

The Virgin talks like we do?

The first day she said nothing. It was the second day, June 25, that she began to speak. She responded to Ivanka when Ivanka wanted to know about her recently deceased mother. The Virgin said her mother was in heaven and that Ivanka should watch over her aging grandmother. There was little else said. At the end of the apparition Mary said, *"Go in the peace of God."* She speaks Croatian in a perfect local dialect.

How many times do they claim she's appeared since 1981?

Four of the visionaries still see her every day, which would come to roughly five thousand formal apparitions since 1981—apparitions that the group participates in and which occur at a set time, usually around 6:40 p.m. (and 5:40 p.m. in the winter). When a seer is traveling, he or she will still experience the apparition wherever he or she happens to be. There are also secondary apparitions that occur to the individual visionaries. These happen spontaneously, while the seers are at home or somewhere else. They also occur up on Mount Krizevac. At first, in the early days, the Blessed Mother gave more involved messages. Now she comes for a briefer time and mainly to pray with the visionaries.

You mean Our Blessed Mother can be seen at the same time by one visionary who is at the church and another who is elsewhere?

Yes, and sometimes she speaks to each seer individually, even when the visionaries are having the apparition together. She can hold several different conversations at once. She can carry on separate conversations. This is no surprise. Spirits are not limited to our time-space continuum. Other times Mary addresses the seers together. She has even shown some of them the afterlife—heaven and purgatory—together.

It was most impressive back when all six visionaries were receiving the apparitions together. You can watch videos of it. When the Virgin appeared, they dropped to their knees with uncanny unity, fixed their eyes on the exact same point, and often became all but totally detached from the real world. Investigators could pick up a visionary or poke at them with fingers, needles, and scientific equipment without causing a reaction from that seer.

When the Virgin appeared, they dropped to their knees with uncanny unity, fixed their eyes on the exact same point, and often became all but totally detached from the real world. Investigators could pick up a visionary or poke at them with fingers, needles, and scientific equipment without causing a reaction from that seer.

Two of the seers didn't blink during the often lengthy apparitions, while the others blinked far less frequently than normal. Tests with an electro-oculogram indicated that their eye movement came to a simultaneous halt during the apparitions, and while their lips moved—while they continued to articulate words with their mouths—no sound could be heard.

Tests showed that their voice boxes, their larynxes, were simultaneously disengaged. Observers could spot no signs or cues to account for the seers' reacting at the same moment in the same way, nor could scientists account for a gaze that was so fixed and motionless. The simultaneity was precise to the second, and at the end of the apparition their voices would reappear in synchronization as they joined Our Lady in reciting the Lord's Prayer.

The frequency of these experiences is unprecedented. There are still four visionaries who see Mary on a daily basis, and the other two experience visitations on special occasions. To me it's inconceivable that anyone, let alone a group of unsophisticated teenagers, could perpetrate a hoax thousands of times over the course of so many years. At Fatima there were only a handful of apparitions; at Lourdes there were eighteen.

Doesn't that seem like too many? Doesn't it become nearly commonplace or frivolous?

Perhaps the number says something about the Virgin's seriousness. It sure doesn't seem frivolous. No matter how many times these young men and women have seen her, they're always awed by the experience. They say she's more real than we are. They say she brings light and joy, that she leaves them happy, although she also has many strong things to say about the world. They can't get enough of her. Where once the apparitions lasted for up to forty-five minutes, these days she comes for a few minutes and simply prays with them. They pray for sinners. They pray for an end to the war. They implore God, Jesus, and the Holy Spirit. There isn't anything commonplace or frivolous about her.

But why Medjugorje? Why such a remote hamlet?

When Vicka asked that same question, the Virgin replied, "*I came because there are many good believers here. I want to be with you, to convert and reconcile everyone.*" She comes where there is prayer. She comes where there is sacrifice. She comes where she's needed and welcome.

In the parish of Medjugorje are many who are dedicated to her, who are devoted to Christ and have been purified through sufferings. War. Poverty. The oppression of Communism. "Happy the man who holds out to the end through trial!" says Sacred Scripture. "God resists the proud but bestows His favor on the lowly" (see James 1:12, 4:6).

So she comes because they have suffered?

And also because she likes humility and simplicity. Our Blessed Mother is at home in peasant territory. She herself was a peasant girl. She came from a rugged land. The complexion of her skin, as described at

Medjugorje, is similar to the complexion of skin in Israel. And she too was a mere teenager when she experienced an apparition (see Luke 1:26).

But why not appear in the capital? Why not in Washington, D.C. or at the Kremlin? For that matter, why not on network TV?

God doesn't usually force the issue. He doesn't violate our free will. He wants to be invited. He is most noticeable where there is prayer. He comes when beseeched. He's subtle. He wants faith. He isn't going to send Mary to do *The Tonight Show*.

When He prods, He does so with subtlety and grandeur.

The main mission of Our Blessed Mother has been to prod us toward prayer, penance, and conversion. She has come to let us know that God not only exists but is ever watchful.

That's the main message, that the supernatural exists?

I think the Virgin was also trying to prevent war in Bosnia. Back in 1981, when the first apparition occurred, few could understand why she was making such an issue of "peace," why she was coming with peace in her very title—Queen of Peace—and why she was saying that peace was threatened. Because that's what she kept insisting, that peace was in danger. Though there had been that long-simmering hatred among Croats, Muslims, and Serbs, there was no one in the 1980s who expected it to erupt so soon into a major conflict, into the greatest conflict on European soil since World War II. At the time Yugoslavia was the most "Western" of Communist nations. It was more open than most Communist states and as such it looked like it was going to make the easiest transition to democracy. When I first visited in 1989 there was no wrenching concern about war. Alone among Marxist nations, it had diplomatic relations with the Holy See, including an embassy in Rome and a diplomatic agency in Belgrade.

But Mary knew what we could not: that far from making an easy transition, Yugoslavia would suffer horribly. She said as much. She came as Queen of Peace because she knew that if there was no conversion, if there was no turning back to God, the ethnic tensions—the age-old hatred, however far below the surface—would soon explode with shocking force.

The Blessed Virgin said from the start that she came to reconcile. She told the seers there was an unnatural separation in Medjugorje between the ethnic groups—a separation that was not good, a division that served as a precursor and microcosm for what would occur across Yugoslavia. She warned that without conversion, without a turning back to God, matters would become more hideous than people ever imagined. As we all know now, that prophecy has materialized in the rapes and torture and bombings. Said a third seer, Mirjana Dragicevic, who was with Ivanka on June 24 when the first appearances occurred: "The Madonna always stresses that there is but one God, and that people have enforced unnatural separation."

In fact, the tensions exploded after Croatia declared independence from Serbia on the anniversary of Medjugorje, June 25, 1991.

Is Mary asking for reconciliation with Muslims? Does Mary say it's okay to be non-Catholic, and even a Muslim?

It's not an endorsement of the Islamic faith—which fails to hold Christ as Savior—but neither is it a condemnation. Rather, it's a call to find common ground and the goodness of God with everyone. *"Tell everyone that it is you who are divided on earth,"* she told a locutionist at Medjugorje.

The Muslims and the Orthodox for the same reason as Catholics are equal before my Son and me. You are all my children. Certainly all religions are not equal [but] 'all men are equal before God.' It does not suffice to belong to the Catholic Church to be saved. It is necessary to respect and obey the Commandments of God in following one's conscience. Those who are not Catholics are no less creatures made in the image of God and destined ultimately to live in the house of God our Father. Salvation is available to everyone without exception. My Son Jesus redeemed all people on earth. Only those who refuse God deliberately are condemned by their own choice. It is God alone, in His infinite justice, who determines the degree of responsibility and renders judgment.

Our Lady's message is to convert others through unbounded love—not through antagonism. In God there's no division. In God there's no separation between believers. *"The only mediator is Jesus Christ,"* said the Virgin. *"There are divisions because believers have become separated one from the other. Do not make distinctions between people."*

If a person believes in Jesus Christ, if a person believes in the One True God, we must find brotherhood with that person. And if a person doesn't, we wipe the dust from our shoes, we protect our spiritual space (see Matthew 10:14).

But we continue to reach out with love.

Hasn't there been controversy over Medjugorje? Aren't there those who believe it's a fabrication, or the work of the devil?

While Medjugorje has encountered less controversy than many apparitions, it has seen its share of excitement, and that should hardly surprise us. I'm not aware of any major mystical experiences, including those of Jesus, that have not met with degrees of dispute. We should remember that the Pharisees went so far as to accuse Christ of healing by the power of the devil (see Matthew 12:24). We have always seen controversy rage around charisms like tongues and resting in the Spirit.

Sometimes the critics are right. Sometimes the devil is behind an apparition. Other times the devil is behind the critics. He inspires unnecessary criticism.

But that's getting away from the point. That's shirking the question. Let's admit that until Medjugorje receives the formal approval of the Church, it must still be considered an "alleged" apparition. It's still open to discernment. It's still open to honest questioning. Disputes still hover around Medjugorje, though there is far less controversy than there was years ago.

The major tension was between the Bishop of Mostar and the local Franciscans, who have been at odds for a long time over control of certain parishes in Hercegovina. Franciscans operate St. James and, as a result, the bishop has been antagonistic toward Medjugorje. He submitted a negative report in 1986. In normal circumstances, that would have spelled doom for the apparitions. It would have constituted an ecclesiastical disapproval or condemnation. The local bishop normally has jurisdiction over apparitions in his diocese, and Medjugorje is in the diocese of Mostar. But the Vatican took the matter out of local hands and it's now under investigation by a national commission of bishops. On April 10, 1991, the commission came out with a statement saying that the investigation is ongoing and that "on the basis of the investigations so far, it cannot be affirmed that one is deal-ing with supernatural apparitions and revelations."

So that's the judgment?

No. It's what they call a *non constat de supernaturalitate*, more or less a preliminary statement saying that so far there has been no objective proof. The war broke out right after the commission was appointed, and ever since that time its attention has been diverted. In Mostar Bishop Zanic has resigned; but his successor, Ratko Peric, is even more antagonistic towards Medjugorje.

Wasn't there an archbishop who came out in favor?

That was Frane Franic, who is now retired but who was Ordinary of the Metropolitan See that includes Medjugorje. He's strongly convinced that the happenings at Medjugorje are supernatural. He has never wavered from this stance. It seems that something unusual happened to the Archbishop when he visited Medjugorje. He told a reporter that he documented the incident and has sealed it in his personal archives, to be disclosed thirty years after his death. He proclaimed that Medjugorje is "the continuation of Our Lady's messages in Lourdes and Fatima."

In America, Mother Angelica, one of the most powerful U.S. Catholics, has openly promoted Medjugorje on her Eternal Word Television Network. One of the country's most prominent priests, Fr. Michael Scanlan, a Harvard-educated lawyer who is president of Franciscan University in Steubenville, is likewise favorable. "I found the message important, powerful, and consistent with the gospels and the teaching of the Catholic Church," he once wrote in the preface of a book about Medjugorje. "I could find no evidence that would motivate me to question the authenticity of the reports given by the six teenage visionaries."

The same convictions are held by a slew of bishops and cardinals, along with Pope John Paul II, who, during *ad limina* visits, has not only indicat-ed his belief but has said he prays for Medjugorje's success and believes it's good for people to go there. He has in effect given Medjugorje informal approval. He's said to have stated that if he wasn't Pope, he would have visited there by now, and recently he has begun expressing a desire to go there in the near future. There are many accounts of priests, bishops, and pilgrims meeting the pope and hearing encouragement. He has described Medjugorje as "a great center of spirituality." When a friend of mine blurted out, "Medjugorje! Medjugorje!" during a general papal audience a couple of years ago, to see what he would do, John Paul smiled and nodded his head knowingly. "Nowadays the world has lost its interest in the supernatural, but many people are seeking these values that we find in Medjugorje, through prayer and penance," the pope told a group of Italian doctors in 1989. That same year he mentioned to Bishop Silvester Treinen of Boise, Idaho, that "it's good for people to go to Medjugorje and pray." In November of 1994, when Archbishop Felipe Santiago Benitez of Paraguay asked the pope if he should allow Fr. Slavko Barbaric, a priest from St. James, to preach the message in South America, the pope reportedly replied, "Authorize everything that concerns Medjugorje." On June 17, 1992, the pope told Fr. Jozo Zovko, who was pastor at the time of the apparitions, "I give you my blessing. Take courage. I am with you. Tell Medjugorje I am with you. Protect Medjugorje!"

All such indications are important, because at the Fifth Lateran Council, Pope Leo X said that when it is a question of prophetic revelations, the pope, if he so chooses, can serve as "the sole judge." Usually, popes leave it to the local bishops so as not to involve the idea of papal infallibility with a private revelation. But Pope John Paul II has come close to publicly endorsing it. Although he has to be careful, because the Church has a set protocol for approving or disapproving an apparition site (and usually likes to wait until an apparition has run its course), on April 6, 1995, the pope indicated during the unofficial portion of a meeting with a delegation from Croatia that if he visits Croatia in the future, he would like to visit Medjugorje, along with the city of Split and the Marian Shrine of Marija Bistrica near Zagreb. In November 1994 Archbishop Jean Chabbert of Perpignan, France, publicly stated that the pope "is truly convinced of the authenticity of the apparitions," according to one report.

Remember, Pope John Paul II is very Marian and mystical. As a mere boy he paid homage to Our Lady of Perpetual Help. He was also a member of the Marian Sodality, a nationwide association of Catholic youths devoted to the Virgin Mary. His appreciation for how Mary brings us to

> *If the Church were to rule against Medjugorje, which could happen after John Paul II is gone, we would have to accept that verdict. We would have to show obedience.... [But] rare is the person who has been to Medjugorje and hasn't returned a different person. Rare is the visitor who prays in the village or trudges up Krizevac and is not touched in a most profound way.*

her Son came from studying St. Louis de Montfort. The pope's first doctorate was in mystical theology, and in a recent book, *Crossing the Threshold of Hope*, he declares that his devotion is *Totus Tuus*—signifying "total abandonment to Mary." He believes Mary intervenes in world affairs. He sees her behind the world stage. He often attends functions holding a rosary. He believes she helps bring us closer to Jesus. And he prays up to seven hours a day. When Archbishop Angelo Kim, president of the Korean Episcopal Conference, visited John Paul II and told the pontiff it was because of his work—his support of Solidarity, and his international pressure—that Poland and then all of Eastern Europe was freed from Communism, the pope replied, "No, not me, but by the works of the Blessed Virgin, according to her affirmations at Fatima and Medjugorje."

It is said that in 1984 the pope, fore-echoing Archbishop Franic, indicated that Medjugorje is the "continuation and fulfillment" of Fatima.

These are weighty words, but still we wait for formal approval. We still wait for final discernment. In any mysticism we must always obey Church elders. We must remain open to the possibility of human or diabolical deception. If the Church were to rule against Medjugorje, which could happen after John Paul II is gone, we would have to accept that verdict. We would have to show obedience.

But what's your personal feeling? How do you feel in your heart?

After the four visits there, and having met all the seers, as well as interviewing several in some depth or appearing with them at various conferences—having met literally thousands who have been there, and seeing the fruits, which is how we're supposed to judge an apparition (see Matthew 12:33)—I feel very confident about Medjugorje. It profoundly affected me and by all indications has deeply affected the vast majority of those millions who have made the pilgrimage from all corners of the world, from paupers to prime ministers.

Rare is the person who has been to Medjugorje and hasn't returned a different person. Rare is the visitor who prays in the village or trudges up Krizevac and is not touched in a most profound way. Rare is the visiting disbeliever. When there is criticism, it's usually from afar. It's from someone who has never visited.

Medjugorje is a uniquely powerful place. It's already the most important apparition since Fatima. If it stands the test of time, if it meets with formal approval, if its authenticity is accepted by the Vatican, and if its prophecies hold true, Medjugorje will turn out to be not just bigger than Fatima but the most important manifestation of the Virgin Mary, at least since the apparitions at Guadalupe, Mexico, in 1531—and more likely the most important of all time.

EIGHT

~

NATURE OF THE PHENOMENA

You've mentioned the secrets of Medjugorje, the messages that are said to contain prophecies. The same happened at Fatima, where such predictions were given to the pope in the form of what became known as the "Third Secret." Does Pope John Paul II know something about the future? Has the pope seen the secrets of Medjugorje?

By all indications the pope is himself a contemplative. He gets his own "messages." And yes, he is very familiar with Medjugorje. He has read books about it, he has spoken with at least one of the visionaries, and he has also met Fr. Jozo, the former pastor there. He understands the nature of the phenomena, which we too must understand if we're to comprehend the worldwide spiritual eruption.

And the secrets?

The pope doesn't know the secrets. No one knows them, except the visionaries. But he knows about them in general. He was sent a memorandum about the secrets on December 2, 1983, by Fr. Vlasic. The letter was written at the request of the Madonna, who told Marija Pavlovic, another seer, that the Bishop and Supreme Pontiff were to be notified "of the urgency and great importance of the message of Medjugorje." World peace, said the letter, was at "a critical stage." There was the call, the repeated, maternal call, for reconciliation and conversion. Vlasic explained that each visionary is to be given ten secrets pertaining to the future and that the visionary Mirjana had already received her ten. Included was a secret that has to do with some kind of great sign or miracle, a sign that will be left at the site of apparitions to convert non-believers. But it's not the first secret. The prophecy from Medjugorje is that this sign won't occur until a couple of other secrets unfold.

"Before the visible sign is given to humanity, there will be three warnings to the world," wrote Vlasic. "The warnings will be in the form of events on earth. Mirjana will be a witness to them. Three days before one of the admonitions, Mirjana will notify a priest of her choice. The witness of Mirjana will be a confirmation of the apparitions and a stimulus for the conversion of the world. After the admonitions, the visible sign will appear on the site of the apparitions in Medjugorje for all the world to see. The sign will be given as a testimony to the apparitions and in order to call people back to faith. The ninth and tenth secrets are serious. They concern chastisement for the sins of the world."

The period preceding the visible sign, wrote Vlasic, "is a time of grace for conversion and deepening of the faith."

The letter also claimed that Satan has been given special powers in our century, power to try the Church, to create divisions among priests. And the power to cause obsessions and murder.

But at the onset of the secrets, said Mary, Satan's special power, his extended grip, would be broken.

This is something that will be seen around the world? There will be a sign that everyone can witness?

We have to be careful how we phrase it. We have to be careful not to distort such things into science fiction. Sometimes the true meaning of words doesn't make it through translation. There will be a sign at Medjugorje. That's the prophecy. There will be a manifestation that I would guess will be accessible to those who go there, just as Medjugorje has already been a stimulus to the world. And just as there already have been some extraordinary signs there. Later we'll discuss previously unpublished hints by Mirjana about what the first "secret" may be, but the important thing to remember is the immediate call for love and conversion.

What exactly do you mean by "conversion"?

Conversion is putting God foremost in our lives.

And how do we do that?

By confessing our sins. By invoking Jesus.

Do you really believe the devil is now more powerful? That he has been given our century? Hasn't he always been around?

In any age, in any era, there's a lot of evil. The devil is always in the shadows. We see him as the serpent. We see him in temptation. Throughout the ages we see him in occultism and paganism. We see him in cannibals and Attila the Hun and at the Coliseum in Rome, feeding Christians to the lions.

But he's really showing his face right now, he's really blatant in our time, and especially of late. According to the Virgin, his time is short. He's becoming aggressive. We have only to pick up a newspaper to see his eyes, to track his footprints.

Is it true that news of Medjugorje has reached leaders like Gorbachev and Reagan?

Yes. In 1987, Alfred Kingon, who was U.S. ambassador to the European Communities and had also served as assistant secretary of the Treasury, visited Medjugorje as a pilgrim. Although he's not Catholic—his mother was Jewish, his father a Christian Scientist—he went to see what Medjugorje was about. He'd long had an interest in apparitions, like those reported at Garabandal, Spain, during the sixties and at Fatima in 1917.

When Ambassador Kingon got to Medjugorje, he was very impressed by what he saw. He was taken by the Spirit. He watched as pilgrims struggled to the top of Mount Krizevac, negotiating those treacherous rocks, even in the rain. In fact, the ambassador was so impressed that he sent President Reagan a personal two-and-a-half page summary.

Reagan responded favorably. He had his secretary call. He was moved by what he had read. The secretary asked how to contact Marija Pavlovic, the seer who receives a monthly message for the world, and though they never did talk, Reagan's secretary also sought her address. Soon after, Ambassador Kingon sent a similar report about Medjugorje to Mikhail Gorbachev. This was done with the help of the Austrian ambassador's office and also Jack Matlock, who was U.S. ambassador to the U.S.S.R. Kingon took thirty-nine pages of Mary's messages and reduced them to a one-page memorandum. The Austrians helped with translation. Then Matlock guided it to the inner circle. "There was no answer from

Gorbachev, but it was indicated that he got it," said Kingon, who strongly believes in the apparitions and told me there is "something of great import going on." He senses that in some fashion "the whole world is going to change."

Another major official, Margaret Heckler, the former congresswoman who served as Secretary of Health and Human Services—a Cabinet-level post—has a similarly strong interest in Marian phenomena. She related this in 1993, when we had lunch in Washington, and then in 1995 when we traveled together to Ireland, where she had served as American ambassador. She told me she has seen the metal links in three of her own rosaries mysteriously turn gold—a common phenomenon at Medjugorje, thought to represent purification. She has discussed the significance of reported phenomena with some of the most prominent names in American politics. I'm in touch with many folks—medical doctors, politicians, psychiatrists, television producers, and businessmen—who in years past would have ignored reports of the supernatural, but who now show a keen interest in apparitions.

What exactly is an apparition? What's the difference between an apparition and a vision?

As I have stressed, a vision is chiefly something we see in the mind's eye, most often during prayer, meditation, or dreams. They're images. They're ideas. They're like photographs, slide shows, or surreal movies.

An apparition is another matter. An apparition is seen by the physical eyes. It's corporeal. It's almost physical. It's like interacting with a living person. It's something that's perceived with the eyes and ears and even, as in the case of Medjugorje, with the sense of touch: the visionaries claim they can reach out and feel the apparition, which is like nothing earthly, nothing they can describe in human terminology.

That's the problem with mysticism: words don't adequately tell the story. There are certain phenomena that can't be related to anything in our normal experience. At Medjugorje they often say the Blessed Virgin can be compared to no statue, nor even to the most beautiful painting. There's nothing like her in the museums. She's far more exquisite. She's transcendental. Her beauty is arrayed in an unearthly light that far surpasses any known luminosity.

We call the experiences with Mary "apparitions" but in the classic sense an apparition is more like a ghostlike form. What's seen at Medjugorje would more accurately be described as a "materialization." The visionaries see Our Blessed Mother as clearly and fully, as materially, as they see a human being.

> *That's the problem with mysticism: words don't adequately tell the story. There are certain phenomena that can't be related to anything in our normal experience.*

And a locution is a voice, correct?

That's right. An inner locution is in the head, sort of like a poignant thought, heard internally. In other cases voices are heard by the physical ear. Those are known as auricular or auditory locutions. When Moses heard God at Sinai, and when witnesses heard God speak from a cloud during Christ's baptism, those were examples of auditory locutions.

What about the brilliant flash of light that comes before or during an apparition? Why light? What's the function of it?

Heaven is light. The spirit world is a world of light. The light serves as a vehicle or signal. It's a non-physical energy. It seems to be a medium of supernatural transference. It opens a porthole, parts the curtain. It's like heaven saying: Pay attention, folks, because here we go. This is the big time.

In many apparitions the light forms a vortex, sort of like a dull spotlight. There's a pillar of light, or a globule of light, and next is seen a figure that looks like it's sculpted in a luminous haze. This is often the second stage of materialization. At Fatima an angel who preceded the Blessed Virgin was described as a light over the trees and in that light was something of "strange whiteness," like somebody "wrapped in a sheet." Those are the words of Fatima visionary Lucia dos Santos, who described the Virgin as "a Lady all of white, more brilliant than the sun, dispensing light, clearer and more intense than a crystal cup full of crystalline water penetrated by the rays of the most glaring sun."

When Mary first appeared at Medjugorje it was likewise as a rather nebu-

> *When Vicka looked up, the apparition suddenly materialized. "I saw her standing there just as clearly as I can see you now.... She wore a gray dress with a white veil, a crown of stars, blue eyes, dark hair, and rosy cheeks. And she was floating on a gray cloud, not touching the ground."*

lous luminosity. The story has been told countless times—how Ivanka, who was fifteen at the time, and Mirjana, sixteen, were taking a walk along the bottom of Mount Podbrdo, a short distance from Mount Krizevac, when Ivanka spotted that luminous form on the hillside. Although it was rather indistinct, Ivanka could make out a female form in the light, hovering about a yard above the ground, in a gray robe. At first Mirjana ignored it and kept heading home; but when she got to the first house on the way back to the village, suddenly she felt compelled to go back for Ivanka, who was still focused on the phenomenon. A bit afraid, they scurried away that first time but later returned with a friend named Milka, who was tending sheep. All three saw the Madonna. Ivanka described Mary as holding the Infant Jesus in her arms, as at Saragossa.

Another friend, Vicka, came looking for them. When she found the three, they told her what was happening, and Vicka ran away without really looking. She's the seer whose brother found the mysterious rosaries. She made a dash toward a place called Cilici.

There Vicka came upon two villagers who were both named Ivan. One was Ivan Ivankovic, an older fellow, and the other was sixteen-year-old Ivan Dragicevic. They'd been picking apples, but when Vicka told them what was going on they went back to see for themselves. The older Ivan said he saw "something completely white, turning." When Vicka looked up, the apparition suddenly materialized. "I saw her standing there just as clearly as I can see you now," she told an interviewer for the British Broadcasting Company. "She wore a gray dress with a white veil, a crown of stars, blue eyes, dark hair, and rosy cheeks. And she was floating on a gray cloud, not touching the ground."

The Blessed Mother was covering and uncovering the Infant, Who was in her left arm. There was nothing said. It was the June 24 experience. The next day, matters became clearer. Ivanka, Mirjana, and Vicka, along with Ivan Dragicevic, decided to return to the hill. Two other youngsters, Marija Pavlovic, who was fifteen at the time, and Jakov Colo, ten, also joined them. These six would become the permanent visionaries. At first Marija could discern only a vague outline, but it gradually came into better focus, "like a mist clearing." Then she could make out the outline of the Virgin's face, even though the Virgin was at the top of Mount Podbrdo, which is a bit of a distance away.

When the apparition beckoned them, the youngsters were able to make what is normally a twelve-minute climb in but two minutes. It was like they were floating. It was like partial levitation. "We ran up that hill," recalled Vicka. "It didn't seem like we were walking on the ground, and we didn't bother to look for the path. We just ran towards the Madonna, as if something was pulling us through the air."

They described Our Holy Mother as slender and about five feet and three inches tall. The cloud on which she hovered reminds us of the cloud that took Jesus out of His disciples' sight in Acts 1:9.

What's the first thing she says?
Her greeting is always three words: *"Praised be Jesus."*

Do the visionaries describe her the same way?
All the visionaries say her beauty is different than the beauty of an actress or fashion model. The Virgin is "beautiful" because she radiates love and holiness. It reminds us of Lourdes, where Bernadette said Our Lady was "young and beautiful, exceedingly beautiful, the like of whom I had never seen." They say she appears to be only nineteen or twenty—but at the same time ancient. They say they can't really describe her, and emphasize that it's futile to try to compare her to any statues or paintings. I mentioned how Vicka saw her in a gray robe, but they describe it as a bright, luminous gray and really not a color of our world. Her complexion is like that of country women in the region. She's olive in hue with reddish cheeks. There's a small black curl at the left side of her face. She holds her hands up as if in charismatic prayer, invoking her Son, invoking the Holy Spirit.

> *The Virgin comes in many different ways, according to the culture and the occasion. She looks like the people to whom she is appearing. She speaks their dialect.*

At Fatima I thought she was all in white?

The Virgin comes in many different ways, according to the culture and the occasion. She looks like the people to whom she is appearing. She speaks their dialect. She speaks Spanish, French, or Croatian. She can speak English more eloquently than a literature teacher. Even the color of her eyes and the complexion of her skin can be different, depending on where she's appearing. She does this so there's an immediate warmth and affinity with the local people. At Guadalupe her eyes were green, while at Medjugorje they're described as blue—although, again, visionaries grope to describe her. She's not of earthly pigmentation. They see her the same way they see anyone—in three dimensions.

Most impressive is Mary's luminous nature. The descriptions remind us of the brightness of Moses when he spoke to the Lord, or that of Christ during the Transfiguration. Or like the radiant angel who was at Jesus' tomb after His resurrection. The angel was described as "like lightning, and his raiment white as snow" (Mt 28:3, KJV), which brings to mind Lucia's description at Fatima.

Do you believe that Mary is actually coming to us from another realm, bodily? Do you believe she's actually there?

Yes. From another realm. But spirits don't have physical bodies. They assume the characteristics of bodies.

She has left heaven?

I doubt she has left heaven as a physical body leaves a physical location. But she's certainly projecting or extending her spirit in a multi-sensory way. Those of you who know about lasers know they can create three-dimensional images called holograms. An apparition is far beyond a hologram.

What about the flashes of light?

At Medjugorje they usually see three flashes just before the Virgin materializes, flashes they compare to lightning. These lights have also been seen by villagers and pilgrims. According to Fr. Svetozar Kraljevic, a priest from nearby Ljubuski, on the third day of apparitions there was a light that shone on the entire area. Another observer described so much light that it was like heaven joining the earth. I don't know if they're speaking about the same event, but yet another time a villager named Marinko Ivankovic saw the sky open and a bright light, perhaps fifteen feet across, heading to Krizevac, where a luminous globe seemed like it was bursting into thousands of bright little stars—so bright he claims he had to turn away. A priest named Fr. Luka Susac saw huge red and violet clouds hovering over Mount Krizevac. Others have seen great auras quite unlike what we might explain away as stereoscopic images. They extend far beyond the mountain. It's not like the aura you see when you let your eyes go out of focus. It's an extensive luminosity that can move quickly like the cloud in Isaiah 19:1, the cloud that brought the Lord to Egypt where the idols were made to tremble and where the Lord began a purification.

NINE

~

FIRE ON THE HILLSIDE

In Isaiah 19:2-5 God allows a great drought to occur in Egypt, and also a civil war—"city against city, neighbor against neighbor." Are you making a comparison to what's going on in Bosnia-Hercegovina?

I believe that when we sin, when we reject God, we reject His protective power. We reject His Holy Spirit. And the result is chaos. Bloodshed and chaos. In 1985, when the visionary Mirjana was privately interviewed by her spiritual confidant, Fr. Petar Ljubicic, she expressed special concern for the future of Sarajevo. She specifically named Sarajevo and indicated that Our Blessed Mother had given her some kind of a prophecy about it; not as part of the secrets, not as one of her ten secrets, but something peripheral. "Father, I wish you only knew how I feel on some days!" she told Ljubicic. "There are times when I feel that I could go mad. If Mary wasn't here, if she didn't fill me with strength, by now I would surely have gone mad. Could you imagine, knowing precisely everything that will occur in the future, just how enormously stressful that alone is to me? So then, when I see how people behave, especially in Sarajevo, how they use God and His Name in their swearing, how thoughtless they are, how they curse God: These wretched ones have no idea what awaits them in the near future. I take pity on them. I feel so sorry for them and pray and cry and pray—pray so much for them."

That prophecy was in 1985?

Correct. I heard a tape of it right before the siege of Sarajevo—before April of 1992, when the Serbs began bombarding it.

We've seen the prediction materialize right there on our televisions: Serbs, Croats, and Muslims turning wildly on each other in a place where they once lived as neighbors, this city where the international community once joined together for the Olympics. Raping, pillaging. Dismembering their victims. It's been neighbor against neighbor, city against city, with certain sections of the region warring against each other, as in ancient Egypt.

Why didn't the public hear of Mirjana's warning?

There are many aspects of Medjugorje that have not been adequately publicized. That's why I'm spending time with it here and will be revealing more of Mirjana's unreported remarks.

Are there any other predictions that have been realized?

Once, in 1981, when the Virgin was asked about Poland, she replied that *"there will be great conflicts but in the end the just will take over."* That prophecy was realized eight years later when the democratic movement known as Solidarity was finally able to wrest control of Poland from the Communists. As prophesied, the just took over. Poland led to the fall of Communism in Eastern Europe.

There have also been personal prophecies. There have been private prophecies concerning people connected with Medjugorje. Most striking was a prediction Vicka received. It was a prophecy about her health. For years Vicka had suffered headaches and blackouts, even daylong comas. She was in and out of the Rebro Clinic in Zagreb. It was a rather mysterious disease. It seems Vicka is a victim-soul.

Then came a prophecy from Mary, who said Vicka would be healed on September 25, 1988. She gave that date. Vicka wrote it down and sent the date to a priest, Fr. Janko Bubalo, who had been interviewing her. And seven months later, on September 25, the illness suddenly left her.

God often forecasts personal events to His prophets. He grants them glimpses into their own futures. Look at some of the prophecies given to biblical figures like Mary herself, or Zechariah. Zechariah was struck mute—unable to speak—when he doubted a prophecy. The message was given to him by an angel who told Zechariah his wife Elizabeth would conceive a child despite her great age and sterility.

Sure enough, Elizabeth became pregnant, and it wasn't your run-of-the-mill child. She gave birth to John the Baptist, and at the appointed time—on the day John was baptized—Zechariah regained his ability to talk and began praising God (see Luke 1:6-64).

Many things in the current episode can be correlated with the Bible. That's true of any legitimate mysticism. If it doesn't have a biblical precedent, it's more difficult to accept and measure. I'm particularly interested in the visible phenomena we discussed in the last chapter. At Medjugorje the Virgin comes on a cloud, which is similar to prophecies in Luke which say that after the tribulation, "men will see the Son of Man coming in a cloud" (21:27). The same was foretold in Revelation, when John saw a white cloud "and on the cloud sat One like a Son of Man" (14:14). I also note that many pilgrims have spotted strange smoke coming from the summit of Mount Krizevac, curls of smoke as from several large fireplaces. That reminds us of Exodus, when Mount Sinai was "all wrapped in smoke for the Lord came down upon it in fire. The smoke rose from it as though from a furnace" (19:18). On October 28, 1981, a large fire was spotted by the villagers near Medjugorje, a fire that burned very brightly on MountPodbrdo and lasted for about fifteen minutes. It was seen by several hundred people, including nuns and priests, right there where Ivanka and Mirjana first encountered Our Blessed Mother.

At the time, Mount Podbrdo was guarded by Communist agents who were attempting to halt the phenomena, but when a guard went to investigate, he found no signs whatsoever of a fire.

Nothing had burned. Nothing was consumed. There were no charred brambles, no charred ground. It reminds us of the famous bush Moses saw, which looked like it was aflame but "was not consumed" (Ex 3:2).

As for the apparitions, I would relate them to the description in Revelation of "a great sign" in the sky, "a woman clothed with the sun, with the moon under her feet, and on her head a crown of twelve stars" (12:1). At Medjugorje Mary is even described as having twelve stars around her head, and we have alluded to the miracles of the sun, wherein the solar orb pulsates or gyrates or spins off splendiferous colors.

I'm not alone in making this comparison. It's said that Pope John Paul II has also related our times to a moral apocalypse.

What has been the single most spectacular sign?

On August 2, 1981, the sun seemed like it was falling to the earth, ready to crash onto Medjugorje. It acted very much like what was reported dur-

On August 2, 1981, the sun seemed like it was falling to the earth, ready to crash on Medjugorje. Witnesses claimed that as the sun was drawing close to St. James, they could see the Sacred Host in it and a company of angels with trumpets. They also saw a cross.

ing the "great miracle" at Fatima sixty-four years before. Witnesses claimed that as the sun was drawing close to St. James, they could see the Sacred Host in it and a company of angels with trumpets.

They also saw a cross.

Later, many pilgrims—many of you out there reading this—reported identical phenomena.

You've seen the cross atop Mount Krizevac spin or turn into a column of light, a light recalling the one that led the Israelites out of Egypt—an unworldly pink or white light which later gives way to the outline of a luminous woman. One poor man was imprisoned by the Communists for two months for telling everyone in the early days that the cross on Krizevac was spinning.

"The turning of the cross and the white light and the figure of Our Lady... were often seen by hundreds, sometimes thousands of people," said one priest who published a report about it.

There have also been funnel-shaped lights and meteorites. Stars seem to move or turn colors. We recall the significance of a strange star upon the birth of Jesus (see Matthew 2:2).

One evening during the summer of 1981, a bright inscription of the word *MIR* appeared in fiery letters above Mount Krizevac. "The inscription was seen by the pastor and several people from the village," said Father Svetozar. Others have seen violet hearts and luminous doves.

In Croation, *Mir* means "peace." The emphasis is always peace. As one writer pointed out, if you take apart Mirjana's first name, you have *mir* and *jana*, which means John and connects with the first day of apparitions, which was the feast day of John the Baptist.

Peace, peace, and more peace. Peace of mind and heart. The Virgin has said that Satan's first maneuver is to cause anxiety and friction in families, which grow to societal conflict and war.

Prayer, fasting, and penance are needed to prevent disasters, she stresses. Prayer from deep within. Prayer to Christ.

"Be reconciled!" the Madonna implored in various messages. *"Only peace. Make your peace with God and among yourselves. For that, it is necessary to believe, to pray, to fast, and to go to Confession.*

"You know that I love you and am coming here out of love, so I can show you the path of peace and salvation for your souls. There is only one mediator between God and man, and it is Jesus Christ. My Son struggles for each of you. The devil tries to impose his power on you, but you must remain strong and persevere in your faith. God does not have a hard heart. Look around you and see what men do, then you will no longer say that God has a hard heart. You will see how greatly sin has dominated this earth. How many people come to church, to the house of God, with respect, a strong faith, and love of God? Very few! Here you have a time of grace and conversion. It is necessary to use it well. Let prayer be life for you. The most important thing in the spiritual life is to ask for the gift of the Holy Spirit. Pray, pray, pray. Ask the Holy Spirit to renew your souls, to renew the entire world. Raise your hands, yearn for Jesus because in His Resurrection He wants to fill you with graces. Through prayer you can prevent wars from happening; with prayer you can stop wars. With prayer you can change the laws of nature.

"I am often at Krizevac, at the foot of the cross, to pray there. Now I pray to my Son to forgive the world its sins. The cross was in God's plan when you built it. These days especially, go up on the mountain and pray at the foot of the cross.

"I need your prayers. Open your hearts to me. I desire to bless them fully. I

> *"You know that I love you and am coming here out of love, so I can show you the path of peace and salvation for your souls. There is only one mediator between God and man, and it is Jesus Christ. My Son struggles for each of you.... Ask the Holy Spirit to renew your souls, to renew the entire world. Raise your hands, yearn for Jesus because in His Resurrection He wants to fill you with graces.*

wish to engrave in every heart the sign of love. I call you always to bring harmony and peace. Peace, peace, peace! Be reconciled. Only peace. The world must find salvation while there is time. I invite you. I need you. I chose you. You are important. Without you I am not able to help the world.

"Today I call you to approach prayer actively. In prayer you shall find the way out of every situation that has no exit. Let prayer be life for you. I want you to comprehend that God has chosen each one of you, in order to use you in a great plan for the salvation of mankind. You are not able to comprehend how great your role is in God's design. I have come to call the world to conversion for the last time. After that, I will not appear any more on this earth. The peace of the world is in danger. This is the reason for my presence among you for such a long time, to lead you on the path to Jesus.

"Without unceasing prayer you cannot experience the beauty and greatness of the grace which God is offering you. May prayer reign in the whole world. The devil tries to impose his power on you, but you must remain strong and persevere in your faith.

"Hasten your conversion. Do not wait for the sign which has been announced for those who do not believe. It will be too late.

"The fire, seen by the faithful, was of a supernatural character. It is one of the signs, a forerunner of the Great Sign. Pray especially on Sunday so that the Great Sign, the gift of God, will come. Pray with fervor and a constancy so that God may have mercy on His great children. The sign will come when you are converted.

"Pray in order that you may be able to comprehend all that I am giving here. Do not be afraid. I am close to you and I watch over you. I want you to understand that I am your mother, that I want to help you and call you to prayer. Only by prayer can you accept my messages and practice them in your life. Read Sacred Scripture, live it, and pray to understand the signs of the time.

"This is a special time. Therefore, I am with you to draw you close to my heart and the Heart of my Son, Jesus.

"Dear little children, I want you to be children of the light and not of the darkness."

TEN

~

HER LAST APPEARANCE

Signs. Secrets. Isn't that apocalyptical?

If by "apocalyptical" you mean full of doom and gloom, the end of the world, then no, our episode is not apocalyptical. On the other hand, if you use "apocalyptical" as defined in the dictionary—as an "uncovering" or "revealing"—then events like Medjugorje are indeed apocalyptical. They reveal that we're in a special time, a time of grace as well as a time of special struggle. The seers were told that the current period was given to the devil as a special test of mankind, and when Satan comes, when he exercises extended power, and when, succumbing to his temptations, a society wanders from God, then heaven offers an equal increment in grace and does so in part with miracles.

They are to feed the sheep, to show that God exists in a way that we usually don't appreciate.

The Lord is watching. He is all around us. He is the only source of true peace and the fullness of life itself.

Isn't belief in Him supposed to be an act of faith without miracles?

Of course. But there are times when faith is all but extinguished. That's when the Holy Spirit is sent.

How would you define the "special struggle" of our time?

We struggle against our flesh. We struggle against our failings. We struggle against powers and principalities. Although many don't want to recognize it, we struggle against forces aligned with an actual malefic entity. The Blessed Mother has come to make sure we realize that Satan is no myth, that he exists, that he is more prevalent than a secular society—a "feel good" society—wishes to acknowledge, and that he seeks only to destroy. *"You are ready to commit sin, and to put yourselves in the hands of Satan without reflecting,"* said Our Holy Mother on May 25, 1987.

There is crime. There's abortion. Each year at least thirty-seven million infants are destroyed, which is more than a third the number of people who lived on the planet at the time of Jesus 2,000 years ago. There are horrible atrocities in places like Rwanda and Nigeria. There is also great evil perpetrated by the media—through movies, music, television.

Satan is responsible for far more than modernists think. He's the source, Mary has said, of emotional disorder. He's perverted and perverting, cunning, a shadowy intelligence who works best when left in the dark. *"This is the time of the devil,"* says Our Blessed Mother. *"Darkness reigns over the whole world. Many people now live without faith. Some don't even want to hear about Jesus, but they still want peace and satisfaction. Children, here is the reason why I need your prayer. Prayer is the only way to save the human race."*

In 1985, during the secluded interview, when she was asked to assess the world situation, Mirjana replied, "There was never an age such as this one, never before was God honored and respected less than now, never before have so few prayed to Him. Everything seems more important than God. This is the reason [Our Blessed Mother] cries so much. The number of unbelievers is becoming greater and greater. As they endeavor for a better life, to such people, God Himself is superfluous and dispensable. This is why I feel deeply sorry for them and for the world. They have no idea what awaits them. If they could only take a tiny peek at these secrets, if they could see [here Mirjana pauses]... they would convert in time. Still, Our Lady gave us God's secrets. They may still convert. Certainly God always forgives those who genuinely convert."

It is necessary, said Mirjana, "to pray a great deal until the first secret is revealed. But in addition to that, it is necessary to make sacrifices as much as possible, to help others as much as it is within our abilities, to fast especially now, before the first secret. [Our Blessed Mother] stated that we are *obliged* to prepare ourselves."

It was Fr. Vlasic's impression that "with revelation of the secrets entrusted to them by Our Lady, life in the world will be changed, that people will believe as in ancient times." We should meditate on that phrase—"as in ancient times." It's a key to how we'll be purified.

How many secrets have been given?

Two of the visionaries have ten, the rest nine.

Which visionaries have all ten?

I've mentioned Mirjana. As of this writing the other is Ivanka. They were also the first to encounter the apparition. They still see Mary on special occasions but after they received the tenth secret their daily apparitions came to a halt.

Do they all have the same secrets?

No, except for the first three secrets, which were given to them together. After that, it's a mixed bag. We can't be certain how many they share because they've never spoken about the secrets with each other. While some visionaries have personal secrets, none of Mirjana's secrets are for her personally but rather for the world, for mankind in general, for Medjugorje, and for some other regions. The first three involve events that will be sent as warnings, along with the visible sign or wonder. This is most intriguing to people, the fact that some kind of supernatural sign will be presented. A sign can be anything from a weeping statue to something in the sky. "The sign will only appear after the first two secrets," explained Mirjana. "After each of the first two secrets, the people will realize that [the Blessed Virgin Mary] was indeed appearing here. The sign will just serve as an additional confirmation. It will be a reminder to the world. It will be a gift to the people who pray."

But before any sign, mankind will experience warnings?

Yes, events sent as warnings. If I may quote her again, Mirjana said that the first two secrets "are not all that severe and harsh. What I mean is, they are severe, but not as much as the remaining ones." When Fr. Ljubicic asked if the first secrets would be a catastrophe, Mirjana replied, "No, it will not be anything as huge as that. That will come later." And yet during another interview on October 26, 1985, she described her consternation upon actually being shown a supernatural picture or "slide" of the first secret. Even a regional event—any disaster—can be overwhelming if seen up close. When the priest asked if the first secrets would be visible or more

> *After each of the first two secrets, the people will realize that [the Blessed Virgin Mary] was indeed appearing here. The sign will just serve as an additional confirmation. It will be a reminder to the world. It will be a gift to the people who pray.*

of a spiritual nature, Mirjana replied, "Distinct, distinct. It will be visible. It is necessary in order to shake up the world a little. It will make the world pause and think. It will be something that will give the world something to think about seriously, allow the world to see that she was indeed here, to see and realize that there is a God, that He exists." Asked how long the first secret will last, Mirjana said simply, "It will last for a little while."

Mirjana said there would be those who explain away the first two secrets as natural phenomena. What will make them seem miraculous to those following the situation, she claims, is that they will be announced three days in advance by Fr. Ljubicic if he so chooses. He will be told of the occurrence a week before that. He will decide who to tell. I assume he'll inform the bishop and those at Medjugorje, among others.

But it's still unclear: The first secret is a warning, but is it a natural or supernatural event?

Who knows? I would say it sounds like a natural event and yet one that will confirm Medjugorje because, if matters go according to what we're told, it will be prophesied there. That seems like the supernatural confirmation. Mirjana said there will be no signs leading up to it. "You can see that there are some rather peculiar things going on in the world," she told her priest-friend. "People are unhappy, dissatisfied. Avarice reigns everywhere. Hardly anyone admits that they ever have enough of anything. Yet, none of this gives any clues about the secret. This secret stands on its own. The secret will abundantly speak for itself on its own and it requires no prior clues or signals."

I believe that the first secret may be a regional event of some kind, a disaster on a regional scale. When asked who would see the event, Mirjana said, "All those who will be here or in the place where the secret will unfold." When asked if she was still pro-hibited from giving a location, she said, "I am not allowed [to say], because that is in direct connection with the secret." When asked if it would take place in Medjugorje, she replied, "That is a 'maybe.'" When Ljubicic pressed her further, asking if people would go to the place where the event occurs, Mirjana said, "Father, surely no one wishes to watch disasters, distress, and misfortune. I don't think this kind of thing attracts people at all. Why would people go to see something of that sort? It is one thing to go and see a sign, quite another to go and see suffering or a disaster. Who would, for example, go to Italy to see a dam collapse? Who has that kind of a

> *Time will tell. The Church will discern. At Fatima there were three secrets and the first two took more than thirty years to become discernible. To this day the third secret may not yet have completely unfolded.... We shouldn't become obsessed with secrets. We should focus on the other messages.*

desire? I don't think anyone does—and that is how it will be with this secret. Whatever is in the secret, it will, of course, be something that everyone everywhere will immediately hear about."

That does indeed sound like a regional disaster. How does it stack up against other prophecies?

There were prophecies from a reputed apparition in Garabandal, Spain, which asserted that there will come from God three major events: a warning, a great miracle, and a great chastisement which can be lessened by prayer. This is of course in general agreement with the structure of the Medjugorje secrets, but at Medjugorje there's not a single, spectacular, world-stopping warning. There is a *series* of warnings. And where the warning from Garabandal is supposed to be something worldwide—seen in the air everywhere and "immediately transmitted into the interior of our souls" (in the words of one seer)—the first warning from Medjugorje sounds more like something that will occur regionally and be communicated by the media. Mirjana says it will be "something that [people] will hear [about] very far."

As a journalist you truly believe in those secrets?

If the secrets are bogus, so are the apparitions. Or at the least, there is trickery. The devil has slipped in a few counterfeits. Time will tell. The Church will discern. At Fatima there were three secrets and the first two took more than thirty years to become discernible. To this day the third secret may not yet have completely unfolded. That's eighty years now. As for La Salette, that prophecy has been like a time-release capsule. Its predictions continue to materialize in our own time, more than a century later.

Let me make clear that we shouldn't become obsessed with secrets. We should focus on the other messages. I'm spending a lot of time discussing the secrets here because I'm probably asked more about them and other such prophecies than anything else, and because a lack of discussion about them has only fueled the wilder levels of speculation. Hopefully, a discussion and airing out here will settle some of the issues, and ease some of the obsessions. Many assume we're talking about the end of the world, when in fact a study of what little we do know about the secrets may yield a less final but no less interesting scenario. And when we begin to fathom their relevance to world events, we begin to better focus our prayers on avoiding negative future circumstances. The secrets are pertinent to every person because we're told they concern the entire world. Our Blessed Mother is trying to marshal our supplications.

How did you form your belief in places like Fatima and Medjugorje?

For what it's worth, I formed it in my heart, in my spirit. It wasn't "objective." I'm not going to feign objectivity, which we were trained to do in the newspaper business. It's not true. It's not sincere. I don't believe there's any such thing as pure objectivity. While I had a certain wariness at first, I felt something extraordinary at Medjugorje; I was immensely drawn and connected to it. That feeling is not mechanical, nor is it intellectual, and once my initial questions were answered, I was extremely impressed. I've never doubted since that something extraordinary is going on. Recently I was with a Medjugorje seer and his wife in Massachusetts, just hanging out with them in a hospitality room during a retreat, and afterwards, I felt something. So did my wife, who was also there. It had been just the four of us and so you saw things up close. The same thing happened in one-on-one interviews. And when I watched a homemade video about Medjugorje, or read about it, a powerful feeling overcame me. The place resonated of the Holy Spirit.

When I first arrived at Medjugorje and saw all the people so revved up... I began to fear that it was a case of collective hysteria.... But then I went to Mass and prayed. I said Rosaries. I saw phenomena myself, but more than anything I felt the Holy Spirit.... There was an indescribable peace, an authenticity in its very texture.

You had initial doubts?

When I first arrived at Medjugorje and saw all the people so revved up—talking about so many miracles, staring at the sun, gawking at the mountain—I began to fear that it was a case of collective hysteria. For a while that first morning the old journalist in me took over, the cynicism. I wanted to leave. I decided it was probably just a frenzy, and I couldn't believe I'd traveled that far and now had to spend several more days in this remote place of barren hills.

But then I went to Mass and prayed. I said Rosaries. I saw phenomena myself, but more than anything I felt the Holy Spirit. I felt Mary, to whom I'd had a special devotion since my conversion, since my days as an author in New York. I felt her like never before. There was an indescribable peace, an authenticity in its very texture. I felt I was halfway between heaven and earth. Suddenly I didn't want to leave. The tranquility was like nothing in my previous experience.

So it was an inner discernment?

It was a matter of external observation and inner discernment. The fruits are astounding. An estimated seven to twenty million people have visited Medjugorje and the vast majority find it a life-changing pilgrimage. I bet a third to a half of the pilgrims go back to Medjugorje, and it's common to meet people who have been there four or five times. I know at least four people who, leading pilgrimages, have been there more than *forty* times. Millions more have never visited but follow it very closely.

Call it conversion. Call it whatever you want. They're on fire for Jesus and the Blessed Mother. It's similar to what I've witnessed during what charismatica call "baptism in the Holy Spirit." It's similar to the sudden conversions that take place when individuals are "born again."

But Medjugorje is more powerful than anything I've witnessed elsewhere. It's overflowing with grace. It's charged with the Holy Spirit. According to Sr. Emmanuel Maillard, a nun there since 1989, the parish maintains a list of more than forty thousand priests who have visited. She also presents a partial list of ninety cardinals and bishops; one theologian writes that actually two hundred bishops have visited. "To say nothing is happening there is to deny the living, prayerful witness of hundreds of thousands who have gone there," said Bishop Michael Pfeifer of San Angelo, Texas. Even the renowned Pentecostal leader David du Plessis, a non-Catholic, discerned a great presence of the Paraclete.

I don't base my faith on Medjugorje. My eschatology and view of reality are based on the New Testament. If a shocking finding were to be announced next week, a finding which demonstrates that despite the many positive indicators, despite the overwhelming endorsements, despite the conversions, Medjugorje is false—if Medjugorje suddenly fell apart as an elaborate or demonic deception—yes, it would surprise me. It would deeply hurt, it would shake me up—but it wouldn't affect my Catholic belief system.

Nor would it discredit the entire supernatural episode. The episode extends way beyond Bosnia-Hercegovina. And one must be cautious because false visions and false prophecy are part of any major episode.

This may sound like a strange question, but is Medjugorje connected to the charismatic movement?

Like Protestants, a number of charismatics are wary of Marian devotion. This is in part because their training may have come from Protestants, who spearheaded much of the beautiful revival. Charismatics worry—sometimes with ample reason—about straying from Christ and about demonic deception. But there is indeed a strong connection between the charismatic movement and Mariology. I've already mentioned the prophecies from charismatics in Rome; and Fr. Jozo, who was the pastor at St. James when the apparitions began, is a charismatic. Pilgrims go to see him as part of the Medjugorje experience, and the highlight is his praying with them by the "laying on of hands," which causes a good many to experience a strong "slaying" or "resting" in the Spirit.

They spin or lean and then softly land on their backs, in a semi-conscious and blissful state for long minutes.

I've never seen anyone exercise that charism more powerfully than Fr. Jozo, who, according to René Laurentin, experienced the Virgin several times. His encounters occurred in the chapel and also while Fr. Jozo was in jail, imprisoned by Communists for supporting the visionaries. There is a force field around him. Folks fall down before he even touches them. Many of those who visit Medjugorje end up speaking in tongues or developing other charismatic gifts, and indeed some of the first visitors included well-known charismatics like Sr. Briege McKenna and Fr. Michael Scanlan. During one of my own visits a flapping white light was seen between the spires of St. James. It reminded me of the "dove" that alighted upon Jesus during His baptism (see Matthew 3:16). As at charismatic services, many are delivered from demons at Medjugorje, and as is abundantly evident with Mirjana, there is also the element of prophecy, which is central to the charismatic movement.

Those who ignore it, who don't really believe in prophecy, or who view it as too "sensational," ignore the part of Scripture which tells us that "he who speaks in a tongue edifies himself, but he who prophesies edifies the Church. I wish you all spoke with tongues, but even more that you prophesied" (1 Cor 14:4). We're also told in the Book of Revelation (19:10, KJV) that the "testimony of Jesus is the spirit of Prophecy."

When the Virgin comes, she prays with hands facing upward, like a charismatic. She prays to the Holy Spirit. *"The most important thing in the spiritual life is to ask for the gift of the Holy Spirit,"* says Mary. *"When the Holy Spirit comes, the peace will be established."* She says all we need is the Holy Spirit because when we have Him we have everything.

That's the central prayer? That's what Medjugorje has to say about praying?
Our Blessed Mother emphasizes direct conversation with God. We must

Our Blessed Mother emphasizes direct conversation with God. We must speak to Him as Our Father. We must go to Him and talk like children, expressing our needs and problems.... Asking Him in faith to do what it is that needs to be done. When we go to Him directly,... we're connected to the ultimate power.

speak to Him as Our Father. We must go to Him and talk like children, expressing our needs and problems. Making our requests. Asking Him in faith to do what it is that needs to be done. When we go to Him directly, in the name of Jesus, with the prayer support of Our Blessed Mother, we're connected to the ultimate power.

"Let me put it this way," said Mirjana. "Naturally, it is necessary to pray the Rosary, to say Our Fathers and other prayers, but it is very important to much more frequently engage in simple conversations with God. [One must] present Him with things that come from the depth of one's soul. It is not enough to just present Him the 'established' "Our Father Who art in heaven..." After praying in this manner it is also essential that we open our souls to Him. It is good to bare one's soul to God and tell Him what hurts you. You see, it should be a simple conversation, just as the one you and I are having now. Certainly, this is what I usually do. I like that a great deal and I feel that God responds."

God wants us to act like His children. When we do we feel the joy of His incomparable love.

So Mary is praying for us?

That's what we ask of her in the Hail Mary: pray for us sinners. When I spoke at a retreat with Mirjana in California, she told those gathered how Mary had defined her own role in the simplest way: *"I ask my Son for you."* As if to hint at something, Mirjana says that "when the time comes we'll see the respect and reverence her own Son has for her."

There are many reputed miracles at Medjugorje—healings, rosaries turning gold, the so-called sun miracles. When the sun is acting in a strange way, why isn't that seen by millions around the world? Why isn't it seen everywhere? Doesn't that prove that it's just an illusion or a localized natural phenomenon?

Obviously the sun is not really moving around in the sky or it would make for some huge headlines. Astronomers and meteorologists would be going haywire. But something is happening at places like Medjugorje, something that alters the perceptual landscape.

God can create whatever effects He likes. He can cause an entire vicinity or group of people to be elevated an inch above normal reality. He can send the Spirit upon a region. This happened in Israel and at Fatima, where movements of the sun were seen by observers in a thirty-two-mile radius but especially within six miles.

When I've visited Medjugorje I myself have seen the sun react in a way I'd never seen before, surrounded by large auras of red, purple, and orange. It was shooting out striations of various color. The auras were twice as large as the sun itself and couldn't have been natural phenomena such as sun pillars, sun dogs, or mother-of-pearl clouds—optical effects caused by ice crystals in the atmosphere. Many pilgrims, myself included, have seen the sun expand to half again its normal size and were able to stare at the sun for upwards of ten minutes—when, according to one astronomer I consulted, Dr. Joseph Patterson of Columbia University, ten *seconds* should be enough to begin a burn into the retina.

In the course of four trips to Medjugorje I stared at the sun on a dozen occasions. It moved around as it was described as having done during the great "miracle of the sun" at Fatima. Not once can I remember experiencing sun spots. Dr. Patterson said he could think of no normal explanation for the sun pulsating the way I described, nor could he think of anything that would account for an off-white disc-like object—reminding some observers of a Communion host—that seems to move in front of the solar orb.

That's not to say he and the other scientists buy into the supernatural hypothesis. When I further consulted James Cornell, spokesman for Harvard University's astronomical observatory, he proclaimed that those who see such things are simply victims of "mass hallucination."

It's an effect of the atmosphere, he said, or something that's "in their brains."

"You can get pulsations of the sun from atmospheric effects," he told me. "In Yugoslavia you have thermals—warm air—over the Adriatic Sea and mountains near the sea. Obviously you do get some interesting atmospheric effects."

Cornell pointed out that the sun's rays can be distorted by a temperature inversion or an erupting volcano.

But there seems to be no astrophysical explanation for humans witnessing the sun pulse on a daily basis—there are not volcanos every year—and if it was only an atmospheric effect, it would have been noted by the people who live there. Such large effects happen nowhere else on such a regular basis. Nor do I believe it's a stereoscopic effect. It isn't the result of the eyes blurring. Nor does it fit descriptions of what they call noctilucent clouds, or the crepuscular rays that come after a sunset.

Spectacular natural displays do happen in the sky, but not, as far as I can tell, day in and day out, during the evening as well as in the morning or afternoon. When I look at the sun in upstate New York around the same time, in early evening, for only a few seconds, I get sun spots. That doesn't happen at Medjugorje.

But more relevant is the sense of peace—peace and well-being—that comes with the experience. It's just tremendous. And when the sun pulses, coincidentally, it's often at the moment of the apparitions.

Let's remain scientific just for another moment. You've mentioned tests of eye movement. What other tests have been performed on the visionaries?

The seers have undergone a number of psychological evaluations, and even the Communists, in the early days, found them sane and normal. Electroencephalographs, which are used to monitor brainwave activity, have eliminated the possibility that the visionaries are asleep or epileptic during the apparitions. "We saw no signs of hallucination, pretense, or invention," concluded Professor Henri Joyeux, a surgeon and professor from the University of Montpellier who led a team of French researchers. Intensive psychiatric tests showed no neurosis, no pathological ecstasy, no catalepsy or hysteria. The apparitions are not dreams. They're not illusions. In 1983 a Yugoslavian psychiatrist named Dr. Ludvik Stopar hypnotized Marija and reported that what she said under hypnosis was identical to what she claimed in a waking state. After neuropsychiatric examinations he declared all the visionaries "absolutely normal adolescents with no psychopathological symptoms." A dozen Italian physicians found the situation free of drugs, hypnosis, or any form of manipulation.

> *When an engineer traced the nerve impulses from the visionaries' eyes and ears to the cortex of their brains, he found that their consciousness was elsewhere. It was like a phone ringing in an empty apartment.*

The visionaries seem to be in another space and time while they're seeing Mary. When Vicka was pricked by a needle, she wasn't aware of it until afterwards, when someone pointed out to her that there was a spot of blood on her clothes. Researchers also tried to startle Ivan using a sudden sound of ninety decibels, which is just about as loud as the sound of a circular saw. He showed no reaction. When an engineer traced the nerve impulses from the visionaries' eyes and ears to the cortex of their brains, he found that their consciousness was elsewhere. It was like a phone ringing in an empty apartment. The researchers went so far as to use a sophisticated polygraph and also to touch the visionaries' eyes with a nylon thread during their ecstasies. The visionaries did not so much as flinch when the thread was placed on their corneas. An ophthalmologist excluded the possibility of hallucination.

There was even a test with a BT 400 electroscope that seemed to measure an unusually high level of energy. The electroscope, which measures electrical charge and usually picks up a background level of zero to fifteen millirads per hour, reportedly recorded twenty thousand in the church and one hundred thousand millirads during prayer in the chapel of the apparitions.

Since that level of radiation would normally kill those exposed to it, certain observers postulated that instead of normal radiation it was a *spiritual* energy which exerted certain characteristics of radiation upon our limited instruments—thousands of times the energy that would have been registered at, say, a crowded hockey arena.

But other tests registered no such force, and really, these phenomena can't be captured by scientific equipment. We'll never prove them through physics, chemistry, psychiatry, or biology. You can't put an apparition under a microscope.

You can't use material tools to gauge something that by definition is non-material. You can't "prove" Mary is there.

All the French team could conclude was that the situation is "scientifically inexplicable."

Why doesn't the Church end all the debate and just approve it?

The Vatican appears to be letting Medjugorje run its natural course. These matters take time. In most cases a final ruling is not issued until the apparitions cease, and obviously Medjugorje is still an ongoing situation. While La Salette was approved by the Church in 1851—five years after the apparition there—and Lourdes was declared worthy of the assent of the faithful a mere three years after the apparitions, it took Fatima thirteen years to gain formal approval. In an official approval the local bishop deems the messages to be in conformity with Sacred Scripture and Church tradition, states that the apparitions are of a "supernatural nature," and sanctions devotions and pilgrimages for the site of miracles. Historically, a key part of the sanction has been the statement that an apparition is "worthy of the assent of the faithful," but that language hasn't been used recently. A site gains yet more credibility when, as with Lourdes, Fatima, and Guadalupe, a pope pays a visit. That really legitimizes it. But the highest level of approval is when one of the visionaries is canonized as a saint—as at Lourdes, for example, and the chapel on Rue du Bac in Paris, where devotion to the Miraculous Medal began.

It's much too soon to know what will happen in Medjugorje. Mother Teresa invokes the Queen of Peace, and Bishop Francesco Colasuono, apostolic pro-nuncio in Yugoslavia, has been quoted as saying that "Medjugorje represents the event of the century."

And yet it may take years for it to win formal approval, if it ever does. The war in Bosnia-Hercegovina has stymied efforts at ecclesiastical investigation, as has the series of controversies with the local bishop. Recently the pope has sent out additional indications that he wants to visit there, and in February 1995, he saw retired Bishop Zanic, who has been so antagonistic to the apparitions, at a meeting with a number of Croatian bishops. Zanic asked, "Holy Father, when are you coming to Sarajevo?" and it's reported that the pope replied, "Oh, I thought you were going to ask me: 'When are you coming to Medjugorje?'"

But let me hasten to repeat here that Medjugorje is not officially approved. While the Vatican took the matter away from the local bishop when it appeared he was going to move to condemn Medjugorje, the apparitions are still in the hands of those bishops who form the national investigating commission and, from what I hear, certain of them share a skepticism or antagonism for Medjugorje. For whatever reasons, they incline to side with Bishop Peric.

If the national commission currently looking into Medjugorje were to rule negatively, I'm not sure if the Vatican would overrule again. It might accept the judgment, which of course would cause tremendous consternation for the millions in dozens of countries who believe in it, a real dark night of the soul. But if the Vatican were to go along with such a judgment, we would have to obey the ruling. We would have to be obedient. Obedience is a test of spirituality and is important.

This book is meant, in part, as a participation in the current discussion. As a journalist, I'm certainly free to express a viewpoint, whatever may happen. And I believe Medjugorje is real.

But I also believe that the commission will probably seek neutral ground and maintain its current position, the one expressed in 1991, that there is no proof of the supernatural, that authentic revelation can not yet be affirmed at Medjugorje. That's neither approval nor condemnation.

There is always a chance that an apparition like Medjugorje might be outright disapproved by the commission. A formal disapproval is when Catholics are forbidden from taking pilgrimages to a site and the apparition is deemed contrary to Catholic faith and morals. Right or wrong, such a disapproval would remind many of the times when mystics such as Padre Pio and Sr. Faustina Kowalska were silenced. There would be suffering. There would be darkness. It would be a test of obedience and faith.

Medjugorje would disappear unless a future pope lifted the prohibitions.

If Medjugorje does not meet with formal approval during the reign of Pope John Paul II, then I'm not sure what will happen. How it is handled by the next pope could well indicate many things about the direction of the Church.

Is it true that Scott O'Grady, the American pilot shot down over Bosnia, had some form of spiritual contact?

On June 13, 1995, a Fatima anniversary day, Captain O'Grady, a devout Catholic, appeared on NBC's *Dateline*. He described how, after miraculously surviving an attack by a Bosnian Serb missile, he encountered equal miracles in his ability to survive without the Serbs' finding him after he parachuted from his destroyed F-16. It was like some mysterious force made him invisible to the enemy. He was hiding about twenty miles south of Bihac, well behind Serbian lines. He told Jane Pauley that his faith in God sustained him, along with everyone's prayers. And he saw something, a phenomenon of some sort, that he connected with Medjugorje but could not verbalize. "A friend of my mom's, she told me about Medjugorje, which is a place in Bosnia where Mother Mary has been seen by people," he said. "I considered myself religious before, but not, you know, not to where I believe any of that. But she was right, because I don't know what I saw, but I saw something." During another interview he said that when he prayed to Our Lady of Medjugorje he could "see" her, but not as a form or image that he can explain. It was more a feeling—and a sense of good battling evil. On his third day in Bosnia, he says, he turned in prayer to Our Lady. "Before long I felt a definite presence," he wrote about his ordeal. "It grew more and more vivid, until I could see it, shimmering in my mind's eye. It's hard to put into words, but I saw the vision through feeling it, and the feeling was very warm and good."

Other well-known personages have had experiences with the Virgin of Medjugorje. Martin Sheen narrated a video about the place and starred in a movie about Fr. Jozo, and once, in Chicago, I had a little chat with the owner of a huge pizza chain, who told me the highlights of his life included his own visit to Medjugorje.

How long do you think the apparitions there will last?

Vicka has indicated that the Madonna may appear in some way, perhaps in less frequent fashion but in some way, during the manifestation of the first three secrets. "She said she would continue to appear to us," said Vicka, "even when she leaves her sign." Others have indicated that her apparitions will end before the secrets.

Obviously, we don't know when that will be. We can only speculate. We don't know what's in the secrets.

But the pope takes it seriously?

The pope takes it seriously. He mentions Medjugorje in the same breath as Fatima. And the Virgin hints at Medjugorje's significance when she says that at least for the current era, the apparitions at Medjugorje, the sightings there in the hinterlands of Bosnia-Hercegovina, the sightings that have gone on far longer and more powerfully than any other serial apparition, will be her finale.

According to Vicka, "The Virgin said this was her last appearance."

ELEVEN

~

OTHER VOICES

So Medjugorje was the start of the explosion?

There have been apparitions every century. There probably have been apparitions every year since 1830.

But the line on the chart goes through the roof after Medjugorje. The proliferation began right there in the former Yugoslavia. Soon others, including a Muslim, caught a glimpse of the Virgin or claimed to hear her voice interiorly. Her sweet voice. So many heard her voice! One of the first locutionists was a ten-year-old girl named Jelena Vasilj, whose home was on the road from St. James to Mount Krizevac and whose messages, if austere, were so powerful that the local clergy began filing them with the messages from the original six visionaries.

Jelena's phenomenon began on December 15, 1982, when a voice spoke to her at school, while she was sitting in a classroom. Soon it pulled the girl into deeper prayer. It taught her spiritual discipline. It was the inner voice of Mary, and it asked Jelena to fast and pray more. *"Be converted!"* said the Virgin. *"It will be too late when the Sign comes. Beforehand, several warnings will be given to the world. Have people hurry to be converted. I need your prayers and penance."*

It was impressive that a ten-year-old would relate words so similar to the other seers' phraseology (*Be converted... several warnings... prayers and penance*), and soon another youngster from the area, Marijana Vasilj, joined Jelena in receiving locutionary messages.

But Jelena's were those that would later find themselves in wide circulation. They were beautiful, striking words, in some instances more poignant than those coming from actual apparitions. The messages continued through the 1980s and 1990s, with Our Blessed Mother asking Jelena and members of her prayer group to avoid television, *"particularly evil programs,"* and to withdraw from excessive sports and the unreasonable enjoyment of food, drink, and tobacco. *"Abandon yourselves to God without any*

"Be converted!" *said the Virgin.* "It will be too late when the Sign comes. Beforehand, several warnings will be given to the world. Have people hurry to be converted. I need your prayers and penance."

restrictions," said the Virgin. *"Definitely eliminate all anguish. Whoever abandons himself to God does not have room in his heart for anguish. Difficulties will persist, but they will serve for spiritual growth and will render glory to God.*

"Love your enemies. Banish from your heart hatred, bitterness, and preconceived judgments. Pray for your enemies and call the divine blessing over them. Fast twice a week on bread and water. Devote at least three hours a day to prayer, a minimum of half an hour in the morning and half an hour in the evening. Holy Mass and the prayer of the Rosary are included in this time of prayer. Set aside moments of prayer in the course of the day, and each time that circumstances permit it, receive Holy Communion. Pray with great meditation. Do not look at your watch all the time, but allow yourself to be led by the grace of God. Do not concern yourself too much with the things of this world, but entrust all that in prayer to Our Heavenly Father. If one is too preoccupied he will not be able to pray well because internal serenity is lacking. God will con-tribute His share to a successful end to the things here below if one strives to do his utmost in working on his own. Those who attend school or go to work must pray half an hour in the morning and in the evening and if possible participate in the Eucharist. It is necessary to extend the spirit of prayer to daily work.

"Be prudent because the devil tempts all those who have made a resolution to consecrate themselves to God—most particularly those people.

"My children, pray! I cannot tell you anything other than pray. Know that in your life there is nothing more important than prayer. My children, pray and fast. I wish to strengthen you, but prayer alone is your strength.

"If you want to be stronger against evil, have an active conscience. For that, pray very much in the morning and read a passage from the Gospel. Plant the divine Word in your heart and live it during the day. In this special way you will be very strong in trials. Always have the love of God in you, because without this love, you are not able to convert yourselves completely. Let the rosary be

in your hands in memory of Jesus.

"I have come to tell the world that God is truth. He exists. True happiness and the fullness of life are in Him. I have come here as Queen of Peace to tell the world that peace is necessary for the salvation of the world. In God, one finds true joy from which true peace is derived."

That was some of what the Virgin said. They weren't just beautiful messages, but powerful, with an economy of language, an eloquence, that sounded like the same voice as that of the formal apparitions. Although they were locutions, which must be treated with special caution, and are not at the same level as the messages of the six seers, they seemed to bear the ring of authenticity. Or should I say, they had the Spirit's resonance. They were much more akin to the apparitions than most of the locutions that soon flowed from elsewhere.

From there the locutions spread?

That was the beginning of the great eruption. Medjugorje triggered an avalanche. No one could ever tabulate how many people have since claimed to experience locutions. I gave you figures on how many were reported earlier in the century, but that was just the beginning. That was just a prelude to Medjugorje, the tip of the iceberg. Pilgrims would visit Medjugorje and upon return to the United States begin to log their own heavenly messages. I saw this happen in Texas, California, Arizona, and—well, every state, except maybe Alaska. I never got up there.

Prayer groups based upon Medjugorje sprung up in every part of the nation. There was also the phenomenon of "peace centers," organizations of lay ministers formed to spread the messages of Medjugorje. The first newsletters were out at least as early as 1985. Within ten years, by 1995, one prominent Catholic newspaper listed 184 such peace centers in North America. Others are not listed but add to the number. These groups, which often rent office space and issue newsletters or faxed messages, are constantly reporting locutionists in their own prayer circles and trying to figure them out. Trying to discern them. Could so many be hearing Mary? It got to be a little hectic, a little overwhelming. And sometimes more than a little. I have visited many of these centers, and I saw the struggle of these good people for discernment.

Did any of the locutions impress you?

In the early stage a number were interesting. Later, many fizzled and fell away. That was one thing, locutions. Even priests were turning into locutionists. Even clergy heard voices. But there was also the remarkable proliferation of apparitions—remarkable because apparitions are a giant step up in mysticism.

Although not nearly as common as locutionists, in the 1980s there were suddenly more visionaries than at any time since the last great episode, which occurred in the 1200s and 1300s. Back then, during that episode, many seers proclaimed the coming of the Anti-Christ and the end of the world, and for those afflicted, it was the end of the world: the Bubonic Plague was in the process of striking the continent in the 1300s and would claim forty million lives before it was over—a third of Europe!

There were also grave problems in the Church, and these problems seemed to propel the prophecies about the Anti-Christ. In the thirteenth century there were so many prophets that St. Bonaventure said he was basically fed up (or as one scholar put it, had complained of hearing to "satiety" all the dire prophecies). And at the end of the fourteenth century, during the Western Schism, more seers arose and their locutions were preached from the pulpit. Many holy men had what were deemed by theologians to be overly dramatic or false revelations.

But if they had gone too far, these folks were still picking up a legitimate spiritual pulse. Although the Anti-Christ was *not* incarnate, there was anti-Christianity; grave evils afflicted the Church, which was now a house divided. There was rancor. There was the schism. There were two popes, one in Rome, one in Avignon, France. For a while, there was even a third. The two key ones had the support of influential secular rulers as well as cardinals. Mystics like St. Bridget implored the papacy to return to Rome, which it eventually did, but not before tremendous tension had been caused.

If that wasn't enough, the Bubonic Plague had also hit the Church, depopulating convents and rectories. There were vandals who sacked monasteries and laid their fields to waste, not only driving out monks but violating the nuns. This period of assault would mark the gradual end of the Middle Ages.

In like manner, there has been a flurry of peripheral apparitions since the early days of Medjugorje. Some are true and many are not; some are from God and some are from deceptive spirits. Others are psychological. Certain interesting ones occurred in Yugoslavia. Not long after the Madonna was first seen in Medjugorje, reports arrived that Mary was also appearing in a place called Gala. The main seer, who is now a cloistered nun in the order of St. Clare, was named Mirjam Munivrana, according to Archbishop Franic of Split; he seemed quite interested in this claim, or at least aware of it, but, perhaps sensing that one major apparition at a time is enough, has rendered no official judgment. There were also children in Izbicno who claimed to be seeing apparitions from 1982 to 1983. At one point eighteen visionaries were reported there. For his part the Bishop of Mostar, the one opposed to Medjugorje, complained that, all told, there were forty-seven visionaries in his diocese.

Do you think any of them were authentic?

When the seers at Medjugorje asked Our Blessed Mother if the Izbicno apparitions were good or evil, she replied, *"They are coming from God."* When asked why there were so many visions in Hercegovina, the Madonna said, *"My children, did you not notice that the faith began to vanish? Many come to church only because they are accustomed to coming. It is necessary to awaken the faith. This is a gift from God. If it is necessary, I will appear in each home."* She further said, *"I appear to you [the six seers] often and in every place. To others, I appear from time to time and briefly."* On Holy Thursday in 1985, she said her wish was *"to keep on giving you messages as it has never been done in history from the beginning of the world."* That's quite a dramatic statement and it may soon be the case. Our episode is already bigger than the one in the 1300s, which was the last mega-upsurge.

Didn't the Madonna say that after Medjugorje there will be no more authentic visionaries?

Our Blessed Mother has said that after Medjugorje there will no longer be genuine visitations, *"only some false apparitions."* On May 2, 1982, the Virgin was quoted as saying, *"I have come to call the world to conversion for the last time."*

> *"I have come to call the world to conversion for the last time."*

Such a statement buttresses the claim from Vicka and also Mirjana that the apparitions at Medjugorje are "the last on earth." However, I'm still not sure she's talking about the last apparitions forever or the last ones in this Age of Mary, which began in 1830 with the Miraculous Medal apparitions. Other of the seers said Medjugorje will be the last apparitions *for this period of the Church*. Not for all time. The issue remains up in the air, misunderstood. When Fr. Vlasic brought it up with Mirjana, she replied, "It is the last time that Jesus or Mary will appear on earth, the last time they will appear as they have, so that you can speak with them. [The Blessed Mother] said she would not appear again on earth. I do not know if this means in this era. I did not think that I should have questioned her on that subject."

When, during that other interview, with Fr. Ljubicic, Mirjana was asked what she thought of visionaries elsewhere, she said, "I believe that they, too, were chosen by Mary, just as we were. All of us were not chosen because we are somehow better than the rest—not at all. I simply mean that all of them were chosen to help people, to divert the people's attention [to God], to tell people [about God and all that will happen], to instruct the ones around them in some way, to talk with them and to tell them what Mary says. To do and say the same things that she tells us. Perhaps people will listen to them. The main task for all of us is to spread faith in God."

Doesn't that contradict those who deny and disparage apparitions other than those at Medjugorje?

In saying that if necessary she would appear in every home, and in indicating that Izbicno was real, as well as mentioning that others see her but for briefer times, the Queen of Peace was clearly verifying that there are indeed other genuine—if lesser—apparitions.

The key word is "genuine." When Mirjana was asked to comment on other seers, she was asked to comment on those having "genuine mystical experiences." Her answer does not address those that may be demonic or psychological. But the visionaries were warned about other seers and Our

Blessed Mother preferred that they not meet with the seers from Izbicno, even though those seers said they had been instructed from heaven to meet with the Medjugorje visionaries. How complex it gets! Mirjana said she was told to be on the lookout for "many false prophets throughout the world in our time, who lie, claiming to see the Madonna or Jesus. This is a great sin, and we should pray for such people. In fact, [the Madonna] and I prayed for fourteen days exclusively for false prophets. They do not understand how grave a sin it is to lie about having visions."

Soon after the initial apparitions in Yugoslavia there were similar reports from Africa, Syria, Venezuela, Korea, and Argentina. They occurred before 1985. I've always taken special note of those that occurred prior to 1985 because that was before Medjugorje had gained any form of real international publicity, which tends to generate copycats. Therefore, those prior to 1985 have that much more legitimacy, although it certainly doesn't guarantee authenticity. From 1985 on, the apparitions spread to Italy, Ireland, the U.S.S.R., and then everywhere. A minimum of forty countries.

Forty countries?
Yes. At least that many.

What about the U.S.?
The United States has always been home to a certain degree of mysticism. If you want, you can go as far back as George Washington, who supposedly experienced seeing a woman in a vision during the winter of 1777. I don't know the reliability of that—it was reported long after the event, in Volume 4, Number 12, of *The National Tribune.* In our own time there have been reputed mystics like Eileen George in Massachusetts, and, up across the border in Montreal, Georgette Faniel, an aging mystic who has been receiving messages since 1921. During the 1970s there were apparitions reported in places like New York and California.

But they *surged* from 1987 on, and it's interesting that the pope had declared a special "Marian year" from June 7, 1987, to August 15, 1988. That was *precisely* when the proliferation of apparitions, the rumbling mountain, turned into a volcano. It was the lava. It was the episode looking like it was beginning to rise toward a crescendo.

The pope had declared a special "Marian year" from June 7, 1987, to August 15, 1988. That was precisely when the proliferation of apparitions, the rumbling mountain, turned into a volcano.

In this particular upwelling, of certain interest to me were the reports of a woman from Ohio, a young mother in her thirties, who to maintain anonymity went by the pseudonym "Mariamante" (Latin for "lover of Mary"). Beginning in February of 1987, Mariamante claimed to experience visions of the Christ Child, the Virgin Mary, and various saints. The Infant wore a grayish, off-white tunic, reminding us of the "gray" but not really gray garb Mary wears at Medjugorje. He spoke gently and yet with impressive authority. *"Behold My mother!"* said the apparitional Jesus. *"I have given her this power and mission to intercede for the world. She acts on your behalf. She acts as the spouse of the Holy Spirit beckoning My return. It is true that I alone have saved the world, but she continually intercedes for you before the throne of God. Listen to what she has told you at Fatima and other major apparitions. These will help you to follow My Gospel. Her intercession is a blessing to the world. Only God could conceive of such mercy, to give you such a tender mother to intercede on your behalf. She makes recompense for your sins by her intercessions. But it is true that you must still atone for them. My Father is too offended. This cannot go on. Call upon the saints in your present struggle. They and the holy angels will assist you. Now go in peace as We bless you from Our Hearts."*

Our Blessed Mother appeared to Mariamante in varied dress, often with a white veil over her head and across her shoulders, or in the time-honored image of Our Lady of Sorrows or Our Lady of Mount Carmel. *"Heaven is most distressed with the state the world is in,"* Our Blessed Mother told Mariamante in 1987. *"It is very bad right now. Only prayer and penance can change this. Be attentive to your children. They are most important. They will live during the reign of my Immaculate Heart. This is a prelude to the ushering in of the reign of the Sacred Heart.*

"Humility and purity are what is needed now in the world. Without them there can be no true love. Love your neighbor. Charity must prevail. There is

no time for pettiness. Be forgiving towards one another."

Mariamante's messages received an imprimatur from Most Reverend Albert H. Ottenweller, the Bishop of Steubenville. They also received an endorsement of sorts from Mother Teresa of Calcutta, who read portions and declared the messages to be "an authentic spirituality of what being a mother means in today's world." The themes of Mariamante's visions were to become the themes of many visions and locutions. They underscored the importance of contemplative prayer, Eucharistic adoration, recitation of the Rosary, prayers for purity in the world, pursuit of God's Will, devotion to the family—especially in an era when the family is under so much assault—and devotion to both the Sacred Heart of Christ and the Immaculate Heart of Mary.

I'm not saying they're infallible—no lengthy locution is—and I have my questions. But after a full reading one can sense a flow of grace, and I'm impressed that Mariamante has maintained anonymity.

By 1987 and 1988, apparitions were occurring at many places in Yugoslavia, especially at the western end. Typical were those reported in the city of Split, Croatia, where a nine-year-old girl named Andrijana Bocina began seeing what she took to be Our Holy Mother on March 18, 1988. *"My dear children, this is my year and my times have come,"* the Virgin, referring to the Marian Year, allegedly told the girl on May 8, 1988. On February 17, 1990, Mary added that *"the punishment is approaching. Pray for the salvation of souls and for many other intentions. My dear angels, my Son Jesus comes with me so that He might give you messages as well. Soon He will be giving you messages. Dear angels, I am begging my Son so that the punishment does not take place—but it will take place. Dear angels, I am blessing you in the Name of the Father, Son, and Holy Spirit."*

Do you think that was Mary?

I'm not quite sure what to make of the message. It's an interesting message. It bears some similarities to Medjugorje. But like so many others, it lacks Medjugorje's resonance. Whether that's because of the translation, because of the girl's speech patterns, or because it's simply not as strong as Medjugorje—it's at a lower mystical tier—is something for the Church to determine. What I do know, and the reason I quote it, is that the theme of an imminent "punishment" is one that would come to dominate the lesser peripheral apparitions. It's discussed much more frequently and with far greater detail in the newer apparitions than at Medjugorje. From 1988 onward many self-proclaimed seers began having spectacular visions that sounded more like the Last Judgment than like a renewal or purification. There was one fellow in Yugoslavia who claimed he'd received ten secrets on the way home from Medjugorje!

Many locutions became lurid. They became sensational. They included every conceivable calamity.

Looking back, that was understandable. For there was indeed a chastisement coming for Yugoslavia. A year after Andrijana's warning, Croatia declared its independence from Yugoslavia, which was in essence run by Serbians.

Serbia didn't like that. It wanted to control all of former Yugoslavia. At the least, it wanted much more land. It didn't like to see Croatia and Bosnia-Hercegovina going off on their own. And that was when the Serbs began their hideous and forewarned assault.

TWELVE

~

PERCHED ON OUR SHOULDERS

So you're saying that the events in Yugoslavia were announced by the flurry of visionaries?

I think a number of folks were picking up a legitimate prophetic impulse. Some had better "receivers" than others. Some got strong reception, like the folks in Medjugorje, while others could barely hear the messages and added a lot of their own thoughts and interpretations.

So you do believe in other apparitions?

Some I find more interesting than others.

Didn't Pope Urban VIII say that in cases which concern private revelations, "it is better to believe than not to believe"?

That's what they claim, and the quote, widespread today in certain Catholic circles, has survived as an oral tradition. Pope Urban did issue decrees that pertained to private revelation on March 13, 1625, but from what I can tell, they were more a guidance from Rome saying that we can believe in private revelations with real faith, provided there is evidence or proof of authenticity. I have not been able to track down the specific quote you see in Marian magazines and newsletters. It's a very popular quote, and so is the directive of Pope Paul VI on October 14, 1966 that publications about new appearances, revelations, prophecies, and miracles can be distributed and read by the faithful without express permission by the Church and no longer require what they call an imprimatur or nihil obstat as long as such revelations do not contravene Catholic faith and morals.

But we have to be careful, because if we go off to an apparition half-cocked, we can fall into deception. I think we should always strive for a balanced attitude, an attitude that involves both open-mindedness and some deep questioning.

Notice I didn't use the word "skeptical." I don't like that word because it implies using doubt as the starting point of an investigation. Doubt is the opposite of faith. And faith provides the power for miraculous occurrences. The very presence of doubt tends to inhibit if not strangle even the most authentic phenomena.

But we do have a duty to be discerning and questioning. "Beloved," says 1 John 4:1, "do not trust every spirit, but put the spirits to a test to see if they belong to God." We have a duty to check the spirits. We have a duty to guard against false prophets who in the end may discourage the faithful and discredit the real prophets.

We must be on guard against evil spirits that masquerade as angels of light (see 2 Corinthians 11:14). I note that when the apparitions first began at Medjugorje, villagers and priests alike were immediately on guard against demons. Holy water was tossed toward the apparition and according to one report, the first reaction of Fr. Tomislav Pervan, another local priest, was to suggest an exorcism. The same had been true at Lourdes, where on February 14, 1858, St. Bernadette and two friends brought along a vial of holy water to ward off any malign influences.

You've seen demonism?

I have. But the greatest problem is human embellishment.

So you're saying that folks can get a little inspiration, a little spark from heaven, and blow it out of proportion?

God speaks to all of us all the time. Christ and the Holy Spirit speak to us. Our angels are perched on our proverbial shoulders trying to feed us the right thoughts.

But on the other shoulder is the evil imp who tries with great persistence to blind us, to blur our spiritual eyes, or to distort our thoughts. We always have a free choice as to what voice we'll listen to.

When a sinful suggestion or fantasy runs through our minds, we must immediately expel it or it will take root faster than a dandelion. It's up to us to police our minds.

The same is true of mysticism. The devil loves to play games. He loves to lead us on wild goose chases. He loves to make us listen to his wild meanderings instead of meditating on the words of Jesus. Like he does in other areas, he tempts us into false prophecy.

We can't go half-cocked with mysticism. If we're not praying for long periods each day, if we don't know how to cast away evil spirits, if we're not fasting—and for Catholics, if we're not receiving frequent Communion and going to Confession—if we have pride in our spirits, whether obvious or far under the surface that we haven't specifically prayed about, then we shouldn't become involved in mysticism. We may be susceptible to psychological trickery or deceptive spirits.

What are the best indicators of a true spirit?

Look for fruits. Look to see if the seer radiates peace and humility, as well as love. Look for fruits in the pilgrims—fruits that last over a period of time. That's the first standard. "A sound tree cannot bear bad fruit any more than a decayed tree can bear good fruit," said Christ (Mt 7:18). "You can tell a tree by its fruit" (Mt 7:20).

Then look to see if the ecstasy is normal or somehow suspicious. Look to see if the visionary has a stable personality. Look to see if there are questions and niggling doubts—any form of uneasiness—in your own intuition. If a message is long and meandering, I'd become immediately suspicious. If it lacks special power, a feeling of grace, why mess with it? Also, watch out for locutionists who can receive messages at will. According to St. Teresa of Avila, that's a sign that the message is coming from the mind's own subconscious, or what she called its own "understanding." St. Teresa said she could listen for days and not hear a locution. She usually heard them when she didn't desire to do so. But when she did get one, it would come no matter how much she resisted it—"impossible to fail to hear them."

"When a locution comes from the devil," added St. Teresa, "it not only fails to leave behind good effects but leaves bad ones.... Besides being left in a state of great aridity, the soul suffers a disquiet such as I have experienced on many other occasions when the Lord has allowed me to be exposed to many kinds of sore temptation and spiritual trial."

She said a true locution is unforgettable and every syllable counts, "whereas the words that come from our own understanding are like the first movement of thought, which passes and is forgotten."

False locutions are usually fantastic and lack the clarity of what we hear from a place like Medjugorje. A real locution costs no labor. It's not something we spend energy obtaining. "A further indication, which is surer than any other, is that these false locutions affect nothing, whereas, when the Lord speaks, the words are accompanied by effects," said St. Teresa.

Does that make you wary of everyone who claims to have become a seer?

I've seen some alarming things, especially in America. In 1992 I turned down an offer from Doubleday to do a book I'd proposed about American mystics because right around that time I began traveling around the country. I began to see some things I hadn't expected, some things behind the scenes. I certainly didn't want to promote anything dubious, or to spend an entire book exposing false apparitions.

There are problems out there. The human personality is a powerful thing. It can overwhelm and dominate a person who has not yet purged his or her ego. I've seen a number of instances where people visited Medjugorje and grew obsessed with being a seer, or getting close to one. There is ambition. There is envy. There's an unhealthy fixation on visionaries. But there shouldn't be. Visionaries are nothing but vessels. Chosen, yes. But no better and no worse than anyone else. They have the same trials. They're judged the same. They are no more loved by Our Father.

Nowadays, there are so many visionaries! They're sprouting like locutionists! I have one list of sixty-nine publicly known seers receiving messages in twenty-six nations, but that list is already a few years old, which means it was done before the latest peak in reports. Using other lists or my own research I can add at least fourteen nations for a minimum total of forty countries reporting such things as apparitions. There have been more purported apparitions since Medjugorje than at any other time in recorded history. One newspaper story claimed that there are two hundred accounts a year reported to the Vatican.

They're really that prevalent?

It's hard to confirm any number. What we can say, what we can deduce at this point, is that Medjugorje is a truly special event in mystical history, unique in its reach—not just another place where the Virgin decided to touch down. It's an urgent call to salvation. It's a chosen place. It's capping off an episode that has deep roots, that goes back to the 1800s. And while there may be lulls, while there may be periods of quiet in the future, it's my bet that it hasn't yet reached its crescendo.

THIRTEEN

~

BEYOND COINCIDENCE

Other than Medjugorje, what claimed apparition have you found most interesting?

Perhaps the apparitions in Rwanda, Africa. They're about as engaging as you get. There were seven visionaries who claimed separate but very similar phenomena. The apparitions started just five months after Medjugorje, on November 28, 1981, in the town of Kibeho.

What sets Kibeho apart is that it involves prophecy that has come true. An apparition of the Virgin warned of immorality in Africa and showed what would happen if there wasn't mass conversion. This took place in a vision lasting eight hours, and it was quite specific. During the revelation one of the visionaries saw what was later described as "a river of blood, people who were killing each other, abandoned corpses with no one to bury them, a tree all in flames, bodies without their heads." *Bodies without their heads.* The vision occurred during the 1980s and its impression was inescapable: something horribly violent, something involving civil unrest, loomed in Rwanda's future if there wasn't a turning back to God. It left an immense feeling of fear and sadness.

We know now what the seers meant. During the spring of 1994 a horrifying civil war erupted in Rwanda. It was caused by the assassination of President Juvénal Habyarimana, a Christian whose family followed the apparitions and who as a result reportedly consecrated his country to Jesus and Mary. President Habyarimana died in an apparently sabotaged aircraft and that led, as in Bosnia, to what was basically a series of tribal massacres.

The war appalled the world and fulfilled the Kibeho prophecy in all its grisly detail. It was a genocide more intense than what was transpiring up there in the former Yugoslavia. In fact, this genocide proceeded at the fastest known rate—day to day—in history. In just three months an estimated five hundred thousand to one million Rwandans were killed as Hutus attacked the largely Christian Tutsis. Many of the nation's Catholics—including priests, nuns, and a couple of bishops—were gruesomely martyred. There were so many corpses that many were simply left to decay under the tropical sun ("abandoned corpses with no one to bury them"). Others were thrown into the Kagera River ("a river of blood") or bulldozed into mass graves. Exact words from the prophecy made it into the newspapers. On May 18, 1994, *The New York Times* even had a sub-head that said, "Blood in the River." An estimated ten thousand bodies floated toward Lake Victoria, and many of them had been decapitated with machetes—"bodies without their heads."

There was actual mention of "decapitation"?

It was shown in the vision. The gruesome scene was shown to at least one of the visionaries. I published part of the prophecy a couple of years before the war in *The Final Hour.*

And there were other prescient aspects. When Our Blessed Mother appeared at Kibeho she requested that a chapel be named "The Gathering of the Displaced." It was an odd name for a chapel, but it now makes perfect sense: the war created an unprecedented 2.2 million refugees. Most fled to Tanzania and Zaire. It was the largest single exodus in human history. More interesting still, one of the camps for displaced people ended up being in Kibeho! Like Medjugorje, where peacekeepers and refugees have likewise been tended to, Kibeho became a center for relief efforts.

But the devil was also around, and on April 22, 1995, there was a massacre in Kibeho. Perhaps this too was part of the horrifying prophecy. "Troops began screening Kibeho's one hundred thousand displaced people to identify those involved in last year's genocide," reported *Time.* "When some tried to break through the cordon, soldiers opened fire. As many as two thousand people died on the steep hillsides."

As at Medjugorje, the basic message had been the message of John the Baptist. And as in former Yugoslavia, the message was largely ignored.

People scoffed at the apparitions?

Yes. Too many. The seers were always complaining about that. They told the Blessed Virgin that people were calling them nutty, calling them insane, and Mary responded: *"Blessed are the crazy of the Lord."*

So you believe Mary appeared in Rwanda?

I believe something happened there. I'll let the Church rule on what it was. The apparitions, it seems, were alluded to by Joseph Ratzinger, cardinal prefect of the Sacred Congregation for the Doctrine of the Faith. It was during an interview in 1985 when Ratzinger, who may well be the second most powerful man in the Vatican, spoke about the multiplication of Marian apparitions. He specifically mentioned reports from Africa. So far the bishop, John-Baptist Gahamanyi, has made no formal ruling. In 1988 he did give his approbation to public gatherings at the site of the apparitions, and when I had a translator call him, he was quick to recount the

When Our Blessed Mother appeared at Kibeho she requested that a chapel be named "The Gathering of the Displaced." It was an odd name for a chapel, but it now makes perfect sense: the war created an unprecedented 2.2 million refugees.... More interesting still, one of the camps for displaced people ended up being in Kibeho!

apparitions, which he obviously found of significance. But in a pastoral letter he said, "because of the complexity of the facts and the number of the visionaries, it is hard to scrutinize each case. There should be no surprise if the Church expresses its judgment only after a relatively long period of time. Many years are often needed to clearly see the truth. We invite you therefore to be patient."

The "complexity" springs in part from the fact that Kibeho had seven main seers with independent apparitions. It was a cluster of individual mysticism. For instance, one began in November, the next during January. They were connected and yet they were not connected. It was very interesting. I suppose the most unusual aspect was the manner of ecstasy. When the main visionary, Alphonsine Mumureka, who was the first to see Mary, went into ecstasy, she flailed her arms and whipped around and fell to the ground with her eyes straining. The gestural expressions were very flamboyant. Whirling. Twisting. Falling. When ecstasies appear unusual, a red flag goes up, because peculiar ecstasies are also common in voodoo dances, shamanistic rituals, and instances of diabolical possession.

But in the case of Kibeho, such commotion may be an offspring of the culture. Rwandans have very colorful means of expression. We picture tribesmen in feathery costume during their dramatic ceremonies. They're very spontaneous. It's a part of their upbringing. And so maybe there's no cause for concern. The seers certainly seemed like devout young people. Five of the seven were raised Catholics, while another was Muslim and the seventh pagan until he converted. It's interesting that at Kibeho, as at Medjugorje, there was a strong ecumenical message. The seers were told that God honors all authentic religions but wants His Son and His Mother to be loved and respected. Our Lady never asked the Protestant and Muslim students at the local school (where many events occurred) to become Catholics—only to recognize her. She was particularly insistent about materialism. *"You are distracted by the goods of this world,"* she said. *"I have seen many of my children getting lost and I have come to show them the true way."* When asked who she was, Our Lady replied, *"Ndi Nyina wa Jambo,"* that she was "Mother of the Word."

Aside from the date, which sets the occurrences right around the same time, and the link with John the Baptist, plus the war, were there any other connections with Medjugorje?

It was said that on June 25, 1993, when Ivanka Ivankovic received her annual visitation, Mary was crying. She showed the Medjugorje seer "awful, horrible pictures." Black people were dying terribly. Ivanka was told the event was close and would be a sign or warning for all of us that we must pray much more.

Afterward, overwhelmed, Ivanka broke down, sobbing.

Ivanka was never told it was Rwanda but that was less than a year before the war and holocaust there.

You indicated that Our Lady appears in whatever way most conforms with the local culture. Did she come in Africa as a black woman?

Alphonsine said she couldn't determine the color of Mary's skin. "But she was of incomparable beauty," said the seer. "She was barefoot with a white dress with no seams and a white veil on her head. Her hands were joined together and her fingers turned toward heaven." Her voice was described as sweet like music, and sometimes she stood with her hands down, as in the Miraculous Medal appearance. When she ascended, it was again as Christ ascended in Acts 1:9.

Was there anything leading up to the apparitions? Was there anything like the thunderstorm at Medjugorje or the discovery of those rosaries?

Before Mary arrived there was what seemed like a demonic attack. We don't know enough about it yet, but according to one bishop, Aloys Bigirumwami of Nyundo, "In Rwanda, between 1979 and 1981, a diabolic fury destroying all pictures and statues inside and outside of churches occurred throughout the country with no intervention by the authorities to stop them."

This is interesting because November 28, the day the Kibeho apparitions began, is also the feast day of St. Stephen the Younger. St. Stephen was born in Constantinople during the eighth century and stood up against the emperor Constantine Copronymus, an iconoclast who was obsessed with stamping out use of sacred images. Ruining holy objects is what vandals in Rwanda were doing, as had also been done during the French Revolution. For his stand St. Stephen was martyred.

What about other messages at Kibeho? Did they contain any additional predictions?

The Virgin seemed especially concerned with moral purity. She told Rwandan women not to be loose with their sexuality. They were warned to seek God's love before serving men and money. They were warned, especially the young, that the wrong way of living, including fornication, would weigh heavily on their futures. The apparitionists were conveying the same theme as Medjugorje. "We must turn to God and abandon evil," was the way seer Anathalie Mukamazimpaka summarized the message. "Wake up, stand up, wash yourselves, and look at Our Blessed Mother tenderly. We must dedicate ourselves to prayer. We must develop the virtues of charity and humility. If Mary comes it is because she loves us. A child playing in the mud does not know he will get dirty and that it is not good for him. But Mary, like a mother, comes to us because she loves us." She told them to "cleanse" their bodies and spirits.

Rwandans were urged to convert while there was still time. They were warned away from material things again and again. Indeed, Mary said she chose to go to Kibeho precisely because it was not yet consumed by materialism. The path to hell is wide and easy, she explained, and has few obstacles. She urged them to take the harder, narrower, non-materialistic road and explained the value of suffering. She said suffering is a means of purification. *"Nothing is more beautiful than a heart which offers its sufferings to God,"* said one message. *"Pray, pray, pray. Follow the Gospel of my Son. Do not forget that God is more powerful than all the evil in the world. Share. Do not kill. Do not persecute. Respect the rights of man because if you act contrary to those rights, you will not succeed and it will come back against you."*

This last message was prophetic in light of the coming war.

As at Medjugorje, there was a strong emphasis on Confession—the sacrament of reconciliation.

But the seers knew the odds were that the messages would not take effect in time. They knew that too many people still scoffed at religion, treated it languidly. "I understand that what makes you suffer is the fact that the day will come when we will want to follow what you are saying—about loving, serving, and doing your will—but it will be too late," the seer Anathalie was heard fretting to Mary during an apparition. "The day will come when we will long for you and we will not find you."

Such was said in a region which would soon be ravaged not only by war but also by AIDS, which turned whole villages into ghost towns.

Were there other visions?

Like Medjugorje, the seers were taken on visions of heaven, hell, and purgatory. They were unconscious for up to forty hours during their "mystical journeys." It reminds us of Vicka's comas. The seers also incurred mystical sufferings. For instance the Muslim woman, Vestine Salima, was blind for fifteen days after her first apparition—reminding us of Saul (see Acts 9:8)—while a seer named Marie-Clare Mukangano experienced her last apparition on the Feast of the Seven Sorrows. This is interesting not only because it tied in with "seven" seers—each representing a sorrow—but also because, at the very same time, up in Bosnia-Hercegovina, which these visionaries had almost certainly never heard of, Our Lady was promoting the exact same meditations on her Seven Sorrows.

The devotion, a recitation of beads, begins with a prayer: *"My God, I offer to you these little beads of sorrow for your greatest glory in honor of Your*

Holy Mother. I will meditate and share Your suffering. I beg for the tears that You spread in those moments to grant me and all sinners repentance for my sins."

Then three times: *"To me a sinner and to all sinners, grant us perfect contrition for our sins."*

And then an *Our Father* and seven *Hail Marys* after announcing each of the Seven Sorrows.

The sorrows are these: Simeon telling Mary that a sword will pierce her soul; the flight of Jesus, Mary, and Joseph into Egypt; losing Jesus in the temple; Mary meeting her Son on the way to the cross; Mary at the foot of the cross; the Virgin receiving the corpse of her son; and Mary at the tomb of Our Savior.

After each sorrow, instead of the *Glory Be*, they repeated *"Mary, full of mercy, remind our hearts of the suffering of Jesus during His passion."* After the Seventh Sorrow there are three *Our Fathers* and three *Hail Marys*.

The message at Kibeho was reconciliation. The message was that when we suffer well we are purified. And we suffer well when we transcend pain and when, instead of seeking false utopias here on earth, we see life as a journey in the footsteps of Jesus.

But what about the prophecies? Didn't one mention that the world is approaching some sort of huge calamity?

On March 27, 1982, the Virgin supposedly told visionary Marie-Clare Mukangano, who at twenty was one of the older seers, that the world *"is on the edge of catastrophe."* The Kibeho seers called the current time a period of "recall." They said it's a time of reflection and mercy. A time to become apostles. They said the Virgin had arrived to help renew us and to prepare the way for her Son.

Such was directly expressed by all the visionaries but perhaps most memorably by the pagan fellow, Emmanuel Segatashya, who was returning from a bean field—resting under a tree—when he supposedly heard a voice say, "Child, if you receive a mission, will you be able to accomplish it?"

From his heart Emmanuel answered yes for some reason—and with no hesitation. I guess it was an auricular locution, heard through the ear. The voice told him to head toward a crowd of villagers in the distance. When Jesus appeared to Emmanuel, it was as a black man dressed in Rwandan garb and set before a brilliant light. *"Tell them to purify their hearts because the time is near,"* said the voice, and when Emmanuel asked who it was, the voice replied, *"If I told you My name, no one would believe you."* When Emmanuel persisted, the voice allegedly told the pagan boy, *"My name is Jesus. Go and bring the message to the people."*

From then on, Emmanuel seemed to have been given a genius for religion. The pagan boy was suddenly conversant with profound Christian wisdom. He answered questions like a walking catechism. And he issued warnings like a prophet out of the Old Testament. He warned against the sins of hypocrisy and slander, which he said were "fornication of the tongue." He said Jesus reprimanded His consecrated people for being too absorbed by the world, reminding everyone that we are poor on this earth no matter what material objects we own and that the only wealth is to be found in the heart and spirit.

"Too many people treat their neighbors dishonestly," Emmanuel quoted Jesus as saying. *"The world is full of hatred. You will know My Second Coming is at hand when you see the outbreak of religious wars."*

Emmanuel was apocalyptical. No doubt about it. He had this wonderful, peaceful smile, but his message was most serious. "Do not lose time in doing good," he warned. "There is not much time. Jesus will come." He spoke about the state of souls and how eternal destinations are decided. "We must prepare while there is still time," Segatashya repeated. "Those who did well will go to heaven. If they did evil, they will condemn themselves with no hope for appeal. Jesus will come and He will find everyone. In preparing for the last judgment be vigilant. You who know that Jesus came on earth have no doubt that He will come again. If you have not yet done anything for everlasting life, this should make you think and you should change your way of living. Real poverty is to be deprived of the grace that leads to God."

Did the crowds see anything?

They claimed that during apparitions to yet another seer, Agnes Kamagaju, the sun spun as at Medjugorje. Other times a cross would appear on the right side of the sun. "God wants to show us that He holds the world in His hands and He can bring it to an end at His Will," Agnes explained. Often, after the seers asked for a blessing from Jesus and Mary, a light rain would fall. On other occasions they saw two suns. This caused a certain degree of consternation, for in tribal lore signs in the sky mean something great and terrible is coming.

Did the visionaries all foresee calamity?

From what I can tell, it was a strong theme of the messages. Among those who saw their end, who were killed, in fact, were several of the Kibeho seers. According to Bishop Gahamanyi, in the end there were eight seers and as many as four may have been killed. He was able to confirm that Vestine, Marie-Clare, and Emmanuel were among the dead. Emmanuel was shot in the head. According to another report that has filtered to us through a nun named Sr. Martha Tillient, who was stationed over there, Marie-Clare was slain with her husband in Butare. The others are said to have taken refuge in Zaire with so many thousands of others. It has been reported that Anathalie has been seeing Our Lady privately and Alphonsine, the lively first seer, went into hiding. If accounts are true, perhaps by now the surviving visionaries are back in Kibeho.

Do you think the tragedy in Rwanda could have been forestalled by prayer?

When Ivanka saw her premonition, the "horrible pictures" of black people dying terribly, she said the disaster could be prevented. It could be forestalled by prayer. Of course, it was not. It has now happened. Two apparitions—in Bosnia-Hercegovina and Rwanda—two pleas for peace starting in 1981—and two utter catastrophes.

I think that's beyond the realm of coincidence.

And it was made very clear that the messages were not just for Kibeho and Medjugorje. *"If I am now turning to the parish of Kibeho it does not mean I am concerned only for Kibeho or for the diocese of Butare or for Rwanda, or for the whole of Africa,"* said Mary. *"I am concerned with and turning to the whole world."*

FOURTEEN

~

PLAGUES AND VIRUSES

That's a prophecy we now hear over and over: that Christ is coming after some major calamities. Do you believe Jesus is really coming?

I found the entire situation in Kibeho worthy of further study. Again, we wait for the Church. We wait for the wisdom of the bishop. We also recall, in considering the more reaching prophecies at Kibeho, that there's been expectation of Christ's return in every period of time since the Resurrection. We don't know when He'll come but we're told to always be on guard. "As regards specific times and moments, brothers, we do not need to write you," says Paul "You know very well that the day of the Lord is coming like a thief in the night. Just when people are saying, 'Peace and security,' ruin will fall on them with the suddenness of pains overtaking a woman in labor, and there will be no escape" (1 Thes 5:1-3). In James 5:8, it says, "Steady your hearts, because the coming of the Lord is at hand." In Revelation 3:11 we are inspired toward the same vigilance. "I am coming soon," says Christ. "Hold fast to what you have lest someone rob you of your crown."

Those words were written 1,900 years ago and we know that Christ's formal return was not quite "at hand" back at the time of the writing. It hasn't turned out to be so soon. There are elements of the Matthew prophecy that you could fit into many time periods. Perhaps it's the case that some prophecies are timeless and tend to repeat themselves in various generations. Perhaps prophecy detects trends that repeat themselves on different levels for perpetuity. Like the Bible, an authentic message may have something to say—something to prophesy—to every generation. There are always wars and rumors of wars. There are always plagues and quakes.

But I often wonder if these events pick up at crucial moments in history. I believe a good case can be made that they do. Perhaps they announce the end of an age, just as plague in the 1300s could be seen as announcing the beginning of the end of the Middle Ages. Certain prophecies are more relevant to one age than another. One day they will all be fulfilled according to the description in Matthew 24 and then we will know we're at the Lord's day of reckoning.

But doesn't the urgency of current mysticism indicate that prophecies in the Book of Revelation are finally here?

Perhaps, but we have to be careful not to gauge everything in linear terms. We can't hold heaven to earthly chronology. There's no time, no clocks, in heaven. We also must be cognizant of the devil, who delights in planting dramatic and false speculation, in feeding our curiosity and our yen for excitement. The Deceiver is only too glad to service our insatiable appetite for end-time things. When that happens, when the devil plants a false prediction and when the prophecy fails to materialize, we grow disenchanted and won't listen to the real thing when it finally comes. The curious, the weak of faith, say, "Oh, that prophecy hasn't come true, so I don't believe this stuff any longer." They're discouraged by erroneous predictions, and their discouragement can even affect their faith in God.

So when it comes to prophecy, in feeding the flock, we must be very careful. We all know that in our weakness we possess an almost morbid desire to witness the end of the world, or at least some kind of a titillating calamity. We all remember grade school, when word would sweep through the playlots or class that the world was going to end at noon on such and such a day—precisely at noon.

It never did. Nothing happened. It was a blank. It was just a hangover from Rod Serling.

The key issue is balance. We have to be careful not to be made foolish. At the same time, we must also watch for signs of the times. We can never let false prophets discourage us from prophecy. If we do that, if we do what in fact too many clerics already have done—if we forget or downplay the Church's mystical origin—then we're ignoring the prescription of St. Paul that prophecy edifies the Church. We're also ignoring Christ's admonishment to watch for signs of the age (see Matthew 16:3).

Why is calamity associated with Christ's return?

Well, there has to be purification when He arrives, and such prophecies are in Luke and Matthew. But it's not all bad. Not by any means. There's also good news. Look at Isaiah: "In the days to come, the mountain of the Lord's house shall be established as the highest mountain and raised above the hills. All nations shall stream toward it; many peoples shall come and say: 'Come, let us climb the Lord's mountain, to the house of the God of Jacob, that He may instruct us in His ways, and we may walk in His paths....' He shall judge between the nations, and impose terms on many peoples. They shall beat their swords into plowshares" (2:2-4).

Was Kibeho too sensational? Were some of the prophecies too apocalyptic?

The visionaries strongly warned that people would soon be meeting their final judgment, that the end was in sight, that they would encounter Jesus; and it was certainly a true prophecy for the five hundred thousand to one million who floated down that "river of blood"—who during the war were shot or clubbed or beheaded.

Sometimes mystics are given a limited view of a particular event and then put their own interpretation on it. Blow it out of proportion. If I were given a vision of smoke and fire all over the place, of fire seeming to reach to the skies, of glass exploding, of countless screaming, wailing people rushing onto the streets, and a roar above, I might take such a vision to portray the instant of a nuclear attack or a cosmic event like a comet or asteroid. I might take it to be the end of the world. I might take it to be an event affecting the entire earth, when in reality what I was given in vision, while bad enough, was only the close-up view of a blazing street or single neighborhood during the fiery Los Angeles riots, not the end of the world. The roar was police helicopters.

So prophets can suffer from nearsightedness?

Often they are not able to put an image or "vision" into perspective. They're given only a piece or two of a larger puzzle. When a seer guesses, when a visionary tries to figure out the entire puzzle, especially time frames, there is trouble.

Most prophecies pertain to personal, local, or regional events, not to the kind of global incident most people would prefer announcing. Let me state again that events like the massacres in Bosnia and Rwanda may themselves be prophecies—prophetic microcosms or prefigurations of future events, events that will happen in a much bigger way if we don't turn to God. Perhaps such regional events are indications of what may be in the Medjugorje secrets.

What about the severity of warnings from elsewhere? We hear some dire prophecies.

Assuming they're not simply matters of false prophecy, we can view some of them more as threats from God than prophecies. Actually, I don't like the word "threat." They are more like warnings. God doesn't intimidate. He loves. The last thing He wants to do is scare us. Yet He also has His rules, and His rules are meant to last. He doesn't compromise them. When we reject His Holy Spirit, then the Spirit is withdrawn and matters begin to unravel. They unravel because they are missing the Spirit's great cohesive or bonding force.

In a universe prone to entropy, where the natural trend is for things to become undone, to burn out, to fall into disorder, it's only the Holy Spirit Who keeps us from chaos.

So in effect we're the ones who bring disorder and randomness upon ourselves. We're the ones who, through sin, put the Holy Spirit at a distance. We're the ones who reject the cohesive order. That's not to say God doesn't specifically send things. That's not to say He doesn't send fire or storms. We know better from the Old Testament. He will take such action. But much of what He does is simply to let us wallow in our mistakes and ignorance. To wallow in our wickedness. And that creates both societal and natural disorders.

As St. Alphonsus de Liguori, a doctor of the Church, once said, "God threatens to chastise in order to deliver us from chastisement." The holy fear of God makes man holy, wrote St. Alphonsus. "We should then fear on account of our sins, but this fear ought not to deject us: it should rather excite us to confidence in the divine mercy."

It was St. Alphonsus' view that God "appears with the bow already bent, upon the point of sending off the arrow, but he does not send it off, because He wishes that our terror bring about amendment, and that thus we should escape chastisement." As it says in Hosea 5:15, "in their affliction they shall look for me." Sometimes it takes fear to bring people to God. And if that doesn't work, then comes the actual prophesied chastisement.

At Kibeho there was an urgent appeal for sexual purity. How do sins of the flesh factor into current prophecy?

Very prominently. Such sins carry more weight than the vast majority of us realize. Along with occult practices, including demonic idolatry, illicit sex was central to the destruction of Babylon, Nineveh, and Sodom and Gomorrah. It has always been a mainstay of witchcraft and magic. Today, even within marriages, there are certain sinful practices, practices that degrade or humiliate the husband, the wife, or both. Anything that infringes on human dignity is evil. Anything that replaces love with lust is a sin. At Kibeho there was more than a hint that great suffering would come, that decimation would come, if Rwandans and, for that matter, the entire world didn't renounce sins of idolatry and fornication.

Fornication is sex among the unmarried, something we now accept as standard operating procedure but something about which the Blessed Mother raised a high flag of warning at Kibeho. On August 18, 1983, she said the youth had developed ideas contrary to those of God and that *"they should not use their bodies as an instrument of pleasure. They are using all means to love and be loved and they forget that true love comes from God. Instead of being at the service of God, they are at the service of money. They must make of their bodies instruments destined to the glory of God and not an object of pleasure at the service of men."*

In the years since Kibeho, sub-Saharan Africa has developed the world's highest number of full-blown AIDS cases, many of them caused by heterosexual sodomy and other forms of illicit sex, especially with prostitutes. By 1994 that region of the globe had 70 percent of the world's estimated 4.5 million cases—and many millions more infected with HIV but not yet in the disease's final stage. Children too are victims of the virus. Up to 90 percent of the worldwide childhood cases are in Africa! Note that the definition of "virus" starts out with "venom, as from a snake" and ends with "that which corrupts or poisons the mind or character; evil or harmful influence." A virus is a physical precipitation of something nefarious.

Many believe that AIDS originated in this very part of the Dark Continent. Rwanda isn't far from Lake Victoria, and the shoreline of that lake, especially a fishing village known as Kasensero, is one of the areas where AIDS first appeared. Kasensero looks out to the Sese Islands, a simple boat ride from the Ugandan city of Entebbe.

Kasensero is known for its smugglers, and the Sese Islands are known for their monkeys, many of which are shipped to foreign nations for medical or other purposes. Some speculate that the trapped monkeys—crowded in those awful, inhumane cages—swapped viruses back and forth until one virus mutated into what became infamous as HIV. Sick monkeys have long been dumped on one of the islands that became known as the Isle of the

Plagues. It's believed they have been captured by greedy animal traders and sent abroad when supplies of healthy monkeys ran short.

No wonder Our Lady of the Word warned about greed! Whether or not AIDS started in that precise location, the disease is devastating the region today. Scientists have identified an even more virulent strain of virus known as Marburg, which along with another called Ebola compose a group of potent filoviruses that can spread with tremendous rapidity. These viruses are highly, highly contagious, such that investigators dress up in biohazard space suits just to get near them. Victims suffer from horrible vomiting and hemorrhaging. Ebola kills the vast majority of those infected within a matter of days. It makes AIDS seem like the common cold.

While we've seen strains of viruses portrayed in popular movies and books, the truth isn't that far out. These viruses are about as virulent as anything known to man. In the initial literature, the worst strain of Ebola seemed to be a strain that came out of Zaire, which borders Rwanda.

So you believe the Kibeho warnings were a harbinger of plague also?

Once more the words come back to haunt us, the warning back in 1983 about purifying ourselves, the warning about uncleanliness and seeking money and fornication. AIDS and similar viruses have spread from the rain forest by way of the Kinshasa Highway, which runs directly across Africa. Prostitutes work along such main roads and in some regions 90 percent of them may be carrying HIV. It seems the Virgin Mary knew something we didn't. There was a virus incubating in the rain forest and ready to hitch a ride down the Kinshasa road.

Do you think any of this is related to the secrets of certain other visionaries?

Well, perhaps in the way of being precursors. I believe the massacres in Rwanda, as well as the outbreak of viruses, are mini-chastisements or pre-warnings. Perhaps they are what lead up to the first major warnings—in other words, as I said, events that themselves become prophecies. An indication of what may soon happen on a larger scale.

FIFTEEN

~

TOMORROW'S NEWS

What about the secrets of Fatima? What were they? How did they fit in?

I mentioned that in the flurry of apparitions at the beginning of our century, Fatima came forth in 1917 with a prophecy about the end of World War I and the rise of Communism. Our Blessed Mother said that terrible war would end but if mankind didn't convert, there would be a second war greater than the first. Such a chastisement, she said, would be announced by some sort of luminous phenomenon. *"When you see a night illumined by an unknown light, know that this is the great sign given you by God that He is about to punish the world for its crimes, by means of war, famine, and persecution of the Church and of the Holy Father,"* said Our Lady of Fatima in 1917. *"To prevent this, I shall come to ask for the consecration of Russia to my Immaculate Heart, and the Communion of reparation on the First Saturdays [of the month].*

"If my requests are heeded, Russia will be converted and there will be peace. If not, she will spread her errors throughout the world, causing wars and persecutions of the Church. The good will be martyred, the Holy Father will have much to suffer, various nations will be annihilated.

"In the end, my Immaculate Heart will triumph. The Holy Father will consecrate Russia to me, and she will be converted, and a period of peace will be granted to the world.

"In Portugal, the dogma of the faith will always be preserved...."

That was roughly the first two-thirds of the prophecy.

The last third, or "Third Secret," has not been revealed. That's why I put an ellipsis after those last words. We don't know what else was said. It's confidential. As far as I know only the pope, Joseph Cardinal Ratzinger, who is in charge of a Vatican congregation, and Sr. Lucia dos Santos, the sole surviving Fatima visionary, know what it is, what follows the word "preserved."

In looking back, we see that the first two parts were simple, direct, and stunning predictions. World War I soon ended but as the Virgin warned, a greater war was in the making. And as prophesied, it was announced by a strange light, an unusually powerful display of the northern lights or aurora borealis across Europe and as far as America in 1938, just before the Nazis marched into Austria.

Note that the Holy Mother used the words "great sign," exactly the words used at Medjugorje, which sees another visible sign on the horizon. We have all pondered what this might be: a sign on Mount Podbrdo, the hill of the first apparitions, where Ivanka first saw Mary with the Christ Child. It's said that it will be visible at or above the hill, perhaps something like fire but not really fire; perhaps some kind of manifestation of light. If so, it will bear a certain affinity to the great sign of Fatima, which also involved light. The Fatima sign took the form of the "northern lights," which are supposed to be a natural phenomenon. But according to *The New York Times,* those who saw the lights in 1938 were astonished at their magnitude and lucidity, the way they sent vivid arcs of light from which came pulsating beams of red, purple, and greenish blue, like those of a surreal searchlight. It was the greatest display of the aurora borealis in at least fifty years. It was seen from the United States to Grenoble, which is near La Salette in western France, where Mary gave dramatic prophecies to those two seers in 1846. There, huge beams of blood-red light were witnessed. From a plane it looked like a shimmering curtain of fire.

In Spain, from her cell at a convent, Sr. Lucia was sure the lights were no mere natural happening but a sign that nations would soon be punished, as they most certainly were in the world war that so quickly and devastatingly followed.

"God manifested that sign, which astronomers chose to call an aurora borealis," observed Lucia. "I don't know for certain, but I think if they investigated the matter, they would discover that, in the form in which it appeared, it could not possibly have been an aurora borealis. Be that as it may, God made use of this to make me understand His justice was about to strike the guilty nations."

In meditating on the Fatima sign, which may give us clues about what is to come at Medjugorje, I note that the lights were spectacular yet subtle. They were subtle in that they resembled a natural phenomenon. They were only *slightly* supernatural—subtle and yet at the same time hugely miraculous. An inch above what is common to nature. But an inch that, to those who discern, spoke volumes.

I say that it carried hidden meaning because when we take a close look at the aurora, it bears an uncanny resemblance to certain atmospheric effects caused by a nuclear detonation. According to J. Rand McNally, a nuclear physicist who resigned from Oak Ridge National Laboratory in 1982 so he could freely warn about the perils of nuclear testing, the northern lights of 1938 most resembled the effects of a nuclear test in 1958 over Johnston Island. There were similar atmospheric effects at this test site in the Pacific.

There were strange reflections and refractions, similar striations, and most interesting was the fact that the explosion was accompanied by a red shock wave six hundred miles in diameter—which reminded Dr. McNally of two giant red spots that accompanied the 1938 aurora borealis.

Like Sr. Lucia, Dr. McNally believes that the northern lights seen on the night of January 25-26, 1938, were a supernatural harbinger. In my own opinion, coming as it did right before World War II, and mimicking the effects of a nuclear blast, the aurora seemed indeed to indicate not only that the war was starting but also how it would end, with the bombs at Nagasaki and Hiroshima.

Along with the war were the prophesied persecutions. Communists tortured and murdered Christians throughout the Soviet Union and spread the errors of Marxism around the globe. The good were martyred, and in effect a number of nations—countries like Ukraine, Byelorus, Lithuania, Latvia, and Estonia—were virtually "annihilated." They lost their freedom along with their national identity. So did the rest of Eastern Europe.

Weren't there other signs at Fatima? Wasn't there also a plague associated with that apparition?

That's right. It wasn't part of the secrets, but two of the Fatima youngsters, Francisco Marto and his sister Jacinta, were told they were going to be taken to heaven soon. Indeed, like some of the Kibeho visionaries, they succumbed shortly after the apparitions, in this case to a great plague that swept through Asia and Europe.

It was a form of influenza that killed at least twenty million in just a few years. That's more deaths than AIDS has caused in the entire past decade. It's interesting that the great historian William Thomas Walsh described the epidemic as "one of the concomitant scourges of the almost universal punishment of man's apostasy."

The predictions at La Salette were also relevant, in that they mentioned "plague" and "infectious disease." The prophecy was made, remember, in 1846 and the parts about war took more than fifty years to unfold. Meanwhile the first two parts of the Fatima prophecy—the first two secrets—took over twenty years to reach fulfillment.

But the day did come. The prophecies—unknown or scoffed at in their time—were in retrospect like reading tomorrow's newspaper.

SIXTEEN

~

FULL TO OVERFLOWING

Have any other prophecies come true?

World War II was also prophesied by the great Polish mystic Blessed Faustina Kowalska, who foresaw a "terrible, terrible war" a year before it erupted.

Didn't she also envision a great sign?

Yes, but it seems different than the one indicated at Medjugorje. I don't know if what Faustina saw was a metaphor or a literal vision. If nothing else it certainly implies an enhanced presence of Christ. *"Before I come as the just judge, I am coming first as the King of Mercy,"* she quoted Jesus as saying. *"Before the day of justice arrives, there will be given to people a sign in the heavens of this sort: All light in the heavens will be extinguished, and there will be great darkness over the whole earth. Then the sign of the cross will be seen in the sky, and from the openings where the hands and the feet of the Savior were nailed will come forth great lights which will light up the earth."*

The concept of light also comes from a prophecy by Fr. Stefano Gobbi of Italy, who is the world's most well-known locutionist. Fr. Gobbi began hearing an inner "voice" while praying in the chapel at Fatima twenty years ago. He has experienced locutions ever since, including a remarkable one on August 31, 1988, during a meeting in Vienna with priests from Hungary, Yugoslavia, Austria, and Germany. *"Let the light of Christ be the only light which illumines you, under the gaze of my motherly and merciful eyes, at the moment when you live through the great tribulation,"* he quoted the Virgin as saying. *"My light, as a dawn which is arising, is spreading from the East and becoming ever stronger, until it covers the whole world. Leave this prayer session with the light of Christ and of your Immaculate Mother and go to lighten up the earth, in these days of profound darkness. **With Austria and Germany, from here I bless the surrounding countries which are still under the yoke of a great slavery, and today I announce that the moment of their liberation is close.**"*

I emphasize that last sentence because when I first read it I said to myself, no way. It wasn't a realistic prophecy, I thought, because the "surrounding countries" included nations such as Czechoslovakia and East

Germany. Fr. Gobbi was predicting the fall of Communism in Eastern Europe! I don't remember a single diplomat or CIA analyst, a single professor or television commentator who, back in 1988, would have ventured such an bold prognostication.

The fall of Communism! I mean, there had been rumblings from Solidarity, the freedom movement, for nearly a decade, and there was a wave of union strikes the year of the locution. But I can't think of anyone in 1988 who expected Eastern Europe to become free without going to war with the Soviet Union.

Yet that's what happened. Less than a year after Fr.Gobbi's prophecy—in a series of events that stunned the world—Poland rose against Russia and elected a non-Communist government.

I'm not saying that Fr. Gobbi's locutions are at the level of messages from Fatima, which is a classical, first-tier apparition. He has his misses. He has been wrong. The copyright page of his book makes it clear that the messages "must be understood not as words spoken directly by Our Lady, but received in the form of interior locutions."

But I think there is a degree of real inspiration. I think Fr. Gobbi is more in tune than most other locutionists, whose messages are probably 10 to 20 percent supernatural. A locution should never be read like Scripture! A locutionist's own thoughts are often involved, and that's why many messages sound awkward or contain presumptions. They come, in large part, from a locutionist's own subconscious. The inspiration is filtered through human consciousness. Many locutionists are writing down their own thoughts or "internal dialogue." Some are even conveying confusion from deceptive spirits, who love to give false locutions.

But there are also the authentic messages and when they hit, it's really something. It's edifying to see. I was very impressed by Fr. Gobbi's prediction as I watched Poland turn into a democratic nation.

Let me divert a moment to remind you that the development in Poland was almost immediately followed by the exodus of people from other oppressed parts of Eastern Europe, refugees fleeing to West Germany in 1989 and soon chipping away at the Berlin Wall. With astounding speed Communists were shaken from power in Hungary, Bulgaria, East Germany, and Czechoslovakia. It was impressive. It was astounding. I was in Rome at the time and I remember picking up a copy of the *International Herald*

Tribune and seeing a photo of a smiling Lech Walesa—soon to be the new Polish leader—in front of a statue of the Fatima Virgin. She was positioned in such a way that her eyes looked upon Walesa with endearment.

Fatima, as we know, was where Our Lady predicted Communism in the first place. It was where she warned of Russia. Appearing years later to surviving Fatima seer Sr. Lucia dos Santos, Our Blessed Mother had asked the pope to consecrate Russia to her Immaculate Heart "in union with all the bishops of the world." She promised to save it by this means. She wanted to save it from atheism and prevent persecutions. She was asking for an invitation to intercede as one who is in a powerful position near Jesus.

It was a request that went unfulfilled from June 13, 1929, until March 25, 1984, when, finally, Pope John Paul II followed the Fatima prescription by inviting the world's bishops to join him from their home dioceses in consecrating the

> *A locution should never be read like Scripture! A locutionist's own thoughts are often involved,... [which] come, in large part, from a locutionist's own subconscious. The inspiration is filtered through human consciousness.... Some are even conveying confusion from deceptive spirits, who love to give false locutions. But there are also the authentic messages and when they hit, it's really something. It's edifying to see.*

world and "those individuals and nations which particularly need to be thus entrusted and consecrated" to the Immaculate Heart of Mary. Mention of nations with a particular "need" was an allusion to Russia. The consecration was almost immediately followed by the rise of Mikhail Gorbachev, whose policies led to the fall of Communism.

You really think an act of prayer can have that kind of effect?
Definitely. Without a doubt. Prayer is all-powerful. It can have a chain reaction.

But many people don't think the instructions of Our Lady were actually met. They point out that all the bishops didn't participate, and that it wasn't done in some kind of huge ceremony. They argue that Russia wasn't specifically mentioned in the consecration, which is true, isn't it?

This has been a big issue for mystics, including Fr. Gobbi, but it's also one argument that is now over. We know from Sr. Lucia's own mouth that the consecration of Russia has been accomplished. She says the Virgin has accepted it. Heaven has accepted it. "Yes, yes, yes," Sr. Lucia said when asked about it on October 11, 1992, during a visit with Bishop Francis Michaelappa and Anthony Cardinal Padiyara of India. The same was confirmed a day later during an audience with former Filipino President Corazon Aquino and Howard Q. Dee, who served as ambassador from the Philippines to the Vatican. Dee and his daughter, Angie, who was also present, both told me about it. There is no more doubt. Sr. Lucia says the consecration has been accomplished.

You mentioned that locutionists often miss. When a locutionist is wrong, or when seers are at odds with each other, doesn't that discredit all the messages?

In Deuteronomy 18:21-22 it says that "if you say to yourselves, 'How can we recognize an oracle which the Lord has spoken?' know that, even though a prophet speaks in the name of the Lord, if his oracle is not fulfilled or verified, it is an oracle which the Lord did not speak. The prophet has spoken it presumptuously." Usually you don't find many mistakes or presumptions in the first-tier or primary apparitions like Lourdes, Fatima, and Medjugorje.

But even those have raised certain questions because mysticism is no science. It's not as straightforward as physics, medicine, or chemistry. A chemist can mix two compounds and predict their reaction because he's done it a hundred times and it only involves a couple of well-known and visible factors. A doctor can diagnose a goiter because he has seen it time and again. A rocket scientist knows the exact equations of propulsion.

Mysticism, on the other hand, tries to perceive a reality that goes beyond the physical universe. It tries to glimpse a reality that's unlimited. It peers into eternity. The mind can't quantify such a realm. We can't take microphotos. We can't repeat an inspiration like we can replicate a chemical reaction.

Thus, mysticism is not a hundred percent clear. Never was. Never will be. We can't expect our mystics to hit every time. For example, in 1987 Fr. Gobbi predicted that "great events" contained in the secret communications at Medjugorje would take place that year, but as far as I can tell, they didn't.

Is there a connection between Father Gobbi and Medjugorje?

Only in that Fr. Gobbi was another who seemed to accurately sense Medjugorje coming. On May 13, 1981, a month before the apparitions began, he reported a locution from Our Blessed Mother which was entitled, "I Have Come Down from Heaven." She told the priest that *"with you and through you, I want to manifest myself, to save my children who are in such great need. For this I come down again from heaven to this poor suffering earth."* It was very good, a hit. It was a prediction of all the apparitions. He quoted Our Lady as saying that *"the light of my Immaculate Heart now embraces all areas of the world, and my plan for the salvation and the comfort of all stands out with ever-increasing clarity."*

He hears an interior voice. What about those who hear with their physical ears?

It's rare to meet a locutionist who has what we call auricular or auditory locutions but it does happen. At Medjugorje Fr. Jozo heard a voice on July 2, 1981, that he described as just like his own. It told him to go outside and protect the visionaries, who were being pursued by Communist authorities.

But most locutions are interior?

I would say 99.5 percent of reported locutions are inner experiences.

Has the pope said anything about locutionists like Fr. Gobbi?

There haven't been any official pronouncements and, in fact, from what I understand, authorities requested that the title of Fr. Gobbi's book be changed from *Our Lady Speaks to Her Beloved Priests* to the less definitive, *To the Priests, Our Lady's Beloved Sons.*

I doubt there will ever be formal approval of Fr. Gobbi. Usually the Church doesn't rule on locutions as it does on apparitions. I'm not sure what kind of a decision it will make, if any. But it's reported that the pope has occasionally met with Fr. Gobbi, who has inspired many hundreds of others to become "locutionists" and as such has helped provoke the eruption of mysticism, with messages that use terms such as "last times" and "Second Pentecost." Like other locutionists he has become very apocalyptic, and his dispatches announce that we are in a time of mercy but heading into a time of justice.

The divine cup, the cup of justice, he says, is full to overflowing—a theme that is now repeated by locutionists on every habitable continent.

SEVENTEEN

~

TRUE PROPHECIES

So that sparked the flurry of locutions?

Yes, along with Medjugorje. Starting around 1985 a proliferation was noted in Italy and Ireland. The two nations sent many pilgrims to Medjugorje, pilgrims who brought back inspiring, suggestive literature. It was widely read and led to similar visions. Around 1988 the outbreak reached America, which was now similarly sending many pilgrims who like-wise returned with books, pamphlets, and newsletters. Claims of Medjugorje-like miracles soon came from Lubbock, Texas, and were fol-lowed by claims in states like Arizona and Georgia.

On the one hand this proliferation seemed in line with the apparitions that had spread in former Yugoslavia—and, thought some, began to fulfill Our Lady's pledge that she would appear in every home if she had to. But there were those who worried about a massive deception. They couldn't help but recall Our Blessed Mother's specific warnings at Medjugorje about how *"many pretend to see Jesus and the Mother of God, and to understand their words, but they are, in fact, lying."* Theologians were well aware of the deceptions which had occurred at Lourdes, where false visionaries—perhaps as many as fifty—swarmed around the grotto where Our Blessed Mother was being seen in 1858 and nearly drowned out Bernadette's legitimate apparitions.

Then how are we supposed to approach all this? How can we ever know what attitude to have when we hear claims of miracles?

By simply following Scripture. "Do not stifle the Spirit," says 1 Thessa-lonians 5:19-22. "Do not despise prophecies. Test everything; retain what is good. Avoid any semblance of evil."

Which is difficult, when we hear so much.

Yes. Just as Medjugorje aroused other apparitions, so did Fr. Gobbi spawn locutions. It was a tremendous heightening of eschatology. While much of the phenomena, especially locutions, were naught more than streams of consciousness, if just 10 percent was heavenly verbiage that still boiled down to a whole lot of inspiration. It still represented an historic eruption. And it was good. It was vital. It invigorated the Church, which had been deadened by years of academic sermons.

So Medjugorje brought the Church to life?

It certainly gave it a big boost. Many who returned from Medjugorje or were converted by reading about the apparitions became daily communicants. A few million. They joined prayer groups. They began adoration of the Blessed Sacrament. They started peace centers. They preserved the Church's integrity in many dioceses. Such are the fruits of a primary apparition.

What do you mean by a "primary" apparition? How do you define it?

They're the most powerful cases, where the Church or Pope has approved or where the manifestation is so potent it creates a site of international pilgrimage.

There are only a handful. I've mentioned Guadalupe, Lourdes, and Fatima as classical first-tier apparitions. I would also include Medjugorje as well as Knock and the Miraculous Medal apparitions. In my mind those are primary because of how close the Holy Mother seemed, how clearly she appeared, and because of the powerful and eloquent messages.

They stand alone. They exude a special grace. It's like praying in tongues for hours. At Lourdes you feel the same level of spiritual power as you do in Medjugorje, although perhaps because it's an ongoing situation, the grace at Medjugorje, is felt over a larger area.

And Fatima?

Fatima is special, a classic apparition because of its great sun miracle. Like Medjugorje, a "shield" or "host" moved in front of the solar orb, which seemed to gyrate, spin off colors, and then plummet towards earth on October 13, 1917, in front of fifty thousand to seventy thousand onlookers. Even nonbelievers saw it. It was tremendous. Fatima is also special because of its devotions and prophecies, including the Third Secret.

The pope has visited Fatima and preached about it. Why does Pope John Paul II seem to have an unusual attachment to Fatima? How did the Vicar of Christ develop such a devotion to Mary?

At the age of fifteen John Paul, then known as Karol Wojtyla, had been inducted into a high school branch of Marian Sodality, which as its name implies was devoted to the Virgin. His veneration has been described as absolute—*totus tuus*—and while he later went through a period of wondering if his Marian devotion took the focus off Christ, that changed when he contemplated the matter at a "deeper" level. "Thanks to St. Louis de Montfort, I came to understand that true devotion to the Mother of God is actually Christocentric, indeed, it is very profoundly rooted in the Mystery of the Blessed Trinity, and the mysteries of the Incarnation and Redemption," wrote the pope, who often recites the Rosary.

Also, John Paul believes that during the assassination attempt on him in 1981, Mary saved his life. The pope was shot on the Fatima anniversary date of May 13, and some say he spotted a Fatima medal hanging from a pilgrim's neck just moments before the shots rang out. One bullet took an unusual route which miraculously missed organs and blood vessels like the central aorta that, if hit, would have killed him. "It was a motherly hand that guided the bullet's path, and the agonizing pope, rushed to the Gemelli Polyclinic, halted at the threshold of death," he later said in a message to the bishops.

A year after the shooting John Paul journeyed to Fatima to thank the Virgin. He had the bullet that had entered his body enshrined there. It was offered on the altar and embedded in the statue of the Fatima Virgin—next to the diamonds in its crown. It's a tribute to her sure intercession through Jesus.

The pope has visited any number of Marian shrines, including Guadalupe, Knock, Lourdes, and Czestochowa, in addition to Fatima. Czestochowa is an ancient town in Poland famous for a monastery on top of a hill called Jasna Gora—meaning "luminous mountain." In earlier times the pope was also attracted to the shrine of Kalwaria Zebrzydowska, which drew pilgrims from southern Poland and like Medjugorje had a crucifix at the top of a hill that dominated the area.

The pope told a Venezuelan bishop, Pio Bello Ricardo, that apparitions seem like "signs of the times" and that Our Lady is "an instrument of evangelizing the world."

Is it true the pope has himself experienced visions or locutions?

We don't have any confirmation. A number of seers, including one I know who spent about forty-five minutes in a private meeting with him, believe he has such gifts. He seems to operate on a mystical level. This was even mentioned by reporters during the pope's 1995 trip to New York City.

But we're not sure?

We're sure he has a profound mystical bent. We're sure he's inspired. We're sure that the pope's first doctorate was in mystical theology! We're sure that many of his actions, such as establishment of international "youth days," seem in direct response to messages from Medjugorje. And there is the legend about him and Padre Pio. In 1947, the story goes, Padre Pio prophesied while hearing Karol Wojtyla's confession that Wojtyla would one day be pope and that there would be an attempt on his life; Wojtyla would be both a pope and a martyr. While the pope has never confirmed that account, in the Vatican's dossier on Padre Pio, who is up for beatification, is a letter from then-Bishop Wojtyla, asking the Capuchin to pray for a Krakow woman with cancer. It was followed soon after with another letter thanking Padre Pio and informing him of the woman's sudden recovery.

And "secondary apparitions." Where do they fit in? How do we define those?

They're not quite as direct. They don't have the same heavenly *nearness* of Fatima or Medjugorje. There isn't the same moment. There isn't the same level of majesty. The apparitions may be frequent, but they don't have the same power or proximity. They are not as historically significant. While the primary apparitions are international in character, drawing pilgrims from around the world, a secondary apparition is more hemispheric or regional. It won't attract pilgrims like Guadalupe, which gets 10 million a year, or Lourdes, with 5.5 million. But the secondary apparitions are very important. They're confirmations. They're supports. And they include older sites like La Salette, Pontmain, Saragossa, and more recent ones like Beauraing, which is in Belgium, Betania in Venezuela, and Kibeho in Africa.

Yet don't you hint that more caution is needed with such apparitions?

Yes, because they're not quite as strong as the primary ones. The transmission is weaker. And the further down the scale we go, the more cautious I am. For if a seer has pride, that pride will blind him or her to a demonic deception, especially in cases where the "signal" is weak. Those who think they can discern are usually those who through such pride are most readily hoodwinked. A deceptive spirit can cause optical illusions, can masquerade as a holy voice, and can cause many kinds of materialization and physical phenomena. Such a spirit loves to play with predictions, particularly to give us times and dates for cataclysms that never happen. Once, when asked about catastrophic predictions, Our Lady told Medjugorje locutionist Jelena Vasilj, *"That comes from false prophets. They say, 'Such a day, on a such a date, there will be a catastrophe.' I have always said that misfortune will come if the world does not convert itself. Call the world to conversion. Everything depends on your conversion."*

What about true prophecies?

There have been some *very* intriguing prophecies from secondary sites like Betania in Venezuela and Hrushiw in the Ukraine. At Hrushiw in 1987 the Blessed Mother gave an accurate vision of the coup against Gorbachev that followed four years later, right down to the number of conspirators. The vision said there would be eight men involved and on August 19, 1991, eight iron-faced bureaucrats named Yanayev, Tizakov, Baklanov, Kruchkov, Pavlov, Yazov, Starodubtsev, and Pugo staged a coup that toppled Gorbachev from power.

In Betania, a hillside near Caracas where apparitions have occurred since 1976, the main seer, Maria Esperanza, has given us a number of interesting predictions. I remember how on December 9, 1992, she told a group of visiting Americans that she saw "two huge towers with black smoke all around them." She said they were in New York and asked the pilgrims to pray about the situation. Something was going to happen in America, she said, and indeed, a couple of months later, on February 26, 1993, there was the terrorist bombing of the World Trade Center, which includes the two huge, towering skyscrapers.

In another prophecy spoken during April of 1993, while in Lowell, Massachusetts, Esperanza made a prediction about world politics. It had to do with Bosnia. It had to do with the war. Esperanza prophesied that within three months there would be "movements in the direction of peace" but that obstacles would remain if there wasn't enough prayer. That was the forecast: movements toward peace. And it excited a number of people in the Medjugorje movement. Everyone was waiting for the hostilities, which had stopped most pilgrimages, to finally end. Maybe there was a bit too much anticipation. According to Maria's interpreter, Kathy Chebly, the prophecy was misreported as a flat prediction of the war's end, when what Esperanza was saying was that peace would come only if there was enough prayer. And indeed, there were unexpected diplomatic talks—the first of substance—right after that prophecy.

But in the end the war raged on, and on October 25, 1993, in her monthly message, Our Lady of Medjugorje said, *"These years I have been calling you to pray, to live what I am telling you, but you are living my messages [only] a little. You talk but do not live. That is why, dear little children, this war is lasting so long."*

So you accept Maria Esperanza?

No mystic is infallible. I can't vouch for everything she has ever done or said. The Church doesn't rule on individual phenomena, and Maria is more of a mystic than a visionary, which is probably why there are often misunderstandings. There are aspects of all mysticism that remain controversial. Because mystics are operating at a higher level, they can be exposed to a higher degree of spiritual attack and deception. There can be spiritual admixture. Seers are no more perfect than you or I.

But I find Esperanza to be full of love and fascinating, perhaps a historic mystic. Her gifts go beyond visions. Like Padre Pio, she suffers the wounds of stigmata, which have been witnessed by doctors and other competent witnesses. She hurts. She bleeds. On many occasions a host has materialized on her tongue and people have been healed after her prayers. The bishop told me he holds her in the highest regard and he formally approved the apparitions in 1987. Because the bishop's approval named the Virgin as "Reconciler of Nations"—a title given through Maria—her experiences were part of the pastoral letter. On a couple of occasions I've smelled the odor of sanctity around Maria, a combination of roses and lilies, and I've spoken to witnesses who swear they've seen her feet rise a few inches during

Mass—during consecration—which brings to mind the levitation of historical mystics such as St. Philip Neri and St. Joseph of Cupertino.

What are Esperanza's prophecies? What does she say about the times we're in now?

She says that in 1992 God's justice began to operate in a special way, and she seems to indicate certain events like tremors, storms, or societal uprisings. She has expressed particular concern over a "big, big war" or a nuclear incident. She has alluded to Asia, particularly China, as a trouble spot. She mentions "something in the air" and warns against nuclear testing. She has urged the U.S. to be on particular guard with developments in Russia and to be especially careful when everything seems to be peaceful and quiet. She has seen earthquakes in various places and said America will also suffer.

She's anything but pessimistic, however. She sees what's coming as a "good test." She sees it as making us better people. She sees a coming manifestation of Jesus, Who she told me will make Himself known "from east to west and north to south." She calls it "the light of His new rising."

"It's a crucial time, a decisive time for humanity," says Maria, to use a composite of her quotes. "We cannot be concerned about money or houses or big cars. No. The moment is arriving when we must leave all those things. This moment is coming. Right now man is punishing himself through his egoism, through his lack of charity, through his lack of conscientiousness.

"There will be much upheaval. There will be some societal chaos. Our Lady is coming to lighten the chastisements. They say at the end of this century, everything is going to end. That's impossible. I don't believe it. People are beginning to meditate and reflect, and new ways will be opened. Jesus will be present among us. There will be problems and certain natural calamities. I see little quakes and certain others. The core of the earth, it is not in balance. A very difficult moment will arrive, but there will remain good because the light and the grace of the Holy Spirit will always illumine a few people who desire justice in the world—the truth and the recognition of Jesus with His love throughout all time."

EIGHTEEN

~

TRIAL BY FIRE

***What do the other apparitions say about the future? How else do they relate
to Medjugorje?***

They tend to anticipate what's in the secrets. They're not as subtle as primary apparitions. They're not as circumspect. They seek to provide details. They convey starker warnings. While, publicly, Fatima only hinted at problems in the Church, and while Medjugorje only hints that some of its secrets pertain to the faith, sites such as Akita, Japan, where the Virgin is said to have spoken in 1973 to a deaf nun, and where a statue sheds tears, include vivid forecasts of Church turmoil. "The work of the devil will infiltrate even into the Church in such a way that one will see cardinals opposing cardinals, bishops against other bishops," said the prophecy of Akita. "The priests who venerate me will be scorned and opposed by their confreres, churches and altars sacked. The Church will be full of those who accept compromises and the demon will press many priests and consecrated souls to leave the service of the Lord."

At La Salette the Blessed Mother said similarly tough things, and in San Nicolas, Argentina, she expressed distress over the paucity of true believers. *"Many are those who claim to be with God, but few are wholeheartedly in the Church of Christ,"* she told a visionary named Gladys Quiroga, whose messages were granted the Bishop's imprimatur.

As usual, there is also Fr. Gobbi. From the very beginning Mary has lamented to him over priests who no longer love her, who no longer listen to the words of Christ, who ignore Jesus' presence in the Eucharist. She continually uses the word "apostasy."

These themes run through a good number of the secondary prophecies: the Church in crisis. It will be afflicted by the arrival of a great anti-Christian force. At Betania, Maria Esperanza has asked us to pray for seminarians, and at Hrushiw the message is loyalty to Rome. "A great task awaits you," said the Ukrainian apparition. "There is a greater need for lay apostles than ever before. Help the pope and the Third Secret of Fatima will be revealed to you. We are living in the times of the Father. The Third Secret is all around you."

Many believe that, in starting with the words *"in Portugal the dogma of the faith will always be preserved,"* and thus implying that elsewhere faith would *not* be preserved, the Third Secret is clearly about Church problems. Many believe that segments of the Church, especially in North America, will split from Rome in the near future—provoking political, spiritual, and geophysical disturbances, as seems to have occurred during the last episode in the Middle Ages and other times in the past. The Akita message warned, back in 1973, that if mankind didn't convert there would be a "terrible punishment" on all humanity. This unprecedented calamity would include fire falling from the sky, wiping out a significant number of people. The Akita Virgin went so far as to compare our times with those of Noah.

Such graphic predictions are similar to other prophecies. They're similar to other secondary apparitions. And they're similar to something Pope John Paul II supposedly said during a 1980 trip to Fulda, Germany, where in answer to a question about the Third Secret of Fatima and why it was never released, the Holy Father replied, "Given the gravity of its contents, so as not to encourage the worldwide power of Communism to take certain steps, my predecessors in the chair of Peter preferred, out of diplomacy, to delay its publication. On the other hand, all Christians must be content with this: if it's a question of a message where it is said that the oceans will entirely flood certain parts of the earth, that from moment to moment millions of men will perish, it is really no longer the case that publication of such a secret message should be so strongly desired."

While the pope's words seem grim, we should be quick to note that he has also said, "The situation may appear desperate, and hint at a new 'apocalypse,' but in reality, this is not the case at all. For humanity of the year 2000 there surely exists a hopeful outcome, and many reasons for hope."

Aren't there those who believe the Third Secret is similar to the prophecy of Akita?

Howard Q. Dee, Filipino ambassador to the Vatican, says that when he talked to Joseph Cardinal Ratzinger about the possible correlation between Akita and Fatima, Cardinal Ratzinger, who has read the Third Secret, "confirmed that these two messages were essentially the same." It has been noted that certain phenomena at Fatima, such as the sun "falling" toward the earth on October 13, 1917, could be interpreted as hinting at a nuclear event—as representing a falling warhead—which would tie in with Akita because a nuclear event would certainly involve fire and heat, and Akita warned that "fire will fall from the sky and will wipe out a great part of humanity."

In Chapter 15, I mentioned the similarities between the aurora borealis and a nuclear test blast. The similarity between the aurora and a nuclear bomb's atmospheric effects, along with the similarities between a falling nuclear warhead and the sun miracle of October 13, 1917—when the sun seemed to plunge towards the earth—brings us to the inevitable conclusion that whether or not it was in

> *The Akita message warned that if mankind didn't convert there would be a "terrible punishment" on all humanity. This unprecedented calamity would include fire falling from the sky, wiping out a significant number of people.*

the formal Secret, one of Fatima's chief concerns (and the chief concern at Akita) was that mankind was rushing headlong toward a fiery holocaust.

At Medjugorje the seer Ivan has said that "the greatest threat to humanity was that it could annihilate itself," and a Canadian newspaper claimed that when asked about nuclear war the seer Marija seemed to indicate (at least as far as they were concerned) that something connected to that might be in her secrets. But because the seers all but totally refuse even to approach the topic of their secrets, I haven't been able to confirm such observations.

Is that what we also get from other prophecies?

Yes, the notion of fire. The notion of it falling from the sky. The notion of Church upheaval and chastisements. Let's look at the most famous secondary apparition, La Salette, where Melanie and Maximin saw that circle of brilliant light on a French mountaintop on September 19, 1846. In addition to warning of plagues and infectious disease, in addition to warning of blood that would "flow in the streets" (which materialized during the world wars in Europe), the alleged La Salette "secret," like Akita, also mentions a future time during which "God will strike in an unprecedented way." It says that "water and fire will give the earth convulsions." It says that "the fire of heaven will fall and consume three cities."

That brings to mind 2 Peter 3:7-10: "The present heavens and earth are reserved by God's word for fire; they are kept for the day of judgment, the day when godless men will be destroyed. This point must not be over-looked, dear friends. In the Lord's eyes, one day is as a thousand years and a thousand years are as a day. The Lord does not delay in keeping His promise—though some consider it 'delay.' Rather, He shows you generous patience, since He wants none to perish but all to come to repentance. The day of the Lord will come like a thief, and on that day the heavens will van-ish with a roar; the elements will be destroyed by fire."

NINETEEN

~

NEWS FROM SISTER LUCIA

Are there any prophecies that specifically tie in fire with Russia?

Many years ago, a woman in the Ukrainian village of Dubovytsya had a well-known vision in which the Virgin said, *"Disaster is upon you as in the times of Noah. Not by flood but by fire will the destruction come. An immense flood of fire shall destroy nations for sinning before God."*

At Hrushiw, also in the Ukraine, which was a part of the Soviet Union, Mary purportedly described another conflagration. There was the vision of villages burning. Water burning. The very air on fire. Everything appeared to be in flames and it seemed related to a war, obviously a nuclear war. Hrushiw began on April 26, 1987, the first anniversary of the Chernobyl disaster. That's another hint: something to do with radiation, or perhaps even a star falling as in Revelation 8:11 ("Chernobyl" is the Ukrainian word for the bitter herb referred to in this verse of Revelation, which in English would be called "wormwood").

Fire. That seems again like Akita. That seems like the fire in the Akita prophecy, "falling from the sky and wiping out a great part of humanity." But is Akita sanctioned by the bishop? Has it been approved?

When I checked with the Most Reverend Francis Keiichi Sato, the new Bishop of Niigata, he sent me a letter saying, "As you may know, opinions are divided on both sides of the question. As pastor of the people on both sides of the question, I have tried to maintain a delicate balance between giving freedom to devotions at Akita, and leaving it to time to clarify the nature of the events." With his letter was an official statement affirming that the statue, from which came the prophetic voice, did indeed exhibit inexplicable phenomena. "The fact that the wooden statue of Our Lady shed tears is undeniable," he wrote. "It is something that occurred over and over (101 times) between 1975 and 1981, with a great number of eye-witnesses."

That means there is partial and tentative approval of Akita and that its prophecy is therefore worthy of our consideration. It was given to Sr. Sasagawa on October 13—yet another anniversary of the Fatima miracle and the same day that Fr. Gobbi, whose locutions began during a visit to Fatima, received his warning about fire. In 1973 Our Lady of Akita explained, *"Many men in this world afflict the Lord. I desire souls to console Him to soften the anger of the heavenly Father. I wish, with my Son, for souls who will repair by their suffering and their poverty for the sinners and ingrates. In order that the world might know His anger, the heavenly Father is preparing to inflict a great chastisement on all mankind. With my Son I have intervened so many times to appease the wrath of the Father. I have prevented the coming of calamities by offering Him the sufferings of the Son on the Cross, His precious Blood, and beloved souls who console Him by forming a cohort of victim souls."*

Such prophecies were given at a time of tension between the U.S. and U.S.S.R. They express what could have happened at the time of the apparitions. They express where mankind was headed since the 1970s. But here's some news: Sister Lucia of Fatima says a nuclear war that had been scheduled for the mid-1980s, and which may well have been what was foreseen at Akita, was averted by prayer. In a meeting with Filipino Cardinal Ricardo Vidal on October 11, 1993, Lucia was quoted by interpreter Carlos Evaristo as saying that when the pope and bishops consecrated the world and by implication Russia to the Immaculate Heart in 1984, that action thwarted a major and imminent conflict. "The consecration of 1984," said Lucia, "prevented an atomic war that would have occurred in 1985."

She claims a major war had been scheduled ten years ago but for the time being has been avoided! Whether Lucia is relying on her own intuition or on matters that have been revealed to her in recent apparitions, she believes we narrowly avoided a war in the mid-1980s. That makes sense when we think back to the truly frightening men who were in charge of the U.S.S.R. at the time. Warhawks.

It was also in the 1980s that Mary came as Queen of Peace to Medjugorje. It now makes sense that she came with such urgency, saying peace in the world was in a state of crisis. It now also makes sense that 1985 saw the huge explosion of apparitions in many other places warning of disaster, including fire. There was a legitimate prophetic pulse.

Remarkably, a message from Medjugorje in the early eighties said that a third world war would not take place, deterred at least for the time being. At Medjugorje it was also said that a chastisement in the seventh secret had been averted or lessened, but that we still faced others.

Lucia says that we are currently in the "era of peace" mentioned in the Fatima prophecy, which obviously means peace, however temporary, between the U.S. and Russia. A period of grace and mercy. Our task is to extend the period of grace and prevent what may be equally daunting events from materializing in the future.

Lucia says the triumph of the Immaculate Heart has already begun, that Our Lady "triumphed over the errors that were being spread by Communist Russia."

Didn't the Hrushiw prophecy, which also spoke of fire, take place after 1985?

Yes, perhaps indicating that we're not yet out of the woods.

What about the Third Secret? Where is that message kept, and why wasn't it released in 1960, as Mary requested?

I don't know where Lucia's message, a single handwritten page, is kept at this precise moment. At one time it was in a small safe in the pope's living quarters. Because the first two parts of the message mentioned Church devotions and because the Fatima children reported visions of troubles in Rome, we come to this speculation: the secret mainly has to do with spiritual and societal upheaval, not fire. It has to do with our souls more than any physical chastisement. Lucia has said that the Third Secret "is not intended to be revealed. It was only intended for the pope and immediate Church hierarchy." She says that the year 1960 was mentioned only as a time after which the message would become *clearer.* The pope could release it after 1960 if he so desired because then it would make more sense, and when we look back at 1960 we see that what became clear during that time was the great infiltration, a tremendous surge, of evil.

The sixties ushered in a revolution of drugs, violence, illicit sex, psychic phenomena, irreverent music, and strong trends against church-going. Priests left in droves. So did nuns who joined the women's liberation movement and the sexual revolution. Pews emptied and scandals loomed. Sr. Lucia won't comment on whether the Third Secret has to do with the Second Vatican Council, but she has said that the Fatima message involved "heresy, atheism, and apostasy"—precisely the message from Sr. Sasagawa in Akita and Melanie at La Salette a century before.

To some extent the Third Secret almost surely describes the steep decline of morals and the atmosphere that has legitimized things like abortion. It is also connected with the Medjugorje message of our century being given to the devil. In a letter back in 1970 Sr. Lucia lamented over the diabolical "disorientation" of the times and fretted that the devil had succeeded in presenting evil "under cover of good" and that the blind are now leading the blind, which has also been a major message from all the secondary apparitions.

If there is too much evil, the Lord will have to allow major events to purge it. He allows certain suffering because only in hard times do many return to Him. It's our role to keep calamities away by offering our sufferings and praying for the conversion of sinners.

Is that why there are so many mystics who suffer things like the stigmata?
Yes, the Lord is receiving their dear sacrifices.

So you're implying that more than anything, more than fire from the sky, the Third Secret had to do with spiritual warfare?
What visionaries see are calamities that will be allowed if our evil continues. What mystics see is what is in store for us at the given moment. The scenario of fire from the sky is perhaps something that happens if we *lose* the spiritual war. Or perhaps it's a symbol of God's justice.

It's one of the calamities upon which we could stumble: a war or some kind of nuclear incident. According to Lucia, one such event has already been averted. Now we look to other such threats in the future, the type of events implied at Medjugorje, which goes several steps further than Fatima.

The Third Secret has something to do with Catholicism in particular?
My belief is that it has to do with spirituality and the Church. The declining Mass attendance, the scandals and the disaffection of priests, and the possibility of the good losing control. Perhaps that's why the Church didn't publicize it, and why the pope, at Fulda, when asked why the Secret has never been released, mentioned that it hadn't been publicized for diplomatic reasons. It hadn't been released because the Vatican didn't want to encourage and provoke the Soviet Union, which would have salivated over the prospect of a crisis in Christianity, a weakness in our resolve and moral fiber, and may have been tempted to strike at Western nations. The secret

may also have predicted the fall of Communism, which Soviet hardliners would have found alarming and another reason to move quickly against Christians.

In other words the Third Secret may have been more limited than what many speculated?

Yes, of a more limited nature as far as political or geophysical events is concerned. Its only allusion to politics may have been Communism, which makes it more limited than what many expected, but no less serious.

Lucia still sees Our Blessed Mother? She still gets messages?

In that 1992 conversation there was also a priest, Fr. Francisco V. Pacheco from Brazil, who asked Sr. Lucia if she continues to see the Virgin. Lucia only smiled in reply. When the interpreter, Evaristo, pressed her on the issue, Lucia said she couldn't answer. But when Evaristo requested that the next time she spoke to Our Lady she remember to ask a favor for Fr. Pacheco, she replied, "Yes, I will ask Our Lady."

While the seer has steadfastly refused over these now nearly eighty years to slip us a peek at the Third Secret, Lucia's personal remarks have often resembled messages not only from Akita but also from any number of other apparitions. "Our Lady did not tell me that we are living in the last epoch of the world, but she did give me to understand that, firstly, we are going through a decisive battle, at the end of which we will be either of God or of the evil one," she has said. "There will be no middle way. Secondly, [she said] that the last means God will give to the world for its salvation are the Holy Rosary and the devotion to the Immaculate Heart of Mary. And thirdly, when God, in His providence, is about to chastise the world, He first uses every means to save us, and when He sees we have not made use of them, then He gives us the last anchor of salvation, His Mother." Lucia has said that the devil is carrying on the decisive battle with the Virgin Mary because "he sees that his time is getting short, and he is making every effort to gain as many souls as possible."

So in the end the Secret has to do with spirituality more than a nuclear holocaust?

Whatever may or may not have been said at Fulda, there's no denying that another pontiff, Pope Paul VI, alluded to the "apocalyptic" themes of the Third Secret and that, in referring to Fatima, Cardinal Ratzinger said, "A stern warning has been launched from that place that is directed against the prevailing frivolity, a summons to the seriousness of life, of history, to the perils that threaten humanity."

TWENTY

~

ACROSS THE UNIVERSE

How are we supposed to pray for a lessening of evil? How do we avoid chastisements?

Every time one of us turns to God—and that's the first step, simply turning to God—we reduce potential trouble. Something good occurs in our spirits, and, believe it or not, reverberates through the universe.

Every person is an important cog in God's machine. We are equally necessary in His plan of salvation. When a person begins to live according to God's will, the entire planet benefits.

Really?

Each person who comes to God mitigates chastisement. We should dedicate prayers every day to our own deliverance and also the world's condition. At Fatima we were asked to recite the prayer, *"Oh my Jesus, forgive us our sins, save us from the fires of hell, lead all souls to heaven, especially those most in need of Thy mercy."*

If each of us can get rid of our own evil and then convert just one other person, we've started a sort of chain reaction. We've twice affected the universe.

But how do we start?

By rooting out vice and developing an active conscience. We start by invoking the Holy Spirit. We ask Him to tell us where we need cleansing. We pray to be purged of all evil. We look inward and through Christ root out greed, selfishness, materialism, impatience, anger, resentment, addictions, insincerity, lack of faith, hatred, and especially any form of occultism or sexual immorality. We dedicate Masses or recitations of the Rosary to the particular cause of reviewing our lives and illuminating past darkness.

We pray regularly to do God's Will, not our own. As the Virgin told Jelena, *"Thus, each day, try to go beyond and to reject every vice from your heart. Find out which are the vices that you most need to reject. Pray, because prayer is life. Pray and fast! Ask the Holy Spirit to renew your souls, to renew the entire world."*

My suggestion would be to begin with a basic sin like pride, which we all have. Locate it. Acknowledge it. Meditate on the many ways you may think of yourself as better than someone else. Think of the times you've considered yourself more advanced or better looking or somehow superior, and ask forgiveness; the times you've taken pride in your clothes or cars; even the times you may have taken pride in your spirituality. Think back on the many times you have been impatient. Impatience often results from pride. Ask the Holy Spirit to let you see yourself as God sees you, to indicate any areas where you're still in bondage.

Break it down. Purge it. Pride leads to so many other sins. When we're proud, we treat our friends and loved ones as inferior. We put them down. We argue. We're testy and we judge others. We focus on everyone's faults but our own. We're negative and temperamental. With pride we become materialistic because we want physical objects to back up our feelings of being above others. We like to showcase ourselves and demonstrate power. We become rude and argumentative.

When pride accumulates it spreads from person to person and can also begin a domino effect. A negative one. Most wars are rooted in pride, which is spiritual aggression.

But aren't there some forms of pride that are good? Aren't we supposed to be proud of certain accomplishments?

There's a difference between feeling satisfaction and harboring conceit or haughtiness. There's a difference between thanking God—Who is actually responsible for any good we do—and thanking ourselves. We should never give ourselves the credit. We should never feel "puffed up" (see 1 Corinthians 4:6, KJV). I've already said that pride blocks grace. It stymies our development. No one who is arrogant can function as an effective Christian. Pride is the real root of all evil because it's pride that leads to materialism, sensualism, and the coarse treatment of others.

Pride is faith in *ourselves*. Pride is magnifying self instead of God. Pride leads to selfishness. Pride causes our prayers to ring hollow.

Pride prevents a closeness to Christ because Jesus is the antithesis of pride. He's the opposite of selfishness. The ultimate humility was His descent into mortality.

So when we have pride, when we're self-seeking, we're the opposite of the way He gave of Himself on the cross.

If we could get rid of all the pride in our lives—just the pride—our world would be on the way to an entirely bright future. There would be fewer wars because we'd be eliminating the kind of pride that can produce obsessive nationalism.

I can't emphasize it enough. The Lord detests pride. He detests arrogance. They are "the evil way" (Prv 8:13) and most often we don't even see it. We're blinded to our own conceit but we bear the consequences.

When pride comes, disgrace comes. Pride goes before a fall (see Proverbs 16:18). Pride is listed among sins from the deep recesses of the heart. It's classified with theft, adultery, and blasphemy (see Mark 7:21-22).

Right now our society is suffering from an enormous epidemic of self-centeredness, which is very dangerous because egotism is self-idolatry and idolatry is a form of witchcraft. It was idolatry that led to the fall of cities like Nineveh and Babylon. *"Pray that Satan does not entice you with his pride and deceptive strength,"* said Our Lady of Medjugorje on November 25, 1987. Two years before she had taught that when we receive a gift from God, *"do not say that it is yours. Say rather that it is God's."*

How would you suggest beginning to root out evil?

Go to Confession. Confessing your sins demonstrates humility and breaks many evil bondages. It also lifts our spiritual blinders. *"Monthly Confession will be a remedy for the Church in the West,"* said Our Lady of Medjugorje, adding that *"every family must pray family prayers and read the Bible."* She says that whenever possible we should attend Mass. The reception of Communion is the single most powerful route to self-deliverance and clears away spirits that cling to us from past transgressions. They cannot stay in God's presence.

There's no prayer more powerful than reception of the Eucharist. *"Let the Holy Mass be your life,"* Our Blessed Mother said. *"Mass is the greatest prayer of God. You will never be able to understand its greatness."*

For Catholics and Protestants alike, a devout regimen of prayer and meditation is the key. Everyone needs a direct dialogue with God in the Name of Jesus and with the prayer of the Blessed Virgin, whose Rosary is a meditation on Scripture (see Luke 1:28).

What about those who say we overdo Mary?

When someone asked Mother Teresa of Calcutta how much devotion we should have to Mary, she replied that we should love the Virgin as much as Jesus loves her.

There's an historical basis for that?

Mary has been written about since 150 A.D. and called the "Mother of God" since the time of Hippolytus.

You mention "spiritual blindness." What do you mean by that term? How does it affect conversion?

Such blindness is the inability to see life for what it is: a battle between good and evil. Once the Holy Spirit comes, we see the world in a different light and we suddenly can see both the movements of grace and the work of evil spirits.

Prayer alerts us to the realities of existence. Prayer is vital because it regulates life's otherwise uneven occurrences. It does that by keeping us in touch with Our Creator.

When we pray, the soot of worldliness, the grime of evil, is cleared away. It's like washing a windshield. Suddenly you can see much more of your surroundings and you have a far better sense of where you and the world are heading.

TWENTY-ONE

~

HOW TO PRAY TO GOD

And the world is heading for a major and possibly unprecedented disaster within our lifetimes, in the next few years or decades, isn't it?

As the Medjugorje visionary Mirjana said in the private interview with Fr. Ljubicic in 1985, "It is necessary to pray a great deal until the first secret is revealed. But in addition to that, it is necessary to make sacrifices as much as possible, to help others as much as it is within our abilities, to fast especially now, before the first secret. We are obliged to prepare ourselves. The Blessed Mother not only asks but pleads with everyone to convert, pray, to fast. They have no idea what awaits them and that is why, as their Mother, she is in deep anguish for them. She stresses again that everyone should pray much, fast, do penance. It is not enough to just simply pray. It is not enough to just quickly say some prayers so that one can say that they prayed and did their duty. What she wants from us is to pray from the depths of our souls, to converse with God. That is her message.

"Naturally, it is necessary to pray the Rosary, to say the *'Our Father'* and other prayers, but it is very important to more frequently engage in simple conversations with God. One must present Him with things that come from the depth of one's soul. It is not enough to just present Him the established *'Our Father Who art in heaven.'* After praying in this manner it's also essential that we open our souls to Him. It is good to bare one's soul to God and tell Him what hurts you. You see, it should be a simple conversation, just as the one you and I are having now. Certainly this is what I usually do and I feel that God responds.

"Most of all I now pray that people will convert, particularly in view of the secrets. My greatest advice to all is to pray for the unbelievers. You see, Mary expends the greatest amount of time talking about that very thing. And we must also not forget the elderly and the infirm."

If every conversion mitigates or lessens a potential chastisement, how many will it take to prevent some of these dramatic prophecies?

It could take one person or one billion. We've seen single saints fend off chastisements. When the Lord was ready to inflict a chastisement upon an

> *Medjugorje visionary Mirjana said, "It is good to bare one's soul to God and tell Him what hurts you. You see, it should be a simple conversation, just as the one you and I are having now. Certainly this is what I usually do and I feel that God responds."*

errant religious community, He spoke to St. Margaret Mary Alacoque. *"I will give thee My Heart, but thou must first constitute thyself Its holocaust, so that, by Its intervention, thou mayest turn aside the chastisements which the Divine Justice of My Father is about to inflict upon a religious community, which in His just wrath He wishes to correct and chastise,"* the Lord told her.

It was during prayer before the Blessed Sacrament that Jesus first revealed His Sacred Heart to Margaret Mary, representing it as a resplendent sun with burning rays, reminding us of the sun miracles. "Flames issued from every part of His Sacred Humanity, especially from His Adorable Bosom, which resembled an open furnace and disclosed to me His most loving and most amiable Heart, which was the living source of those flames," recounted Margaret Mary.

In the late 1920s, Blessed Faustina, the great mystic of Divine Mercy, learned that God was going to cause a chastisement to fall upon what Faustina described as "the most beautiful city in our country," which, since she was in Poland, probably meant Warsaw. "This chastisement would be that with which God had punished Sodom and Gomorrah," she wrote in her diary. "I saw the great wrath of God and a shudder pierced my heart. I prayed in silence. After a moment, Jesus said to me, *'My child, unite yourself closely to Me during the Sacrifice and offer My Blood and My wounds to My Father in expiation for the sins of that city. Repeat this without interruption throughout the entire Holy Mass. Do this for seven days.'*

"On the seventh day I saw Jesus in a bright cloud and began to beg Him to look upon the city and upon our whole country. Jesus looked down graciously. When I saw the kindness of Jesus, I began to beg His blessing. Immediately Jesus said, *'For your sake I bless the entire country.'"*

On another occasion the Lord told Blessed Faustina, *"My daughter, your confidence and love restrain My Justice, and I cannot inflict punishment because you hinder Me from doing so."*

Thus we see that one person can have great consequences. In the time of Abraham God required only ten righteous (see Genesis 18:32).

When there is sin, He gives us a chance to erase it. We are given a chance to do penance. The Virgin of Medjugorje arrived with a warning that the peace of the world was in danger but at the same time that we could suspend natural laws and avert disasters through fasting and prayer. Without prayer, without humility, our society will continue stumbling into the future and there will only be entropy and disorder.

Increasing in intensity, there will be one disaster after another.

Blessed Faustina Kowalska stated, "On the seventh day I saw Jesus in a bright cloud and began to beg Him to look upon the city and upon our whole country. Jesus looked down graciously. When I saw the kindness of Jesus, I began to beg His blessing.
Immediately Jesus said, 'For your sake I bless the entire country.'"

TWENTY-TWO

~

LIKE A THIEF IN THE NIGHT

You mentioned that pride can lead to obsessive nationalism, which then leads to warfare. Is that what you see on the horizon?

I don't like to talk of issues that in any way date prophecy, but based on current mysticism I'll go so far as to speculate that if things keep going as they have, we face an unprecedented war between now and the mid-point of the twenty-first century. A key concern is that the kind of ethnic war currently fought in Bosnia-Hercegovina will either grow in scope or, worse, repeat itself in the former Soviet Union, which has the same ethnic components as former Yugoslavia. The Serbs are akin to the Russians, Croats are like the Ukrainians, and Bosnian Muslims would be analogous to the Muslims who dominate regions such as Turkmenistan and Kazakhstan, which once formed the southern flank of the U.S.S.R. They are every bit as hostile with one another, and so in that sense the conflict in Bosnia-Hercegovina may be like a microcosm or precursor.

A warning of something larger.

Russia could easily drift back into Communism, and suddenly it could engage in new disputes with the U.S. or other nations over issues like the Balkans. If such animosities were kindled, it would be a tremendous military spectacle. Where Yugoslavia had a population of eighteen million, the U.S.S.R. had a population fifteen times as large. And the former republics of the Soviet Union have much more sophisticated armaments, including nuclear weapons.

There are dozens of places where such animosities have erupted or soon could erupt. We've already seen problems in Chechnya and Armenia. Once engaged, a war between the republics, a full-scale conflict, would of necessity drag in first Eastern Europe and then the West. It would certainly affect Germany, which has one of the world's largest economies. We might also see the involvement of nations like Turkey and China, since there are many Turkish Muslims in both the former Soviet Union and western China. All of Eurasia could be embroiled.

Mystics certainly warn of China. They also see conflicts that may erupt in the Baltics or of course the Middle East.

I don't pretend to have worked out the correct scenario, nor do I know what's in the secrets of Medjugorje. What I do know is that when the Virgin first arrived she immediately said the peace of the world is in danger. Mirjana said the Virgin showed her the first secret and explained, *"It is the upheaval of a region of the world."*

There were similar warnings from those nineteenth-century mystics, weren't there?

Yes. In France one known as the Ecstatic of Tours said that there would be earthquakes and "signs in the sun," which is now very intriguing in light of the sun miracles. That was back in the 1800s, and this mystic also said that, toward the end, darkness would cover the earth. "When everyone believes that peace is assured," said the mystic, "when everyone least expects it, the great happenings will begin." This is also what Paul said in 1 Thessalonians 5:1-3: "You know very well that the day of the Lord is coming like a thief in the night. Just when people are saying, 'Peace and security,' ruin will fall on them with the suddenness of pains overtaking a woman in labor."

We are currently in a time when many have heard prophecies but are becoming lax because Medjugorje has been going on since 1981, and aside from the Bosnian war so far nothing has happened. But if we keep it up, the time will come. The day will dawn. It seems to me that while mankind had improved enough to forestall war around 1985, things started back downhill a few short years later—and more swiftly than ever.

Why are there all these indications of war if we're in the Triumph of the Immaculate Heart, if we're in an "era of peace"?

As I said, Sr. Lucia was referring to tensions between the U.S. and Soviet Union, tensions that have decreased since the dissolution of Communism. We're in an era of peace, but it's a tenuous peace.

And the Triumph?

We see the Triumph in the extraordinary manifestations of Marian phenomena. Our Blessed Mother is triumphing. It's a triumphant spectacle. She has been sent by Christ to step on the serpent's head, and she will. The question is how much pain there will be on the way to victory. The Fatima secrets are nearing completion, but the events in the Medjugorje prophecies take us to the next step. And they haven't even started.

Would war relate to the "wars and rumors of war" in Matthew?

All I can say is that we live in a very militaristic time. Since World War II there have been a hundred wars of one kind or another.

But violence is not confined to the battlefield. There is also the prospect of riots, revolutions, and other kinds of social upheaval. Apparitions like the one in Cuapa, Nicaragua, which occurred in 1980, nearly always ask us to implore God for peace and non-violence. They tell us to do so by using the Rosary. They urge us to get back to the Christian basics and open our hearts to the Lord. They implore us to recite the Rosary, to pray for peace, to make sacrifices, to help the poor, and to abandon our lives to God's Will. Especially we're asked to discover humility, faith, and love.

These are the basic messages. These are the moral teachings that are rendered by the totality of apparitional messages—not fantasizing over war. *"Everything is based on faith and love,"* said the Virgin of Cuapa to a man named Bernardo Martinez. *"Love one another. Forgive each other. Make peace. It is not enough to ask for peace. Make peace. If you do not make peace, then there will be no peace."*

"Do not waste time," said the Virgin of San Nicolas, Argentina, where those apparitions began in 1983 and were supported by the bishop. *"The night is coming."*

"But wherever people substitute my Immaculate Heart for their sinful hearts," said the Virgin in Marienfried, *"the devil has no power."*

While the words from a secondary apparition are not as powerful as those from a primary one, what the secondary apparitions like San Nicolas and Cuapa do very well is warn about evil and its consequences. They warn that a society, like an individual, suffers when it is corrupt and unfaithful. A society especially suffers when it wanders throughout the journey of life—which is one huge test—without guidance from the Holy Spirit.

When we go through a day without prayer, when we forget God, things occur that wouldn't happen if we were in a state of grace. We wake up and stub a toe and things degenerate from there, until we can't wait for the day to be over. Work goes badly. Lunch is hectic. There are rude drivers on the way home.

While it's true that no matter how much we pray, every day has its crosses and trials, praying allows us to intuitively anticipate certain events and to respond gracefully and correctly to challenging situations.

When we don't pray, things get out of control. There's "bad luck." There are unfortunate circumstances. It's true for individuals as well as entire communities. When we don't pray, we put ourselves at a distance from the Holy Spirit. We allow openings for evil spirits and when we allow demons around us, they engender problems.

The same is true for entire nations. They have their ups and downs. They're in various states of grace. When they're blessed, as America was once blessed, there is peacefulness and bounty. There's inspiration. There's coherence and happiness and unselfishness. When the Spirit decreases, on the other hand, many negatives begin to play out. A nation becomes unruly and degenerate. It loses grace. Its institutions of law, education, and finance begin to melt down. The prime example is the former Soviet Union, where atheism led to a dark and dismal society where nothing went right. It took years to build a simple, shoddy hotel there. The people were reduced to unhappy robotons because when a nation is distant from the Holy Spirit, it lacks humanness. It lacks inspiration. It's more prone to political trouble. The farther a nation moves from God, the larger and more numerous are the potential disasters.

Of the major recent apparitions, which have the most dramatic and frightening prophecies?

Of the well-known ones some of the most severe warnings have come from a mystic in Ireland named Christina Gallagher, who is currently being put through the discernment process. In other words, we still need to investigate further. Christina is certainly a fine person. I've always enjoyed being around her, but her prophecies can be a bit startling. If her mysticism holds up, it will rank at the level of an Akita or Hrushiw. As happened at both of those places, she saw fire falling. She said fire will fall in three parts of the world but didn't get into further specifics. She has seen many things. She has seen earthquakes and mudslides and a darkness descending on the Church—trouble for the pope. Her spiritual director, Fr. Gerard McGinnity, told me Christina had recently been "shown" a coming purification. He said it's the only time she hasn't shared details with him.

She is very much like the old-school mystics around 1800. In addition to her apparitions, Christina experiences manifestations like the stigmata, with significant quantities of blood issuing from spontaneous "wounds" on her feet. It's not just a little red mark or scab. The blood flows up to six inches from the point of emanation. Christina's phenomena allegedly began in the eruption of 1985 when she and others saw strange aerial images above a Lourdes statue at a shrine in County Sligo. On one visit Christina saw the head of Jesus. It was in the sky. It was crowned with thorns and it reminded her of the Shroud of Turin. Later she experienced apparitions of the Virgin along with Thérèse of Lisieux, St. Joseph, and John the Evangelist.

Have any of her prophecies come true?

Back when I first interviewed Christina in 1991, she said the next year, 1992, would see many people cry out for God's mercy. She liked to say that when God moves His hand, it will be swifter than the wind. Frankly, I expected that if she was on target, that meant 1992 would see some kind of monumental event. As far as I was concerned, that didn't happen.

I asked Christina about that when I visited her a second time on August 13, 1995, in the company of Fr. Michael Scanlan, president of the Franciscan University in Ohio, and Ambassador Margaret Heckler, the former emissary to Ireland. We met Christina at her House of Prayer on Achill Sound, a cold, windswept place in the western part of Ireland. It immediately reminded me of the barren environs of San Giovanni Rotundo, where Padre Pio once lived. It was an electrical meeting. There was the palpable energy you often feel around seers.

While many took the onset of justice to mean an immediate global event, Christina maintained that what she had seen was an intensification of wars and other chastisements beginning in 1992. She saw much upheaval leading up to the year 2000. She was especially concerned for her homeland of Ireland, which she feared would one day allow abortion and divorce (both of which were illegal at that time), and she was also very wary of attempts to unify the economies of European nations. She feared the Maastricht treaties.

Like Esperanza at Betania, Christina saw 1992 as the beginning of various sorrows, when God's mercy would begin to transform into His merciful justice. She saw "more calamities and more disasters worldwide." I can't judge some of Christina's more grievous predictions, and like I said, her mysticism has not yet been discerned. But I will say that America has experienced at least three of its top ten all-time most costly disasters since 1992: Hurricane Andrew, the Mississippi floods, and the Los Angeles earthquake. They total perhaps $60 billion in damages. And they're only part of a recent upsurge. *Six* of the top ten American disasters have occurred since 1989 and are joined by the monsoons, volcanic eruptions, and mudslides in other countries.

During 1995 England experienced its driest summer since records were begun in the 1600s, and there was an enormous quake in Kobe, Japan ("Kobe" means "the door of God"). We have also seen potent blizzards, unusually active hurricane seasons, and terrible brushfires from California to Long Island. Such activity brings to mind the reputed and controversial La Salette prophecy, wherein it was mentioned that thunderstorms would shake cities and "the seasons will be altered." And Christina is another who warns that we must be most vigilant when things seem most peaceful and quiet. She is another who has indicated concern about a war between Russia and China.

TWENTY-THREE

~

A FINAL WARNING

What indications are there that such circumstances may also be contained in the secrets of Medjugorje?

Certainly there are indications of grave events, but it doesn't seem that the first couple of secrets involve any kind of global catastrophe. You may recall that when grilled by Fr. Ljubicic, Mirjana described one event as a more localized or regional disaster. She indicated it would occur at a specific time and place. She compared it to a dam collapsing in Italy. The first two secrets are warnings, followed by what sounds like another warning coupled with the "great sign." Then some seers have messages about the Church, the parish of Medjugorje, and their own personal lives. The last several secrets, at least in the case of Mirjana, seem to be chastisements for the sins of the world. She said the larger-scale events are contained in her later messages.

The Medjugorje visionaries don't all have the same secrets?

The only secret we're sure they share is the third, about a great sign that will appear on the hill of apparitions.

They don't know each other's secrets?

No. They've never discussed the secrets among themselves and often refuse to even broach the subject, especially Ivanka and the youngest seer, Jakov Colo, who have said very little publicly.

They were given times and dates?

Mirjana says she knows the exact times of all her secrets. Others know some of the dates but not all. They handle whatever knowledge they have with great discretion.

When do you think the events will happen?

The seers say they'll live to see them. Most of them are in their early thirties, so if they have an average longevity it means the secrets should begin sometime between now and 2040. If you want to narrow it down further,

Mirjana was told to confide in a priest who will announce the events just before they occur and she chose Fr. Ljubicic, who's in his fifties.

How long will the events last?

Mirjana claims the time between the first and second secrets "is of a certain period" and that the time between the second and third secrets is of a different duration. "For example, and I stress, the first secret may take place today and the second one already tomorrow," she told Fr. Ljubicic.

Once they begin, some of the secrets may be more natural and gradual than many expect. They could take decades to play out. They may transpire in such a way that one or two occur this week and the following one occurs ten years from now. Remember that the first two parts of the Fatima message, including the prediction of World War II, took more than two decades for completion. Meanwhile the Third Secret took more than forty years to become clear and, according to Pope John Paul II, is only now reaching its fulfillment.

So it could be a while.

It could be a while. The secrets may span several decades. On the other hand, events could begin tomorrow.

Many people are waiting for a huge and sudden event, a mega-incident. We hear people conjecture about all kinds of sensational scenarios.

The first secrets are warnings, and warnings are signals. They're not the climax. They're not the grand finale. They sound like mundane events, or at least happenings that have a context within the natural order.

In our reach for the spectacular, we often forget that God just about always works within nature, and Mirjana has even indicated that many people will explain away the first two warnings as normal or natural phenomena, just as happened with the aurora borealis at Fatima.

Because they are within physical laws, the secrets may seem to be wholly natural. The vast majority of God's signs work that way. He speaks powerfully but with exquisite subtlety. Even when He sends momentous events, they tend to arrive in a gradual or at least a natural fashion. He nudges. He whispers. He gives hints that are often seen with eyes of faith. It's the devil who's loud and insistent.

Yet Mirjana indicates the events of the first secrets are nonetheless serious. When the Madonna describes *"the upheaval of a region of the world,"* it reminds us of what already has happened in Sarajevo.

Mirjana said the first secret is a warning that will require no prior signals. "It will be something that people will hear about very far," she had told Fr. Ljubicic, indicating, to repeat myself, that the first secret involves a localized or limited happening that will be reported by the media—as opposed to an event of cosmic proportion.

But as Mirjana said, "If people saw the first secret, as it was shown to me, all of them would most certainly be shaken enough to take a new and different look at themselves and everything around them."

The importance of the secrets is to prepare us spiritually. We're told to step up our prayer and especially to eliminate selfishness. Our Blessed Mother has begged prayers for the unbelievers. Mass. The Rosary. She has made it clear that the Rosary can thwart Satan's designs and that through fasting and prayer we can stop wars and transcend those natural laws. Where there is prayer, there is conversion, and where there is conversion there's reason for optimism.

> *In our reach for the spectacular, we often forget that God just about always works within nature, and Mirjana has even indicated that many people will explain away the first two warnings as normal or natural phenomena, just as happened with the aurora borealis at Fatima.*
>
> *Because they are within physical laws, the secrets may seem to be wholly natural. The vast majority of God's signs work that way. He speaks powerfully but with exquisite subtlety.... He nudges. He whispers... It's the devil who's loud and insistent.*

But the others could have a different first secret?
For all we know.

Did Mirjana ever say how long the first secret will last?
She said it will last "for a little while." That's all we know. A little while.

And then the devil's time will end?

The special period during which Satan has been allowed to use all his power, the current era of evil, which some believe began a century or more ago, will last only until the event of the first secret. And then, the seers say, his insidious hold will be broken.

How?

In a way the seers can't describe, because it's part of the secrets.

Didn't Mirjana see Satan?

I believe a couple of times, including a notable encounter in Sarajevo. He came in a flash as an awful presence who tried to dissuade her from listening to the Virgin, promising her happiness in life while saying that Mary would lead only to suffering.

The secrets will be distinct and visible?

Yes.

And you really believe in such specific prophecy?

I believe in Medjugorje and so I believe in the secrets. If they don't pan out, it will certainly cast serious doubt on the apparitions.

Are there any more indications about when these events could start?

Another hint may lie in the life story of the Virgin, which Mary dictated to Vicka between 1982 and 1985. It's sort of Mary's autobiography. Vicka is waiting for the Virgin's signal to publish it. When I asked whether the account will be released before or after the secrets, Vicka told me it's her feeling it will be published *before* the secrets begin.

Which secrets did you say are the chastisements?

In Mirjana's case the last several, and Vicka seems to have similar knowledge. She and Mirjana may share one of those secrets. Both have spoken about the seventh secret and both have said the severity has been averted or at least lessened by much prayer. Our Blessed Mother spoke to Vicka about the future of the world during much of 1985 and 1986, around the time she was suffering her peculiar ailment—lapsing into comas that lasted for up to fifteen hours, just as the seers in Kibeho went into comas for long periods and then spoke prophecy.

It was a little eerie the night I asked Vicka about the secrets. It was November 5, 1992, at her uncle Stanko Vasilj's house, and that was the night Medjugorje was hit by a thunderstorm that even the residents found unusual. I'm not sure I've ever seen anything quite like it. It sounded like we were inside a bass drum. Coming as it did after the conversation, it seemed like an exclamation point.

Have they said anything about economic collapse? Is the economy a part of the secrets?
Mirjana says she knows nothing about that.

How about the United States?
When asked about the future of the West, Marija Pavlovic flushed, as if the question—posed by a priest from Mostar—impinged on her secrets.

The great sign will happen between the warnings and chastisements?
That's what they claim. After the first two secrets comes some kind of phenomenon that will leave a permanent sign on the hill of the apparitions. According to Fr. René Laurentin, Vicka has had at least three visions of the sign. She believes she'll see the Virgin less than an hour before the sign appears and that the sign will mark the flow of great graces upon the world, causing conversions and healings. Vicka says it's "very beautiful" and that there are those who will be healed miraculously.

Do you have any idea what such a "sign" could be?
Let me put it this way: The secret concerning the sign was given on October 2, 1981. Several weeks later, on October 28, 1981, the villagers saw that strange fire on apparition hill; when asked about it Our Blessed Mother said it was *"one of the signs, a forerunner of the great sign."*
A forerunner can mean a prototype or first indication.
There were also those many instances when villagers saw luminosities around Mount Krizevac, a white light that used to come and cover the cross with an image of the Holy Mother.

When asked about signs such as those and the word *MIR* scrawled in the sky, Our Blessed Mother replied, *"These are advance signs for those who do not believe. The big sign will come later."*

Jakov said it will be "something that has never been on the earth before."

It will be a joy for those who pray, says Mirjana.

For non-believers, says Fr. Laurentin, it will be "a final warning."

TWENTY-FOUR

~

THE OTHER SECRETS

And that will be the end of the apparitions?

Our Blessed Mother told Ivan that the sign would be given at the end of the apparitions.

What about the middle secrets?

At least one has to do with the parish of Medjugorje, perhaps pertaining to the war or to something like a visit from a pope, or to final recognition or rejection of the apparitions. Take your pick. It's just speculation. All we know is that it's something to do with Medjugorje's future. Once the war started I wondered if a major happening would occur in Medjugorje, whether Medjugorje would be destroyed. For a while, it appeared that would happen.

But so far it has been spared. It has been protected. There are many accounts of the Serbs wanting to attack the village but being foiled. As the *Wall Street Journal* reported, "At one point, the war front was only three miles away—so close that Easter Mass was held in a sandbagged cellar. Planes and artillery ravaged nearby towns. But only six shells hit Medjugorje. The casualties: one cow, one chicken, one dog. The sole air raid on the town ended with a few bombs exploding harmlessly."

Famous is the account of several bombs that were dropped but did not even detonate. Villagers took one of them and stuck it in a sewer in front of St. James. There are also those who say a Serb pilot was suddenly caught in an unusual fog—unable to spot the village—when he went on a bombing mission.

Whatever the veracity of individual stories, it's reminiscent of the way Portugal, which was officially consecrated to the Immaculate Heart of Mary, was preserved during World War II. It's definitely unusual that so many nearby places have been bombed but not Medjugorje. I visited twice during the war and I remember the mortars exploding in nearby Mostar. You could hear them from Mount Krizevac, and the house I stayed in, owned by the seer Ivanka, had all its windows taped to prevent glass from shattering.

I snuck into Mostar and saw the devastated churches, the gutted hotel, the funerals for young soldiers, the bullet holes everywhere, including on a road sign for Medjugorje. It's very peculiar how the Serbs targeted Catholic churches and especially liked to spray their gunfire at statues and crucifixes.

The bishop's residence was utterly devastated in 1992, and so was his cathedral across the street. I stood and gawked at the destruction. Then I entered another church, St. Peter and St. Paul Church, that was so totally destroyed all that was left was the altar.

Some saw these as signs. Some saw the damage as omens. It was the Bishop of Mostar, who had been so antagonistic to Medjugorje, whose palace and cathedral went up in flames. "Isn't it a sufficient reminder for us all, when this war has left the Bishop of Mostar without a diocese and without a cathedral?" wrote one man in the Croatian periodical *Nasa Ognisjista*. "The Queen of Peace waited for us for ten years and yet we still scorn her messages."

But all was not lost. While the bishop's magnificent library of fifty thousand books was destroyed, the archives of Medjugorje survived the bombardment. Up in Split, which should have been a major target, Archbishop Frane Franic, who supported Medjugorje, incurred no damage. And the fact was not lost on him. Franic warned that without conversion the war would spread. He pointed out that on April 10, 1991, the bishops of Yugoslavia issued a statement that still refused to acknowledge the supernaturality of Medjugorje and "very soon after, in June of that same year, the Serbs from the town of Knin began their revolt. This was the start of the Serbs' war of aggression on Slovenia and Croatia."

The Virgin was also very much in tune with the situation. On June 25, 1991, in her monthly message, Our Blessed Mother said, *"Dear children! Today I invite you to pray for peace. At this time, peace is threatened in a special way, and I am seeking you to renew fasting and prayer in your families. Dear children, I desire for you to grasp the seriousness of the situation, and that much of what will happen depends on your prayers, and you are praying [only] a little bit."*

Two months later, on August 25, 1991, Mary as Queen of Peace issued one of her strongest messages in all the years of Medjugorje. *"Satan is strong and wants to sweep away plans of peace and joy and make you think my Son is not strong in His decisions,"* she lamented. *"Therefore, I call all of you, dear children, to pray and fast still more firmly. I invite you to renunciation for nine days so that with your help everything I wanted to realize through the secrets I began in Fatima may be fulfilled. I call you, dear children, to grasp the importance of my coming and the seriousness of the situation. I want to save all souls and present them to God. Therefore, let us pray that everything I have begun be fully realized."*

So the archbishop and the seers saw Satan behind the turmoil?

Beyond question. Marija noted that "Satan is present on all sides in this war."

And yet the war wasn't one of their secrets?

They told me it wasn't one of the secrets. I interpret it more as a sign or precursor.

Didn't they say some of the coming chastisements are inevitable?

Anything can be changed by prayer. The most serious of all circumstances can be altered by faith. Our Blessed Mother would not continue to come if the situation were hopeless. She's forming a cohort to stem the tide, and while matters are very serious and even degenerating—a cloud of darkness across the world—there can be much hope if the faithful pull together.

We must all pray in earnest. We must all remember to pray for the world and especially unbelievers, including them in our Masses and Rosaries. We must fast and make sacrifices. We have to converse directly with God. We must implore Him. We have to beg God for a better future. Think about it. Who would want a situation to arise in which we would all have to worry about radiation in our water or food? Who would want to go without electrical power for weeks or months? Who would want our children to face a future of chaos?

You're saying we still have time?

We still have time. We can do it. We can change the world. We can prevent disasters.

In his letter to the pope, Fr. Vlasic said, "Punishment is inevitable, for we cannot expect the whole world to be converted." He said the chastisements would definitely occur.

So did Mirjana. She said, "The tenth secret is totally bad and cannot be lessened whatsoever." Since I'm not privy to the secrets, I can't argue with her. If we continue as we are, her prophecy will prove only too accurate. But when asked about the chastisements, Vicka said, "With prayer and penance they can be substantially lessened." It's like what Jesus said: "I assure you, if you had faith the size of a mustard seed, you would be able to say to this mountain, 'Move from here to there,' and it would move. Nothing would be impossible for you" (Mt 17:20).

Why is fasting so important?

Fasting allows us to transcend our physicality. Jesus Himself had to fast before beginning His public ministry. Fasting unlocks our dormant prayer power. And with prayer we can diminish the coming chastisements.

Remember Blessed Faustina and the city of Warsaw? If one dedicated soul like her can intercede for a city that size, then how much more can thousands and millions of us do?

Marija notes that if we heed the messages of prayer, fasting, and reconciliation, we can "restore God's kingdom of light and love and peace and joy to all people on earth." As Ivanka once said, "We will all have a role to play in the unfolding of the secrets. That is part of God's plan. Each person on the earth will be involved in the unfolding of the secrets. God calls us all to be faithful in all circumstances of our lives. He calls us to be faithful to His Will."

The situation is imperative. As Our Blessed Mother said on November 28, 1990, *"Today like never before I invite you to prayer. Your prayer should be a prayer for peace. Satan is strong and wishes not only to destroy life, but also nature and the planet on which you live. Therefore, dear children, pray that you can protect yourselves through prayer with the blessing of God's peace."*

Five years before, she had said that *"in prayer you will come to know the greatest joy and the way out of every situation that has no way out."*

Every individual, she said, is *"dear to my heart."*

How have the visionaries been able to keep the messages secret all these years?

Mirjana said she has been in the situation many times when she came close to disclosing a secret. "But then, suddenly, something flashes through my head," she said. "It is then that I sober up and ask myself, 'What am I doing, what is the matter with me?' The fact is, we are incapable of divulging the secrets."

Are there any indications the secrets are contained in Scripture?

Well, when asked if they had been revealed in previous generations, Mirjana told Fr. Vlasic, "I can't answer that. Anyway, you know all the secrets that have been told before. But, you do not know all the secrets. You know some of them but not all."

Could the secrets have to do with the Great Tribulation and the Second Coming?

> *Ivanka once said, "We will all have a role to play in the unfolding of the secrets. That is part of God's plan. Each person on the earth will be involved in the unfolding of the secrets. God calls us all to be faithful in all circumstances of our lives. He calls us to be faithful to His Will."*

There are times when I wonder if the secrets are related to what the Bible calls "signs of the times" or the "beginning of calamities." That's in Matthew 24, a chapter that, along with Luke 21, seems especially relevant.

But the Second Coming? The seers have never said they know about that. Neither have they denied it. When interviewed by author Jan Connell, who asked if Medjugorje signaled the End Times and if the Blessed Madonna had spoken to them about the Apocalypse or the Second Coming, Mirjana replied, "That is part of the secrets. I would not like to talk about it." When asked on another occasion, Mirjana said, "The Scriptures have promised us that the reign of God is at hand. The Lord will walk among His people. His covenant is everlasting."

Asked the same question another time, Marija said, "I never speak of the Second Coming of Christ. Christ is alive. He is risen. He is among us."

When asked if Medjugorje could be a preface for the return of Christ, she said, "I do not speak at all in that way."

In 1984 there was a message that said, *"Do not think that Jesus is going to manifest Himself again in the manger."* This seemed to imply that when He comes it will be as it says in Matthew: on the clouds of heaven with power and glory.

The only thing we know for sure is that if the Second Coming is in the secrets, it can't be any of the secrets for which the seers have been given dates. They can't know the time and date of that, for it says in Matthew 24:36: "As for the exact day or hour, no one knows it, neither the angels in heaven nor the Son, but the Father only."

Isn't God merciful? Why chastisements?

Chastisements are admonishments. They're instructive punishment. They're a correction. No doubt our society needs correction. It's like a parent whose child continues to reach for a hot stove, risking injury. The parent first explains the situation to the child, then, if that doesn't work, scolds the youngster, and if that doesn't work, spanks the child—chastises the child—in order to prevent that child from burning himself.

God does the same thing. He instructs us through His prophets. He gives us signs. He indicates the proper course. And then He sends louder warnings. If they don't work He will chastise mankind in order to prevent souls from a different type of burning: the scourge of hell.

Let's be frank. Mirjana says that knowing what she knows would make her "go mad" if she didn't have the consolation of Mary, if the Virgin did not still come to her on occasion. In commenting on the first couple of secrets, when asked if they involved "something like a catastrophe," Mirjana replied, "No. It will not be anything as huge as that. That will come later." She was referring to the final secrets. Mirjana told Fr. Laurentin that the majority of her secrets are "grave, catastrophic." I can't sugarcoat that. I can't downplay it. If the warnings sound like regional events, these sound like they may involve global circumstances. In 1985 Mirjana reported the Virgin to have said, *"My angel, pray for unbelievers. People will tear their hair, brothers will plead with brothers, they will curse their past lives lived without God. They will repent, but it will be too late. Now is the time for conversion."*

The locutionist Jelena also had a strong message on June 24, 1983, when she quoted the Virgin as saying, *"You cannot imagine what is going to happen nor what the Eternal Father will send to earth. That is why you must be converted! Renounce everything. Do penance. Express my acknowledgment to all my children who have prayed and fasted. I carry all this to my divine Son in order to obtain an alleviation of His justice against the sins of mankind."*

The prophecies should serve to invigorate us, not cause a bit of fear. "If we are afraid of these kinds of things, we don't have confidence in God," said Vicka. "Fear of this kind does not come from God. It can only come from Satan who wants to disturb us, so that we close ourselves to God and are not able to pray. With God, you can only have confidence—and strength to go through any troubles."

"The Blessed Mother told us never to focus on bad things," added Ivanka. "She told us always to focus on God—on His love for us and on the future He has planned for us in heaven."

Mirjana says that "if we love God our Father, and Mary our Mother, it is very clear that nothing really bad is going to happen to us."

> *If the Second Coming is in the secrets, it can't be any of the secrets for which the seers have been given dates. They can't know the time and date of that, for it says in Matthew 24:36: "As for the exact day or hour, no one knows it, neither the angels in heaven nor the Son, but the Father only."*

When I think of purification, when I think of tribulation, I think of course of Christ, Who didn't go around trying to lighten or downplay matters but Who gave us His protection. "The day will come when not one stone will be left on another," He prophesied about the temple (Lk 21:6). "Nation will rise against nation and kingdom against kingdom. There will be great earthquakes, plagues, and famines in various places—and in the sky fearful omens and great signs.... You will be delivered up even by your parents, brothers, relatives, and friends, and some will be put to death. All will hate you because of Me, yet not a hair of your head will be harmed" (Lk 21:6, 10-18).

TWENTY-FIVE

~

A GREAT WONDER

Have any recent seers alluded more directly to the Second Coming?

At Betania, it is claimed that more than two dozen competent observers watched an apparition of a male figure they took to be Christ in February of 1995. They saw a figure with a red, pulsing heart and a sword that seemed to symbolize justice. It was observed through something they could only describe as a spiritual "screen" or "window," and it appeared for more than an hour in the rain forest. The main visionary believes that one day Jesus will manifest "in glory with rays of light" and will brighten the whole world. Like Margaret Mary she mentions a resplendent sun. "It's incredible the way He will come in glory." We get more and more of these reports, and I believe they foretell a presence of Christ's power, which will come to break the power of evil (see 2 Thessalonians 2:8). Scripture clearly sees Him arriving next time in light or some form of brightness. As soon as Christ manifests, in whatever way He ends up manifesting—in flesh or spirit, visibly or in an unseen way—it will be the end of the evil period.

I'm more comfortable looking on recent sightings of Him as symbols or representations rather than as full-fledged apparitions. If Jesus appeared with the same presence as Our Lady of Medjugorje, it would be heart-stopping and monumental. It would be a manifestation similar to His appearances after the Resurrection. He has been seen at Medjugorje as the Infant with His mother, and the visionaries have also glimpsed His suffering face as He hung on the cross; but He hasn't appeared as Mary appears, on a cloud delivering public messages—not yet, anyway.

In fact no messages from Jesus are reported at primary apparitions. It's from elsewhere, including several secondary sites, that we hear so many claims. At Kibeho, Emmanuel Segatashya and Agnes Kamagaju reported apparitions of Christ, and His coming is also foreseen in dozens of lesser situations. In every period there have been prophecies about the nearness of the Second Coming. In 1 Thessalonians 4:15, Paul indicates the coming of Jesus, and in James 5:8 it says that Christ's return is "at hand." I think what the Bible is doing is making sure we are always prepared and expectant. When the Second Coming is preached, people convert, and that's a good fruit. It's a fruit of mysticism. And it's true: Christ will come. We better never forget that Christ's return and the gift of His mysticism are at the very root of the Church's existence.

At the same time, we're not to become agitated on the question of His coming. We're not to be terrified by oracular utterances (see 2 Thessalonians 2:1-12). We're not to fall into false prophecy that the day of the Lord is here. Because we don't know much of anything for sure. All we know is that, before He comes, the mass apostasy must occur and the man of lawlessness must be revealed. We're to always be on guard, and there is the need for watchfulness (see Luke 21:34). We are told to watch for the signs of the times. Not to jump the gun, but to pay attention and to keep in mind the supernatural.

Yet there are so many who downplay the supernatural and who have substituted psychology for exorcism. They have shoved out the spiritual explanations when indeed there are valid spiritual explanations for many if not most of our maladies. The demotion of mystical theology has been a near calamity for the Church, and this is where the schism is: between those Christians who believe in the supernatural and those whose faith is on the back burner. As one bishop said in 1995 during a conference at the University of Notre Dame, "Pope John Paul II not only suffers because the message of Medjugorje has not been accepted, and for the war that surrounds that country, but he suffers even more so for the situation existing within the Church, for this division between the bishops and the crisis of acceptance of the supernatural, which he himself has said is evident at Medjugorje. This is why people worldwide are drawn to Medjugorje, to find this atmosphere which is supernatural, of prayer and of sacramental life, which is missing in the Church."

The same thing happened in other periods. Phenomena arrived to bolster the Church and soothe the pains of transition. It seems to be heaven's way of marking or underscoring the end of one period and the beginning of another. It announces change that is both historical and spiritual. It announces the turning of a new corner.

As one scholar, Evelyn Underhill, pointed out, there were three significant waves of mystical activity between the time of Christ and the beginning of our own episode. They seemed to correspond, said Underhill, to the close of the Classical, the Medieval, and the Renaissance periods of history. The major episodes seem to come every five or ten centuries with many minor ones in between. Of special intensity was the one that peaked during the 1200s and 1300s, but there was also a nearly equally significant episode in the fifth and sixth centuries when the Roman Empire was in turmoil and ready to break apart and the Church was under assault by barbarians.

Until our own, those stood as the major episodes since Jesus. They came to remind us of who we are and where we really belong, which is not here on earth.

And I think many detractors will be touched by the current one. Although two centuries old, it's not over yet, not by a long shot. In the 1800s Elizabeth Canori-Mora prophesied "a great light" that will shine upon earth and mark the reconciliation of man and the supernatural. She had a vision of many angels descending from heaven with St. Peter and said that when all seems to be lost,

> *The demotion of mystical theology has been a near calamity for the Church, and this is where the schism is: between those Christians who believe in the supernatural and those whose faith is on the back burner.... This is why people worldwide are drawn to Medjugorje, to find this atmosphere which is supernatural, of prayer and of sacramental life, which is missing in the Church.*

God will intervene. "The Lord showed me how beautiful the world will be after the awful chastisement," said Abbess Maria Steiner, another from the nineteenth century. Fore-echoing the priest from Medjugorje, she added, "The people will be like the Christians of the primitive Church."

After the great trials of the Church, after the evil upheaval, said Pope Pius IX, "there will come a great wonder which will fill the world with astonishment."

TWENTY-SIX

~

WHEN THE TIME COMES

That brings us back again to the prophecy of the great sign. Is such a prodigy forecast at other apparitions?

Yes, several other places, at alleged apparitions in Spain, Ecuador, Slovakia, and America. Our Blessed Lady said she has secured this sign for unbelievers as their mother. According to Revelation 12:1, she is herself a great sign, or *"Signum Magnum,"* which was the title of an apostolic letter by Pope Paul VI that confirmed the Era of Mary on the fiftieth anniversary of Fatima.

Mary herself is the sign?

Mary is a sign heralding her Son. I've already referred to representations of the Sacred Heart at Betania. People claim they've seen a symbol of the Sacred Heart. That's interesting because Betania means Bethany, and Bethany is near where Jesus appeared in apparition to His disciples on the Mount of Olives (see Luke 24:50).

Bethany. The name also evokes the flow of precious ointment, as in the currently oiling statues (see Matthew 26:7). And it sets the stage for entry into a new Jerusalem. Our Blessed Mother told Maria Esperanza that her title should be, *"Mary, Reconciler of Nations,"* and it was under this title that the bishop pronounced Betania as "authentic and of a supernatural character." At the first apparition in 1976, an enormous white cloud appeared along with a light that made it look like a nearby farm was on fire. *"My little daughter, tell my children of all races, of all nations, of all religions that I love all of them,"* the Virgin has told Maria. *"For me, all of my children are the same. There do not exist rich ones or poor ones, ugly ones or beautiful ones, black or white. It doesn't matter. I come to gather all of them to help them go up the high mountain of Zion to my fertile land of Betania in these times so they can be saved, so that they unify, so they will live as brothers."*

It seemed like a preparation. It seemed like an announcement. At times she appears in Venezuela as Our Lady of the Miraculous Medal, hearkening back to the apparitions that initiated the modern Age of Mary in the nineteenth century. It's as if she's indicating that we have now come full circle and that her era, begun with the Miraculous Medal, is reaching a conclusion.

We're on the verge of her finale. It's the Triumph of her Immaculate Heart and that's why she appears near Lourdes grottos in Ireland; it was at Lourdes that she came as the Immaculate Conception.

Her Triumph includes the casting down of the red dragon and is accompanied by the reappearance of the woman's Son (see Revelation 12:5), Who comes as the Sacred Heart and is Light itself, the Light that clothes the Woman, represented by all the sun miracles and resplendence.

St. Louis de Montfort said that Mary is the dawn which precedes Jesus, and Christ is the "Sun of Justice"; that's confirmed in Scripture where it says "the sun of justice with its healing rays" will rise for those who respect the Lord (Mal 3:20).

He is going to bless us. He's going to bless us with His Sacred Heart. I think it's in the secrets of Medjugorje. I think Jesus will in some way descend upon us. During the sun miracles there's that round "shield" that seems to move in front of the sun, blotting out the hottest center rays. Acting as a filter or screen, it looks much like a Communion Host. It draws a link between the sun miracles and Jesus. During the apparitions, Mary is often accompanied by a heart, a cross, and the sun, once more drawing a connection.

And at a recent conference in Modesto, California, when asked about controversies over Mary's role, and how much Our Blessed Mother should or should not be revered, Mirjana replied, "When the time comes, we will see the respect and reverence her own Son has for her."

That seemed like another hint: *When the time comes... her own Son.*

I believe the Sacred Heart follows the Triumph of Mary's Immaculate Heart and that we're in the midst, although not yet the conclusion, of that Triumph. The devil's power will be broken and in the illumination of victory we will in some way see Christ. Perhaps it will be like the experiences of St. Teresa of Avila, who said "the vision of Him passes so quickly that it may be compared to a flash of lightning," or the visions of St. Margaret Mary, who like Esperanza saw His Sacred Heart as a "resplendent sun."

There will be a manifestation. It will introduce the Era of the Sacred Heart. That's my own little prophecy. It will be a time of mercy and justice. It will be a time of great grace. *"My Divine Heart,"* He told St. Margaret, *"is so inflamed with love for men... that, being unable any longer to contain within Itself the flames of Its burning Charity, It must needs spread them abroad by thy means, and manifest Itself to [mankind] in order to enrich them with the precious treasures which I discover to thee, and which contain graces of sanctification and salvation necessary to withdraw them from the abyss of perdition."*

I think that's what we have to look forward to: a special manifestation. Jesus is going to manifest at some level.

But when you say Christ is going to manifest, could you be more specific? What do you mean by "manifest"?

> *"I bear a special love for Poland, and if she will be obedient to My Will, I will exalt her in might and holiness. From her will come forth the spark that will prepare the world for My final coming."*

Perhaps invisibly, through an outpouring of grace—perhaps, as Mother Angelica once told me, through the Blessed Sacrament. Or perhaps in apparition. As in the days of the Apostles, we can only wait with joyful expectation.

Give us the bottom line. Are you saying the secrets may have more to do with a manifestation than the formal Second Coming?

I'd be careful about labeling anything.

Didn't Blessed Faustina say something about the Second Coming and our current pope? Isn't Pope John Paul II supposed to be an omen?

In one entry Blessed Faustina said, "As I was praying, I heard Jesus' words: *'I bear a special love for Poland, and if she will be obedient to My Will, I will exalt her in might and holiness. From her will come forth the spark that will prepare the world for My final coming.'"*

Well, we all know John Paul is from Poland. We're also told that he was handpicked by the Virgin. During an apparition at Medjugorje on September 3, 1981, Our Blessed Mother reportedly went to a large picture of the pope and with a smile firmly hugged it. She told them to look upon John Paul II as everyone's father. Mirjana says "the radiance in his eyes is the same as Our Lady's."

TWENTY-SEVEN

~

Seers Real and Imagined

In every century they've expected the Second Coming. You said many current mystics say the same thing. How do we discern the authentic messages? How do we detect the phonies?

All such prophecies must be taken with extreme caution. It's a confusing time, and even at a legitimate site the devil can infiltrate. He can slip in. He can ape Mary or Jesus. Our Lord has never appeared at a primary site as a full-fledged apparition, and so we must be careful of those who claim to see or hear Him.

That's not to say He doesn't appear to individual mystics or that He doesn't grant fleeting visions, but we're in an age of false prophets and as Jesus Himself said in Matthew 24:23-27: "If anyone tells you at that time, 'Look, the Messiah is here,' or 'He is there,' do not believe it. False messiahs and false prophets will appear, performing signs and wonders so great as to mislead even the chosen if that were possible. Remember, I have told you all about it beforehand; so if they tell you, 'Look, He is in the desert,' do not go there; or 'He is in the innermost rooms,' do not believe it. As the lightning from the east flashes to the west, so will the coming of the Son of Man be."

When I asked Father Jozo of Medjugorje how to discern, he said false sites consist of "words without fruits" and are fashioned to "attract the curious." They give us a few fireworks and engender a faith that's superficial. They spread like wildfire and try to obscure or dilute the message of authentic seers. "We know that evil always follows apparitions, as in the case of Fatima and Lourdes," said Fr. Jozo, referring to those many false seers who swarmed upon Lourdes during St. Bernadette's apparitions.

What exactly happened at Lourdes?

The legitimate apparitions began on February 11, 1858, and proceeded for eighteen formal apparitions in the grotto or small cave. Midway through those apparitions, which are among the most famous in history, others began to claim the same thing. They claimed they too were seeing Mary. This started around April 11 when five women went to an opening in the cliff above the grotto to investigate. Two of them claimed they saw an apparitional woman. A few days later a second group went to the opening and a vague, vaporous figure appeared to a fifty-year-old servant woman.

It was the beginning of a rash of apparitions that would soon create forty-eight seers who are known by name, and others whose names have escaped history. These imitators were often children and while in ecstasy some made bizarre and nearly farcical whirling motions—as if something were mocking Bernadette and her legitimate apparitions. While a few of the visionaries seemed credible, especially a woman named Marie Courrech, others were suspected of showmanship or infestation by the devil. In fact during one frenzy an eerie, high-pitched voice issued from the grotto—thought by some to be the Virgin but, as one observer noted, "more the devil than the devil himself."

The commotion continued until July, when the Bishop of Tarbes condemned accounts coming from the false seers and established a commission to investigate Bernadette, who of course was found to be authentic. Marie Courrech also was not discredited by the inquest, but was never treated as a formal seer. Thank God the attempt at obfuscation didn't ruin the main apparitions.

Are you saying that we're seeing the same thing now?

On a more massive scale because at this stage Medjugorje is much bigger than Lourdes or Fatima were at the beginning.

Why would the devil want to ape Mary? Why would he promote something religious?

It's simple subterfuge. Many seers have messages that seem holy enough but are actually of human origin and may be woven with the whisperings of deception. Instead of the powerful grace you get from authentic messages, the questionable ones often transmit an almost gritty and confused sensation. You become a little uneasy. As John of the Cross warned, "To deceive and introduce lies, the devil first lures a person with truths and verisimilitudes that give assurance; and then he proceeds with his beguilement."

Whether it's apparitions or people who say they've seen angels or other phenomena, how do we know if someone is having a holy experience?

Through the eyes of love. When we love, when we let love fill our hearts, we recognize God because God is love. God gives us peace. He blends with our spirits. And He casts forth an illumination, a spotlight.

Love is the truth of the Light and it's joined by humility, which gives us a clarity of spirit. Humility infuses the soul with perspective and balance. It gives us a wide field of vision while pride and ego lead only to blindness.

Many want a magic bullet for determining apparitions but all I can say is, seek spiritual balance. Don't become too believing—buying into every mystical claim—but neither become overly skeptical, which is even worse. Seek a place in between. Pray for balance. Pray for discernment. Like any talent, it's a gift. And it's special. I've seen many holy people who simply don't have much of it. They have other gifts. They have other attributes. But not the discernment of spirits. As it says in 1 Corinthians 12:4-10, "Through the Spirit one receives faith; by the same Spirit another is given the gift of healing, and still another miraculous powers. Prophecy is given to one; to another power to distinguish one spirit from another."

But all of us are given discernment to some degree and in addition to humility we can augment discernment through prayer and fasting. Those who fast will find a keener sense of discrimination because fasting conquers the flesh—declares the spirit to be supreme—and puts evil at more of a distance. It backs evil away. It separates demons and stops them from influencing us.

If you want to make sure something is not from the evil one, fasting will clear the mind and, if done well, will flush the evil out (see Matthew 17:21). On the other hand, an involvement in mysticism without fasting is an invitation to deception. *"Pray for the gift of love, for the gift of faith, for the gift of fasting,"* says Our Lady of Medjugorje. *"Persevere in prayer and in sacrifice and I will protect you and will hear your prayers."*

How do false apparitions occur? What would make someone want to fake a vision?

Most false visionaries are not deliberate tricksters but rather are plagued by self-deception. Although the thoughts are of the natural order, they begin to think there's a divine origin to all of their thinking. Many people have mental images that are good and may even be *inspired,* but that are misrepresented as apparitions.

How else do we judge? What else do we look for? What else do we avoid?

A high-level locution instructs us without loss of time and with words fuller than our own. It engraves itself almost indelibly upon the seer's memory, whereas the words that come from our own understanding are like the first movement of thought, which passes and is forgotten, said St. Teresa of

Avila. She added, "The divine words resemble something of which with the lapse of time apart may be forgotten but not so completely that one loses the memory of its having been said. Only if a long time has passed, or if the words were words of favor or of instruction, can this happen; words of prophecy, in my opinion, cannot possibly be forgotten—at least, I can never forget them myself, and my memory is a poor one."

Thus, a high-level locution will come to us even if we resist it. Some saints have suggested that in the initial testing we do exactly that: resist locutions to see if they do return. Test them by rejecting them. "No soul who does not deal with them as with an enemy," said John of the Cross, "can possibly escape delusions in a greater or lesser degree in many of them."

If a locution is from the devil it will fade or there will eventually be niggling doubts. St. Ignatius once said that any thought which weakens or troubles us in the least should be suspect. Where there is smoke, where doubts persist, there is often fire—although we must also be cautious that the devil doesn't instill unnecessary doubts. Once more, fasting and prayer are the only ways of purifying our discernment.

There are some other things to look for. There are some intellectual signposts. A false or low-level locution is often rambling and unexceptional. It goes on too long. It is uneconomical. It sounds like it could well be the seer's personal musing, a product of the mind's internal dialogue. Or, it sounds like it may be a mixture of the subconscious with certain inspired ruminations but also the murmurs of a deceptive spirit.

There are many gray areas. We all have good thoughts and bad thoughts and inspired thoughts. We all hear God and also our own subconscious. It's very difficult to separate inspirations unless the locution is a powerful one.

Most locutionists have messages that are low-powered or have been filtered through their personalities and thus are only as pure as the seer himself. I would stay away from messages that go on too long with lurid words or that paint an apocalypse in overly tremendous detail.

Stay away from spectacular language, or what Fr. Joaquin Maria Alonso, the expert on Fatima, called cataclysms of the latter times "predicted in the most grotesque manner."

Trust those who most exhibit faith, humility, and love. Look for goodness. Look at their personal lives. Look at the way they treat people. Look to see if they want to be hidden or if, to the contrary, they crave any form of money or attention. It's when you look backstage that the alarm goes off. It rings at any bit of pride or disharmony in the seers' family or psychological makeup. Any oddities in the way of ecstasy should also cause concern—any peculiar facial expressions or movements of the eyes—and naturally a message that doesn't conform to doctrine or the Bible, and that inspires persistent division, should be immediately cast off.

I could further cite scholars such as Poulain and Tanqueray or documents from Rome but in the end, however valuable certain guidelines can be, discernment is a spiritual and not an intellectual process. There's no academic formula. Most false messages are too cunning for simple logic. I've seen them fool some of the most prominent theologians, and the same has been true throughout history. One Cardinal writing in the seventeenth century enumerated more than twenty condemnations in his time against mystical simulators. In sixteenth-century Spain a nun tricked priests, bishops, and cardinals with mystical gifts—including apparitions and stigmata—that she later admitted were from a demon.

That was in the 1500s. There are more today. They come in all forms, and they can vex the highest intellect. They fool upon first impression. That's why we must discern on a spiritual level and in the end use good old common sense, which is another gift of the Spirit.

How about if we reverse the question. How about if we look at it another way. When a seer is real, when a seer is authentic, does that mean the person is a saint? Are all legitimate seers holy?

Perhaps not at first. As St. Bonaventure said, "Otherwise, one would have to say that Balaam was a saint and his ass as well!"

Many seers don't start out as saints. Christ seeks everyone. But if a person who has received what theologians call gratis datae—visions, ecstasies, or miracles—doesn't begin a profound transformation and especially if the seer maintains a hardness of heart, it's a clear danger signal. The seers we have most trusted have tended to be those who, like Catherine Labouré, Bernadette, and Lucia, sought the seclusion of convents.

What about visionaries who have missed in certain of their prophecies?

It's certainly a cause for concern, but by itself doesn't always disqualify the seer. There may have been an unconscious distortion, a misreporting of what had been said, as once happened to St. Catherine Labouré and other saints such as St. Bridget and St. Joan of Arc.

There are those instances in which a prophecy would be better defined as a conditional warning. On seeing that Nineveh survived after forty days, on seeing that the repentant city had been spared, and not destroyed as he warned, Jonah was very distraught and even angry (see Jonah 4:1). He didn't realize that many of God's prophecies would be better described as warnings based upon our response. Because Nineveh wasn't destroyed, he felt like a false prophet.

Are there some other tips you can give in spotting deception? What have you seen? What have you experienced?

I really don't want to get too negative but when I began to travel around speaking about phenomena and studying seers I was startled by the false ones. Knowingly or unknowingly, some visionaries are using the powers of mediumship and psychic phenomena. Even a legitimate seer, when functioning as a medium, can become the instrument of both good and evil. We must beware because the beginning of an apparition can be from God but the rest may be conjured by the devil. It's said that St. Ignatius once had a true vision of the Blessed Trinity but a few days later, when the Lord appeared again, something about it troubled Ignatius and when he made the sign of the Cross the apparition suddenly transformed into a serpent.

The devil always attempts to spoil legitimate mysticism. He appeared to St. Catherine of Bologna in the form of the Crucified Christ, which should give us yet additional reason for discernment.

The devil leads to division, perplexity, and corruption, while God and His angels eliminate all sadness and produce a genuine lightness of heart. A real seer will inspire joy and conversion. Permanent conversion. Look for the fruits that last! And look for the gentle voice. God speaks as softly as dew on a flower. He tries to communicate with all of us all of the time and especially seeks nonverbal union. He wants our nonverbal thoughts raised up to Him. That's the highest form of mysticism: not a locution or vision but divine union, raising our minds to Him in love.

As John of the Cross put it, "These apprehensions are nobler, safer, and more advantageous than the imaginative corporal visions because they are already interior, purely spiritual, and less exposed to the devil's meddlesomeness."

TWENTY-EIGHT

~

THE GREATEST MYSTICISM

So are apparitions something that perhaps would better be left alone? And where do angels fit in? Do we have the same problem discerning angel experiences?

The highest form of mysticims is not locutions, not angels, not visions. The greatest mysticism is prayerful union, elevating the mind and spirit to our Creator. It's loving God, and wanting to be near Him and allow Him to infuse our minds with knowledge.

This mystical experience is available to *everyone*. We all can feel peace by lifting our thoughts to God.

As for the goodness and historicity of the phenomena, well, it's similar to phenomena throughout the Bible. There are precedents with which to gauge both validity and goodness. There are a number of supernatural episodes in the Bible and several at especially crucial junctures in history that would better be described as "mega-episodes."

The Great Episode of Jesus actually went on for three or four centuries. It may have begun in 200 B.C. with apocalyptic Jewish literature that described the way God would begin a new era by purging evil and creating a world that was more spiritual. In other words, Jesus was preceded by a run of prophecy, and at His conception there was the appearance of an angel. There were dreams, the dreams which instructed Joseph. At His birth there was an unusual star, which reminds us of strange stars seen at places like Betania or Medjugorje.

When Jesus was baptized, onlookers saw a dove. At many sites of apparition, witnesses have spotted or even photographed dove-shaped forms, including a light above St. James in broad daylight. Jesus prophesied, as seers now prophesy, and there were external locutions—"This is My Son, in Whom I am well pleased"—just as today some claim auricular locutions. Jesus cured the sick, as many are cured today at places like Lourdes, and He also cast out demons, as many demons are cast out at Medjugorje or during prayer sessions with the Rosary. Jesus could tell the life history of the woman from Samaria, just as mystics "read" souls, and He walked on water, as certain mystics, including St. Joseph of Cupertino, have been seen in levitation. He calmed the wind and sea, just as construction of the cross atop Mount

Krizevac put an end to hail storms. And as I said, He experienced apparitions of Moses and Elijah.

The episode continued through John's writing of Revelation, which was probably between 81 and 96 A.D., during the reign of the emperor Domitian, which stretches it to a lengthy episode. Before Jesus, around 1300 B.C., was the episode of Moses. Largely through divine revelation, this great prophet—the most prolific locutionist on record—led the Israelites out of their enslavement in Egypt. That major event, the return to Israel, was accompanied and earmarked by phenomena. There was the rod that turned into a serpent. There were the phenomena at Mount Sinai. There were the Ten Commandments, which were expressed among Moses' long and majestic locutions. We look at the burning bush in Exodus and then we pick up a current-day magazine like *Harper's* and see a report on Medjugorje that includes the description of "a shrub on Mount Podbrdo swallowed in a halo of light, outlining the figure of a woman."

In the time of Abraham, the same was true. You had locutions. You had the appearance of angels. You had the wonder of Abraham's wife Sarah giving birth at the age of ninety. The Lord granted Abraham a number of miracles as well as the prediction that his descendants would be as numerous as the stars of heaven. "I will make of you a great nation, and I will bless you," the Lord said (Gn 12:2), a prophecy that was fulfilled when Abraham's descendants formed the nation of Israel.

The very first episode was the episode in the Garden, which *started* with a locution. After Adam and Eve had eaten the fruit, God asked Eve why she had done such a thing. If we remember, Eve replied that the serpent had tricked her. He had convinced her not to heed God's warning. He had tempted her and Adam. And that led to the fall of mankind. They had succumbed to the devil. Immediately, in a supernatural denouement, God turned to the wily serpent and said, "Because you have done this, you shall be banned from all the animals and from all the wild creatures; on your belly shall you crawl, and dirt shall you eat all the days of your life. I will put enmity between you and the woman, and between your offspring and hers. He will strike at your head, while you strike at his heel" (Gn 3:14-15).

Those are the episodes?
Those are the mega-episodes. There have also been a number of smaller ones. There have been other significant upsurges. We're not quite sure yet how ours will fit in.

Where else in Scripture?

It's impossible to summarize a book that's almost fourteen hundred pages, but I think of Daniel and Isaiah as prophets who most fit our times, and possibly Jeremiah. One could also mention Ezekiel and the beautiful and resplendent colors he described, colors like those described at places like Medjugorje; chrysolite and sapphire and the cloud of flashing fire with something that "gleamed like electrum" (Ez 1:4).

Is that what you'd compare Medjugorje to?

Medjugorje has less flourish. It doesn't have Ezekiel's extravagant imagery. And good thing. Can you imagine what people would say if Ezekiel lived today? Can you imagine what they would say about his visions of figures resembling humans but with four faces?

As for angels, they're mentioned more than three hundred times in the Bible, most memorably appearing before the destruction of Sodom (see Genesis 19:1) and to announce the birth of Jesus (see Luke 1:26).

So angels figure in too?
Yes.

And it's better to believe than not to believe, even if there's deception out there?

After His ascent, Jesus sent the Holy Spirit—which tells us to keep an open mind and *expect* the supernatural, expect miracles. They didn't stop when the last word was penned in the New Testament. It was the end of public revelation, but not of private ones.

It's better to believe than to be skeptical. There are graces to be gained. There is spiritual comfort. But let me add that above all else we should seek mental union with God and strenuously avoid any apparition that may involve a deceptive spirit.

In Deuteronomy we're warned of witches, fortunetellers, and those who consult ghosts or seek oracles from the dead. Doesn't that also apply to consulting the Virgin Mary? Aren't apparitions a form of necromancy?

This is a serious question that deserves a serious answer, because it's wrong to seek communication with the deceased, which is the definition of necromancy. It's what "channelers" and spirit mediums do, and it's totally dangerous because evil spirits can mimic or masquerade as a beloved dead person—and even if the spirit actually is a friend or relative, we don't know if the spirit has yet finished its purification. An impure spirit may be prone to mistakes or mischief.

So the danger of necromancy is interaction with an impure spirit. It's seeking an oracle from the dead. It has nothing to do with the communion of saints. It has nothing to do with angels, who are pure spirits and are not conjured but rather come at God's command. It's not a sin to welcome heavenly grace, and it certainly was not necromancy when Christ spoke to Moses and Elijah. What we must be careful of are negative spirits who come in the guise of such holy figures, which can happen.

Have you ever seen a diabolical ecstasy?

Yes, and the awful transfiguration of face, but I'd rather not comment further.

One has to be especially careful of third-level or tertiary apparitions, the ones that are now everywhere, because there is sometimes a mix of spirits. There are all kinds of different energies. Some seem good, some less so. The first major one was the one I mentioned that occurred in Gala, Croatia. After that the number of apparitions quickly escalated and then went beyond tabulation.

What about angels? What about all those people on TV and in the magazines who claim to have experienced angels?

The same rules apply. When Scripture warns of demonic deception it's specifically in the realm of Satan transforming himself into "an angel of light" (2 Cor 11:14). It specifies angels. Today we see many angel accounts that have the ring of something occultic, psychic, or New Age. Those are different ways of saying the same thing: a diabolical source.

But I happen to believe that angels are appearing in a special way and that many are real, just as some of the apparitions are legitimate. In fact angels are said to accompany Our Lady of Medjugorje—arriving during her apparitions as meteorites of light—and Ivanka says that the ones she sees look like classic cherubs.

There are good angels and, unfortunately, evil angels. We pray to keep away the bad ones. There are dozens of books on the topic. So prevalent is this phenomenon that when *Time* did a survey with CNN in 1993, they found that 69 percent of those polled believed in angels, and 32 percent had actually felt an angelic presence in their lives. Nearly half—49 percent—believe in the existence of demons. Angels help us even when we don't sense their presence. They help us pray and they feed our intuitions.

You mention mental prayer and also the "infusion of knowledge." What's that?

An infusion is a sudden inflow of wisdom. And when it comes to mysticism, it's the highest form.

St. Thérèse, the Little Flower, once said that Jesus has no need of books or teachers to instruct souls. He teaches without the noise of words. "Never have I heard Him speak," said this beautiful saint, "but I feel that He is within me at each moment."

It's a matter of acknowledging Him and trusting Him and seeking conversation with Him in constant mental prayer, instead of seeking the spectacular. To do that we have to shed our egos, dispel self-centeredness, and abandon ourselves to God. When we gain humility, God deigns to present us with knowledge. And it's a gift of the highest order. I'd rather have

It's wrong to seek communication with the deceased.... It's what "channelers" and spirit mediums do, and it's totally dangerous because evil spirits can mimic or masquerade as a beloved dead person.... So the danger of necromancy is interaction with an impure spirit.... It has nothing to do with the communion of saints. It has nothing to do with angels, who are pure spirits and are not conjured but rather come at God's command. It's not a sin to welcome heavenly grace; it certainly was not necromancy when Christ spoke to Moses and Elijah.

the gift of knowledge than most spiritual phenomena. I'd rather have an infusion than a miraculous photo or even a locution. I'd rather God grant me insight without all the struggle with verbiage. As John of the Cross wrote, "Although the touch of knowledge and delight that penetrates the substance of the soul is not manifest and clear, as in glory, it is so sublime and lofty that the devil is unable to meddle or produce anything similar, for there is no experience similar or comparable to it, or infuse a savor and delight like it. This knowledge savors of the divine essence and of eternal life, and the devil cannot counterfeit anything so lofty."

TWENTY-NINE

~

A LAST SECRET

There is real mystery in all this. There is real mystery in how God down-loads information, and there still seems to be unexplained mystery in all the apparitions that began after Medjugorje.

Yes, starting with the ones in Croatia at a place called Gala about seventy miles northwest of Medjugorje. What happened here pretty much typified what soon happened elsewhere. The apparitions at Gala began on August 27, 1983. In the beginning there were a few children who, along with Mirjam, saw Mary. Now a nun in Split, Sr. Mirjam has continued to have visions as well as inner locutions, which to her are more deeply spiritual. She says the apparition appears to her as a woman of eighteen on a small bright cloud, and the message is the familiar one of prayer, sacramental life, and conversion. According to Don Alojzije Bavcevic, a Croatian priest who provided me with this information, all the seers received secrets. Some have ten. Sr. Mirjam has twelve. According to another visionary, Ivana Tomasevic, certain secrets pertain to the Church, others to the whole world, and, as at Medjugorje, some to the seers personally. A few of the visionaries spoke of coming "days of darkness" as well as visions of heaven, hell, and purgatory. They also saw a demon in the form of an ugly, "unfamiliar" animal.

Many priests opposed the apparitions and a bishop's commission studied the situation but issued no verdict.

There were also apparitions reported in Zagreb, Pasman, and near Ljubljana. These are all in former Yugoslavia. They were followed by reports in other countries. I refer to all of these as third-level or tertiary apparitions because they have not yet attained the acceptance or prominence of primary or secondary apparitions. There also remain issues of discernment. Such issues have caused initial reluctance among clergy, although at least one priest has gotten over it. "In the beginning I rejected the happenings in Gala as some satanic game of the imitation of Medjugorje," says Fr. Bavcevic, "but when I saw these innocent children who conduct themselves much like those in Medjugorje, that the messages are similar, similar phenomena, similar graces, then I concluded that there is no way I can say 'yes' to Medjugorje and 'no' to Gala."

Were there any other messages?

There were a number of messages. The apparition said we should surrender ourselves to the Blessed Mother and allow her and Jesus to shape us. She requested total abandonment and consecration. *"Dear children, offer up all your suffering, pain, and sorrow to God as a sacrifice and then you will be able to bear everything much more easily. Surrender to me totally and allow me to lead you along the path that I prepared for you long ago."*

The Virgin urged us to *"forgive everyone everything and love all people without any difference."* She said that to obtain healing we need *"a great deal of prayer, penance, and trust."* She advised us to call upon the Holy Spirit.

The theme of abandonment is also what the pope urges, and with that surrender to Mary come great graces not otherwise available. *"If people only knew what my Immaculate Heart can secure for them, they would consecrate themselves in greater number,"* was a message from April 27, 1984.

The following year, on the feast of the Annunciation, Mary came to Gala standing on the globe with one foot crushing the head of a snake, which is precisely the image recorded on the Miraculous Medal.

It seemed an indication that indeed the time of Triumph has arrived. Once more, the Age of Mary seemed to be coming full circle.

"My child, pray for the world a great deal because the great day of chastise-- ment is approaching," she allegedly said on January 9, 1986, adding the next day, *"I came to you today to repeat what I once said at Lourdes: 'Penance, penance, penance!' Hasten your conversion because the end is near!"*

On other occasions she said, *"There are still many who need to offer their sacrifices. Many, many sacrifices are still required to alleviate the just anger of God. This is why you must pray and convert!"*

The Virgin said she is engaged in a "final battle" and that we must help her with our prayers.

Mirjam claimed that on visiting Medjugorje she saw the Risen Jesus atop Mount Krizevac in the midst of great radiance. And she claimed it was then that He entrusted her with her last secret.

So it gets back to what you said about the possibility of Christ manifesting?

It gets back to that. Now, Mirjam isn't one of the Medjugorje seers. She is from a lesser apparition site, and Christ is often seen as such lesser apparitions. But perhaps it's an indication of something that may happen at a major site in the future: Christ as a full-bodied apparition.

What other countries reported apparitions right after Medjugorje?

Around the time of Gala there were reports in Syria, Argentina, and the Philippines. I've mentioned Argentina, but also interesting was the case of a woman in Syria named Mirna Nazour. Starting on November 27, 1982, an icon of the Blessed Mother in Mirna's home, one of those classic Orthodox icons of Mary with the Christ Child, began to exude olive oil. The oil also exuded from Mirna's hands, and on Good Fridays the young woman suffered stigmata. Her descriptions were strikingly similar to La Salette and were especially powerful at a visual level. She said that Mary arrived in a large, luminous white globe that resembled the reflections of a diamond. As the halves of the globe fell away, a bow of light appeared above the globe, and inside was the beautiful lady.

Mirna's experiences have been witnessed by Orthodox, Catholics, and Muslims alike—right there in Damascus, not far from the spot where the light from heaven surrounded Saul (see Acts 9:3). Mirna is a Byzantine Catholic. She was praying with two women, one Orthodox, the other Muslim, when they noticed a light coming from Mirna's hands and then oil emanating from her skin. A few days later, on November 27—which is the anniversary of the Miraculous Medal—oil began flowing from the icon. As at Medjugorje there was a strong ecumenical message. *"The Church is the Kingdom of heaven on earth,"* the Virgin reportedly said. *"Those who divided it have sinned and those who rejoice in the division commit sin. Jesus founded it on small beginnings. When it grew, divisions also grew. Those responsible for these divisions do not have love."* She told Mirna to *"announce my Son, Emmanuel"* and to maintain an awareness of the Father. *"My children, be mindful of God. God is with us. You know a lot, but you know nothing. Your knowledge is incomplete. The day will come when you will know all things as God knows me. Deal kindly with those who do you wrong; do not mistreat anybody. I have given you oil, more than you have asked. I will give you something stronger than oil. Repent and believe. Be mindful of me in your joy."*

The message was love, faith, and unity—not one world religion, but brotherhood. Mirna was also given a beautiful prayer of mental elevation: "Sweet Jesus, grant that I rest in You above anything else, above all creation, above all Your angels, above all praise, above all rejoicing and happiness, above all glory and honor, above all heavenly hosts, for You alone are the Most High, You alone are the Almighty and good above all things."

Can't oil from a picture be demonic?

Any supernatural phenomenon, including tongues and words of knowledge, can be deceptions. And I have seen certain phenomena that seemed rather creepy. It does happen. There has to be a discernment. Pictures and statues are mere reminders to put us in the mood of prayer and focus our invocations. St. Francis de Sales said oil represents gentleness and goodness, which rise above all things and stand out among all the other virtues.

What about Protestants who say statues amount to idolatry?

They need to study the real idols of Egypt, Jerusalem, and Babylon. I remember visiting the National Museum in Cairo. That's where you see idols! When the Bible speaks of idols it's referring to images of snakes, jackals, and man-beasts, not saints or angels. Idolatry is worship of demons. An idol is an occult image. It's a pagan "god." The pagan gods were devils in disguise (see Revelation 9:20). They were "creeping things and abominable beasts" (Ez 8:10, KJV). They have nothing to do with an image of a saintly person whose prayers we are seeking in heaven. We have statues of saints for the same reason that we have family photographs: to remind us, to create a reflective atmosphere. According to tradition, holy images have been painted by the likes of St. Luke and the earliest miracles associated with a statue date at least as far back as the fourth century.

Was Mirna approved by the Church?

Not formally, so I'm not certain yet what to think, but the bishop allowed her to propagate the ecumenical messages.

A lot of people have trouble with ecumenism. A number even have problems with certain messages from Medjugorje, especially when Mary endorsed Islam and said that all religions are equal.

The Holy Madonna didn't endorse Islam and she didn't say all churches are equal. She said that all *men* are equal before God. She said it isn't up to us to judge. She said she doesn't favor any particular culture or skin color.

"In God there is neither division nor religion," said the Madonna. *"It is you in the world who have created these divisions. The only mediator is Jesus Christ. There are divisions because believers have become separated one from the other."*

That's not to say all churches are equal. That's not to deny that some churches have a more direct line to the supernatural, especially churches that take the narrow road and embrace sacrifice and discipline. *"It is not equally efficacious to belong to or pray in any church or community, because the Holy Spirit grants his power differently among the churches and ministers,"* said one message from Medjugorje. *"All believers do not pray the same way. It is intentional that all apparitions are under the auspices of the Catholic Church. The fact that you belong to one religion or another is not without importance. The Spirit is not equally present in each Church."*

The point is that through faith we all have access to the Holy Spirit. Our Blessed Mother is an advocate. She's an intercessor. She's Co-Redemptrix but she has to go through her Son for a supply of graces that she then dispenses with His permission. We ask her to pray for us as we ask people here on earth to pray for our intentions. But obviously Mary is in a much greater position. She's allowed to manifest at certain places in a fashion deemed proper by her Son.

After Syria, you had reports all over, from Kinshasa, Zaire—where nine people claimed apparitions—to Ireland, where phenomena were reported by people like Christina Gallagher at many roadside shrines, little grottos with statues of Bernadette kneeling before the Lourdes Virgin.

Ireland was part of the 1985 eruption. There were at least twenty-five sites. There were pillars of light and strange fogs and moving statues. In some instances the faces of Padre Pio, St. Bridget, and the Little Flower were being superimposed over the face of the Madonna. There were also miraculous images of Jesus. These occurred at the many little roadside shrines or "grottos."

The plot really thickened. Hungary. Korea. It was like someone was pointing a laser and sending holograms. And sun miracles. The most remarkable solar phenomenon was recorded at a place called Oliveto Citra, in Italy, where the sun pulsed with such force that the peasants were literally screeching and collapsing in amazement. I had a video of it.

In Ukraine, which at the time was still part of the Soviet Union, peasants reported strange lambent lights around old abandoned shrines—as if heaven was bringing the long-persecuted Church back to life—and near Buchach I saw an incredible face that was said to have been miraculously etched into a window.

It had occurred at an old farmhouse. I had to trudge on back roads and through muddy pastures to find the place where it had been hidden from the Communists. It looked like the portrait of an Apostle. It just appeared on a pane of glass one day. I'll never forget the peasants pulling the glass from under a bed and unwrapping it for me. It resembled an etching but was really like nothing of this world. The etching of a holy face. I still have trouble explaining it. I fell to my knees in prayer. It exuded holiness. An "etching" but not an etching! It was just *there!*

In Lviv I spoke to the cardinal and he really didn't know what to make of it. He was understandably concerned that much of it was simple hearsay. I interviewed many eyewitnesses and don't see how it could all have been a case of copycatting. Many of these villages had no newspapers, no radio, no phones at the time—and yet the phenomena were consistent with apparitions reported not only in other villages but also in Ireland and South America.

At the village of Hrushiw, Mary appeared in a luminous globe surrounded by tongues of flame and wearing fiery robes, while at Pochaiv she was also seen wrapped in "flames" near an ancient monastery.

Most impressive was a small shrine between Lviv and Kiev called Zarvanystya, an area that had seen much oppression and was only now coming out from under the iron hand of Communism.

There I spoke to eyewitnesses who told of the Virgin in a huge glow at a tiny chapel. Mary was described with a cross hanging from her neck, along with a heart.

One witness was an old woman who had done time in Siberia. I'll never forget her eyes. They were the deepest and most sincere of eyes, imbued with an unearthly wisdom.

There was also a young man who told me the light around Mary had been like the moon and described how the glowing mass, which was twice the height of a tree, moved north over quiet meadows.

THIRTY

~

PAST AND PRESENT

Where did the apparitions, the "glowing mass," move from there?

There were two or three places in the United States that began getting a lot of attention and also a site in the Andes Mountains that claimed apparitions. I never could come to a final mind about the Andes reports. They involved some very dramatic stuff, and witnesses included the postmaster general of Ecuador.

I ran into so many others. Seers sprang forth in the late 1980s and then really came on strong during the early 1990s. No way was it all a spiritual fad. I mean, a lot of it was. But it was too spontaneous, too widespread, to explain as just psychological suggestion. Whether or not you believe it was always Mary, it was *something* of a supernatural nature. In sheer numbers it had become more intense even than the episode in the Middle Ages.

And there were connections. More and more, I started to see connections between past and present. I saw connections between the current episode and the one in the Middle Ages. In 1208, Our Blessed Mother appeared to St. Dominic of Spain. She arrived in a chapel and in her hand was a rosary, which she taught him to pray.

Seven centuries later, at Fatima, the Virgin also held a rosary.

In 1251, Mary appeared to St. Simon Stock with a multitude of angels. She was garbed in brown as Our Lady of Mount Carmel.

On October 13, 1917, during the last apparition at Fatima, Our Blessed Mother likewise came dressed as Our Lady of Mount Carmel.

I think the most intriguing connection occurred in 1385 when, during the height of the Medieval episode, a knight known as D. Nuno Alvares Pereira had an experience in the very vicinity where the Fatima apparitions would later occur. Nuno had been heading for the village of Aljubarrota. On the way, he and his men spotted a small church dedicated to the Mother of God in Ourem County. According to lore, Nuno stopped, got off his horse, and entered. Kneeling before the altar, the knight invoked Our Blessed Mother's help and promised he would return to the church if she helped him gain victory. Then he and his men headed for battle.

As the knights crossed a hill that today overlooks the famous shrine known as Cova da Iria, something very strange was said to have occurred. There was the feeling of a mystical presence. And the horses stopped in their tracks, lowering their front legs as if to kneel.

It was precisely at that spot, 532 years later, that the Virgin appeared to Francisco, Jacinta, and Lucia.

There are also connections to Medjugorje. During the night of March 24, 1400, a group of shepherds near Chalons, France, reported a bright light near a chapel dedicated to John the Baptist. When they approached they saw a thornbush engulfed by flames, yet the leaves and branches seemed unaffected, just like the fire on Mount Podbrdo. In the middle of the little "fire" they found a statue of Mary.

How do you interpret such connections?

Somebody is trying to tell us to take a look back at what happened during the Middle Ages. When I do that, the first thing I recall is societal upheaval. The Middle Ages saw many different tribulations, in keeping with what Christ said about tremors, famine, pestilence, wars, and rumors of wars. The winding down of the Middle Ages was foretold not only by a flurry of prophets in the 1200s and 1300s, but also by the Black Death that killed up to forty million. A third of Europe was dying, and at the same time, in the same convulsion, the Church was under assault by vandals who ranged across the countryside and sacked monasteries and convents.

Persecution. Plague. And Turkish invasions. It had elements of Matthew, and there was also that major schism whereby the Church had two popes.

Complete disarray.

Jesus warned that "as for those things which you see, the days will come in which not one stone shall be left upon another" (Lk 21:6), meaning there will be upheaval and demolition at the end of an era. These are "the early stages of the birth pangs" (Mt 24:8). They accompany not just the End Times but the end of one age and the birth of a new one, along with phenomena such as "signs in the sun, the moon, and the stars" (Lk 21:25).

And such phenomena arrive in proportion to the impending change.

Today we see not only the same kind of phenomena as in Medieval times but also disturbances in nature. No period has yet seen all the signs of the times, but we have witnessed bits and pieces. They come according to the degree of transformation. I know this is hard for rationalists to take, but the

Bible tells us to expect happenings, both natural and supernatural, when we're nearing the end of a historical epoch. And so even if nothing as momentous as the Black Death has yet occurred, we wonder about everything from the quake in Kobe, Japan, to the ravages of Hurricane Andrew. There have always been harsh events caused by nature, but these days it makes for headlines. "Experts Are Baffled by Violent Weather That Has Battered the Globe," said a May 24, 1994, headline in *The New York Times.* There have been unusual floods and fires and viruses.

You're saying those are harbingers?

The greater the change, the more birth pangs. The phenomena in the 1300s prefaced the end of the Middle Ages, as did the Bubonic Plague.

And now we face the end of another period?

We approach the end of a period or age. In some way, we approach a breakdown of the Era of Modernism, which began after the Middle Ages. If it's a minor transformation, if the next stage is not radically different, it will be the end of a "period." If it's a larger metamorphosis, on the other hand, if we face a major overhaul, it'll be the end of an epoch or "age."

Whatever is coming can be softened, can be made more gradual, by simply responding to God's directives. Look at what went on in ancient Nineveh. That city-state, located in what is now northern Iraq, was a caldron of violence, promiscuity, and sorcery. But for many years Nineveh was saved from catastrophe because it had heeded Jonah. When the famous prophet warned that Nineveh had only forty days to repent, even the king donned sackcloth and sat in ashes as a sign of reparation (see Jonah 3:6). God gave them plenty of time. When He wanted to change Nineveh, He gave warnings through Jonah. He tried to reach them through prophecy. He preferred to see them cause their own change.

Today our Jonah is the Virgin Mary, who is telling us to change ourselves so God doesn't have to do it for us, and who recently has even been spotted in Iraq.

There are sightings in the very vicinity of Nineveh.

THIRTY-ONE

~

APPARITIONS IN IRAQ AND INDIA

The Virgin Mary is appearing in Iraq?

At a place called Mozul, the vicinity of which encompasses the ruins of Nineveh. The visions started in 1991 on the Feast of the Assumption to a fourteen-year-old girl named Dina Basher. She also exhibited stigmata. She had been receiving apparitions and exuding oil when a voice told her that "a day will come when blood will come out of your hands," as it indeed did. The stigmatic wounds in her hands have been as large as eight centimeters, and she also has bled from her feet and side. In Baghdad three bishops saw the blood flow. Dina is Syrian Orthodox and claims that on one occasion Our Lord came to her in a bright light and she was blinded like Paul for several days. Dina has seen Jesus with a golden crown and white shining robe or with white rays around His head. She believes the Second Coming is drawing near and repeats the message of repentance. The Patriarch issued a decree referring to the happenings as "astounding miracles and wonders" while the Bishop of Baghdad saw it as a manifestation of God's living power. The message is again love and unity among all people.

Isn't that an ominous signal? Isn't that what was said just before the wars in Bosnia and Rwanda?

The pouring out of the Spirit reminds us yet one more time, a final time, according to Dina, that we are in a period of major transition (see Joel 3:1). It also reminds us of the fate of Nineveh, which, though saved in Jonah's time, was later destroyed when it reverted back to its occultism and materialism.

Nineveh was later destroyed?

Yes, around 612 B.C. It was destroyed by a combination of the Tigris River flooding and enemy invasions.

Was Nineveh like Babylon?

They were sister cities and also one another's great nemeses. In fact it was Babylonians who helped destroy Nineveh before Babylon was itself laid to waste. They were located about two hundred miles apart and flourished in the same period. Babylon is a symbol for the corruption in our major cities. The same is true of Nineveh. Both towns shared the worship of horned idols and had shrines to earth divinities and temples of the great gods like Ishtar, who was portrayed with a serpent.

A nearly identical idolatry also infested the Egyptians, but it was Babylon which was known as "the mother of harlots and abominations of the earth" (Rv 17:5, KJV). Its spirit now pervades our largest cities. We're in the midst of a decisive spiritual war. That's why I entitled one of my books *The Final Hour*—because it's a dramatic spiritual moment. It's the final hour of Satan's century. It's not just a social issue; it's a deeply personal battle. There are actual demons, and in our times they have grown so bold as to openly display themselves just as they did in Babylon. Their visages are now seen as gremlins and the other weird characters in movies, cartoons, comic books, video games, or as toys that are given to our youngest children.

We also note evil in societal confusion. There is currently a diabolical disorientation. A role reversal. Good is made to seem evil, and evils like abortion are made to seem like a good. "Progressive." We see it in the media, in the educational system, and particularly of late in our legal system. We are warned that evil is coming out of the closet and infecting our institutions. *"For now as never before, Satan wants to show his shameful face by which he wants to seduce as many people as possible onto the way of death and sin,"* said the Medjugorje Virgin on September 25, 1991.

In Scripture the unloosing of demons seems to fall again into Revelation 12, when it says "woe to you, earth and sea, for the devil has come down upon you! His fury knows no limits, for he knows his time is short" (12:12). After that the wild beast rises from the sea with the seven heads and ten horns. What does the beast symbolize?

The spirit of anti christ, and possibly the Anti-Christ himself. The spirit of antichrist rears its ugly head in every generation, especially at the end of most epochs. When it infuses a person, when it takes someone over, that person, if powerful enough, becomes a forerunner of the Anti-Christ, an antichrist in miniature.

The Anti-Christ himself, when he comes, will wield an influence over world affairs. He may not be an actual leader, but he certainly will be someone who affects the course of history. Many Protestants believe the ten horns represent ten nations that will compose a new confederacy which will dominate the world, sort of a revived Roman Empire. Or a revived Babylon.

Isn't Saddam Hussein resurrecting Babylon?

He wants to rebuild Babylon and, according to reports, has already done so with the Southern Palace of Nebuchadnezzar and the Ishtar gate, which represents a demigod. But of more concern is the spirit of Babylon. It could also be called the spirit of antichrist (see Revelation 17:3), and it's rising everywhere. We think of all the occultism and New Age, the way it has reached everyone, entering our popular culture, the fact that recently city fathers erected a monument to Quetzalcoatl—the feathered Aztec snake god—in downtown San Jose. Over in India they burn powder to idols that are derived from the idols of Babylon and Nineveh.

> *When demons are invoked they often cause violence because they always sow division. I'm not only speaking of war. I'm speaking of horrible crimes and also the potential for civil strife. Racial hatred. We often get so wrapped up in Armageddon that we forget about the threats of trouble at home.*

Both cities are resurrecting (see Revelation 17:8). Both are making a spiritual comeback. And this time there are no geographical constraints.

Isn't occultism just superstition?

Occultism in any of its many forms is contact with evil spirits, and when demons are invoked they often cause violence because they always sow division. I'm not only speaking of war. I'm speaking of horrible crimes and also the potential for civil strife. Racial hatred. We often get so wrapped up in Armageddon that we forget about the threats of trouble at home.

Remember what Mirjana said about "the upheaval of a region of the world." In this light we watch for nuclear terrorism, or for civil unrest in hot spots like India. There are mystics who have long warned that our social policies haven't worked and that, without true love among all peoples and on all sides, we face bitter and perhaps monumental rioting.

When mystics warn of revolutions and general uprisings I think of South America, Africa, and India—especially India, which is very occultic and which is being warned by yet more apparitions that are being reported in Ajmer, southwest of Delhi, and in Goa, south of Bombay.

The visionary in Ajmer is said to be a victim-soul who actually hails from Niddodi, in South Kanara. There are visions of the Virgin along with other wonders. I've gotten dispatches in the mail. One priest from Ajmer wrote me about the many exorcisms he has performed there. "The devas who are worshipped as gods or goddesses by pagans are actually devils because in hundreds of cases of exorcisms I have come across these devas or devils under various names confessing against their wills that they are coming from the depths of hell," he wrote. Our Blessed Mother often arrives to help deliver us from such occultism.

There are many places aside from India where occultism is practiced. There are centers of satanism in cities like Melbourne, Australia, and Turin, Italy. London too has long stirred the psychic caldron, and in the Caribbean and Africa you have voodoo, which is a more primitive form of satanism. I've heard that some witches actually spend their time aiming curses at activists in the Christian movement. I have spoken before crowds and later learned that witches or New Agers were there to take stock. This should teach us a lesson about what is now going on everywhere: that before armed conflict there is spiritual war.

THIRTY-TWO

~

THE WEAPON OF LOVE

How about war in the Middle East? We've already seen what happened in 1991. Could the apparitions be an omen?

I'm not sure we've heard the last from Iraq—or from Iran, for that matter —but prayer can change them. And anything else. Our Blessed Mother says that she's with us *"even when you think there is no way out and that Satan is in control."*

Aren't there mystics who worry about Russia marching one day with Arab states and overcoming Israel?

That's the classic scenario for Armageddon. Right now, thank God, there's peace with Russia. It will remain only if we keep the situation in prayer. This is certainly another area we must hold in supplication. The political landscape could be changed by a single act of assassination.

Aren't there biblicists who see apocalyptic signs in the recent peace accord between Israel and the Palestinians?

There are Protestants who believe that Israel's future, as portrayed in Daniel 9:24-27, includes a covenant between Israel and the Anti-Christ. I don't know that anyone involved in the current peace accord would qualify as the Anti-Christ.

The peace accord may be but a forerunner of the prophetic accord, a microcosm. Again, our concern right now is the *spirit* of antichrist. I see that spirit in racial division. I see it when blacks hate whites and whites do not accept blacks. I see the spirit anytime that love is absent.

With love, we defeat the spirit of antichrist. With love we rearrange the structure of reality.

You speak as if love is a supernatural force.

It is. Love disarms the enemy. It's the same as union with God. If you can love the person in your life who is most difficult for you to love, if you can love someone you used to hate, then you will begin to feel a joyous love, a miraculous love, for everyone. In this way you'll feel peace in the depths of your soul and that peace will enter into God's line of sight as a prayer for peace in the world.

You think this can happen without physical or verbal action?

As Thérèse, the Little Flower, said, "love attracts love." If you're having trouble with somebody, send him or her love and watch the change. Watch him turn inexplicably into a friend. Watch his or her heart soften. It may take time, it may take persistence—it will certainly take faith—but watch how those who dislike you will end up loving or at least liking you back. It's an irresistible force!

And you think it can also work with whole nations?

Without question. Prayer can move mountains. It's a function of faith, the belief that God is beyond all human systems.

With faith in God, we have no fear of Satan. Next to God, Satan is smaller than a grain of sand. When we have faith, we have God. But when we have fear, especially when we fear evil, we get in trouble because fear of the devil is faith in the devil, and that too unlocks powers. Fear of the devil empowers the devil, while faith in God allows God to act, to a degree commensurate with the trust we place in Him. Faith in God allows us to transcend the storm clouds, instead of sinking our feet in the mud. When we have great trust, we have great and indeed unlimited power, because then we have God. The Lord can affect the course of nations. He does that with a flick of his little finger!

We saw this happen during the revolution a few years back in the Philippines. At the time they were rebelling against the corrupt dictatorship of Ferdinand Marcos, and they were doing so not with guns and mortars but with flowers and prayers—fervent prayers—of the Rosary. The people took over a constabulary and Marcos' troops were blocked from taking it back because thousands of Filipinos—rosaries in hand—were forming a human barrier.

Finally the troops found a way to get back to the encampment and were ready to fire on the people when, according to a number of sources including journalist June Keithley-Castro, a lady dressed in a long white gown suddenly appeared and raised her hands. She said something like, "Please do not shoot my children."

The account is well-known and is also told by His Eminence Jaime Cardinal Sin, whom the soldiers sought out to tell him what happened. The apparition occurred at the corner of Ortigas Avenue and Epifanio de los Santos. The latter means "epiphany of the saints." A church now stands on the site. It's called Our Lady Queen of Peace.

In a military sense, what else are mystics concerned about?

I think like the rest of us that they're wary about how the U.S. and Russia might react with each other if there's a change in leadership and tensions arise over situations like Bosnia. In Ecuador the seer claimed to have been given a vision of war that involved Russia, Germany, China, and Czechoslovakia. In this case she saw the U.S. forming an alliance with Russia.

The mention of Czechoslovakia was interesting because there have also been some interesting apparitions in Litmanova, Slovakia. This nation borders Ukraine and is not all that far from Hrushiw. The apparitions started on August 5, 1990. During the visitations Our Blessed Lady reportedly warned that "a disaster looms over Slovakia" (formerly the eastern part of Czechoslovakia) but that it can be averted if the people pray and devote themselves to God.

One must also keep the Baltic states in prayer, and former republics of the U.S.S.R. like Ukraine and Kazahkstan. There could be an Islamic revolution in the southern republics, which would create enormous tension. It would be a larger rendition of what we are today seeing in Bosnia-Hercegovina. That very conflict is itself a precursor, and it could have been stopped through prayer. During the early stages of the Bosnian conflict the Madonna warned that Satan is strong and that without prayer and fasting he would lead them to destruction. As the war worsened, her pleas for prayer intensified and by 1991 she was sounding as urgent in requesting prayer as she had back in the very beginning. She said she wanted us to understand *"how serious the situation is,"* and she asked us to let the rosary remain in our hands as a sign to Satan that we belong to her.

If there were a single nation that you think needs special prayer now, what would it be?

Along with the Balkans, China. This huge nation continues to hold a fifth of the world's population captive. They honor Babylonian-style idols like the red dragon. They force women to have abortions as a means of birth control, and abortion wasn't tolerated even in Nineveh. You can't have more than one child in China. It's against the law. They regularly check women to make certain they're not pregnant, and do an immediate, forced abortion if they are. There are 10.5 million abortions per year in China, which is ten times our own rate. As Mother Teresa of Calcutta has said, the fruit of abortion will be nuclear war.

I constantly hear about China in prophecies, and it's surprising because while folks worried about a war between Russia and China back in the 1960s, it's been quiet since. I would suppose the biggest concern would be of China siding with one of the bordering Asian nations that was once a republic of the Soviet Union in a war against Russia, or of Muslim extremists in those former republics provoking China by instigating China's own Muslim population. This could also draw in the Middle East.

We must pray for China and also offer up our fasting and sufferings. We need to sacrifice for China. A little bit of sacrifice is a big prayer. We should do this all the time: offer to God the little annoyances of life—the chores we don't like, the things we don't want to do—as prayers for China's conversion. Our Blessed Mother will then bring these sacrifices as gifts to her Son. "Stripped of self-will and clothed in disinterested love," said St. Louis de Montfort, "the little that we give to the Blessed Virgin is truly powerful enough to appease the anger of God."

You seem as concerned about China as Russia.

I mention it because that nation has cropped up in prophecies from around the world. It's a common theme: keep an eye on the Orient. Pray for it. Make sacrifices for China!

And during 1995, guess what? Phenomena were reported in China itself. The Virgin had taken her cause right into the lair of the red dragon.

THIRTY-THREE

~

LAIR OF THE DRAGON

There have been apparitions in China?

In a village known as Dong Lu in the Hebei Province of northern China. The phenomena started during the vigil of Our Lady of China on May 23, 1995, and continued the next day. There was an underground Roman Mass concelebrated by four bishops and 110 priests in an open field. About thirty thousand witnessed the phenomena that began during the opening prayers and recurred during consecration of the Eucharist.

There was a special feeling because the people had braved roadblocks, physical abuse, and other repression to attend the liturgy. Dong Lu is one of China's two famous Marian shrines, and pilgrimages to it are illegal. So is the Roman Church. The only legal Catholicism is practiced by what they call the Chinese Catholic Patriotic Association, whose "bishops" are appointed not in Rome but by the Chinese government.

As described by several witnesses and confirmed by Bishop Su Zhimin of the Baoding Diocese, the sun was seen to move and suddenly lose its over-powering brightness at Dong Lu in 1995. As elsewhere, it seemed to be eclipsed by an off-white Host and surrounded by halos. "Rays of various colors emanated from the sun," said a report by the Cardinal Kung Foundation in Connecticut. "With the passing of the minutes, the sun changed colors, first to yellow, then to red and blue, followed by other colors. Subsequently people saw different apparitions in the core of the sun: a holy Cross, the Holy Family, Holy Mary, and the Holy Eucharist. At times, the sun would approach the crowd and then retreat. People were heard crying out, 'Holy Mother, have pity on us, your children,' and 'Holy Mother, please forgive my sins.'"

The people were all seeing similar things because they shouted out similar observations. ("Yellow! Red! Blue!") This lasted about twenty minutes until a sudden white ray came and the sky returned to normal.

The fact that the sun spun during consecration of the Host ties into Medjugorje and the resplendent Heart of Jesus. The people saw a white dove and the Lord raise His hand to bless the congregation. He appeared after His mother, as if to confirm the prophecies of St. Louis de Montfort, who said that Mary "is the safest, easiest, shortest, and most perfect way of approaching Jesus" and that "as she was the way by which Jesus first came to us, she will again be the way by which He will come to us the second time, though not in the same manner." It reminds us that at Medjugorje Our Blessed Mother indicated there would be no second manger scene but that we should expect something.

What other lessons were there from Dong Lu? Doesn't the fact that it occurred in a country where Roman Catholics are repressed stand as a general warning about persecution?

Yes, because our future is foretold not only by prophecies but also by the events and circumstances—the societal circumstances—surrounding them. Events themselves are harbingers. During many of the apparitions there were attacks on Christianity. During the episode of the Classical Age barbarians assaulted the Roman Empire and there was also a huge dispute between Church factions over Christ's divinity. There was schism. During the episode of the Middle Ages there was also Church division. This time it was called the Great Western Schism. Then came our own episode. In 1808, we come to Napoleon, who seized the Papal States. When he was excommunicated for that, he went so far as to arrest Pope Pius VII that year. It was a spirit of persecution that had started with the French Revolution and soon spread to Russia—as well as places like China.

And so we ask: Will we come full circle as the episode reaches a climax and face similar anti-religious feelings?

Does Our Lady appear in China to remind us of persecution?

In some way will we witness a repeat of the French Revolution?

Already, in our day, there are little persecutions, as when school prayer and nativity scenes are disallowed, as when Germany suddenly bans the crucifix from the public place, or as when a Hollywood studio comes out with a movie defaming priests. Believe me, I know we have certain problems in the clergy. But I also know the percentage of bad priests is very low, that the vast majority are dedicated and sincere, with far more virtue than the rest of society. I've always been pleasantly surprised by their faith and devotion. Priests are amazing, self-sacrificing spirits.

Defamation is one form of persecution. There are others. There is the persecution by cable companies who refuse to carry programs with a Christian theme. There is also persecution, subtler persecution, from within our own Church, such as when a parish prohibits adoration of the Blessed Sacrament or recitation of the Rosary. I constantly meet Catholics who fear that Americans will one day split from Rome and that in such a schism the Holy Sacrifice of the Mass will be compromised. They fear there will be an "American Catholic Church," just as there is a Chinese Catholic Church, and that the old Church will have to go underground. There are sixty-five "catholic" churches in America that have disavowed Rome.

What chances do you give a schism as happening now?

Right now, not much. I don't think American Catholics would separate while Pope John Paul II is in Rome. He's too popular. Even if many Catholics disagree with his stand on issues like birth control, they still give him a phenomenal 86 percent approval rating. And for the most part our bishops are very dedicated and loyal.

But I do wonder what will happen when Pope John Paul's gone. I do wonder what will happen under the next pope if he's not as strong. According to one survey published by *USA Today*, only half of American Catholics think sex outside of marriage is always wrong and, according to another poll in *U.S. News and World Report*, only 31 percent—about the same percent as regularly go to church—think priests should remain unmarried and celibate. Those are disheartening statistics, even more prevalent in places like Holland and Austria, and they indicate that the schism exists on a spiritual level. There's a split between traditionalists, who want the Church to remain above the vagaries of social trends, and lukewarm Christians or modernists who devise new bibles that conform with the movement of the moment. One new bible has changed the Lord's Prayer to say, "Our Father-Mother in heaven...."

Such compromises were supposedly prophesied in the fourth century by St. Anthony of the Desert, who according to devotional literature said, "Men will surrender to the spirit of the age. They will say that if they had lived in our day, faith would be simple and easy. But in their day, they will say, things are complex; the Church must be brought up to date and made meaningful to the day's problems. When the Church and the world are one, then those days are at hand. Because our Divine Master placed a barrier between His things and the things of the world."

The general tenor of modernism is liberal progressivism, which has come to mean a Church more in tune with the world and less in tune with the Bible, the Blessed Sacrament, and Confession.

Influenced by the rampant scientism, modernists look upon the sacraments more as rituals than as something invoking the supernatural. They've stripped Christianity of mysticism, and it's the Virgin who has come to restore that element.

I note that Mary appears in places like Dong Lu, places that are "old-fashioned" and aligned with the pope.

But aren't there even priests who don't believe in the supernatural?

Our poor priests have been put through many trials of faith. They always have. Priests are under tremendous spiritual pressure. The devil really works at harassing them and that is why we need to specially pray for them. They're at the front line. And the greatest problem is that they're no longer taught mystical theology.

Everything is "psychological" now, isn't it?

Supernaturalism has been all but removed from our sermons, and that's what has really emptied the pews: the elimination of mysticism and the turning of homilies into dry lectures. Priests need to talk about active prayer and miracles!

What about the disputes concerning altar girls and taking Communion in the hand?

If the official Church approves something, I would not publicly criticize that decision.

What about churches that have taken out statues or set the tabernacle to the side?

I prefer churches that have the tabernacle containing the Eucharist at the very center of everything, and that have many statues. Artwork brings with it the element of supernaturalism. Many statues were removed in an effort to appease those who criticized them as "idolatry," but as I said, idolatry is the worship of a statue fashioned after creeping things; it has nothing to do with Our Blessed Mother, whom we don't worship but do honor. Holy figures are not only okay but are highly valuable. And yet they are still removed. I've seen it in many places: statues tossed in the garbage bin. The last time so many were taken from churches was during the French Revolution.

Is that where modernism began?

The Age of Modernism actually began at the end of the Middle Ages when the old ideas of Aristotle and the notion that all knowledge can be obtained through the physical senses, without recourse to the spiritual were resurrected. Logic. Rationality. Everything can be explained in physical terms. That view of reality began to dominate after the Middle Ages as the Age of Modernism got under way. It came full force with the French Revolution and our own century of rampant scientism, which simply means elevating science to the level of religion. It's this era of irreligion that's causing our current turmoil and that will soon be broken down.

What else concerns you about the state of the Church?

The infiltration of the occult and New Age. I'd even be careful with things like the enneagram. There's a real spiritual confusion, which for me was best expressed by two bumper stickers on the same car parked for Sunday Mass at a church near my home. One of the bumper stickers said, "Jesus Takes Care of Me," which was great, but the second was a tourist memento that said, "Salem, City of Witches: Stop By and Stay a Spell." We see here a churchgoing Catholic who obviously is not warned about the occult and so sees nothing wrong with witchcraft.

In Salem itself, where there are four thousand practicing witches, the local covens have tried to gain admission into an interfaith clergy association.

The attitude of many intellectuals is that witchcraft and paganism are just other forms of faith, nothing to get squirmy about, and that the devil is greatly exaggerated. Many problems that were once attributed to Satan—depression, obsession, oppression, and possession—are now explained in psychological terms.

But in truth there's a tremendous demonic factor and the public seems to sense as much. By 1990, 55 to 60 percent of Americans believed in the existence of the devil, up from 37 percent in 1964, according to George Gallup of the Gallup Poll. Many realize that the devil is active every day all day, which is also a key message from Medjugorje. Especially he attacks the Church and the family unit, which is the worst form of persecution.

What about more traditional persecution? What about those who foresee a pope chased out of Rome, or assassinated?

There have been prophecies about attacks on the Church in every century, and there seems to be special bouts of persecution during supernatural episodes.

Isn't there also a prophecy that after John Paul II we'll get an "anti-pope," a bad pontiff?

Yes, and it's a prediction we should be extraordinarily cautious about. The devil can feed us false prophecy to predispose us against the next pontiff. Everyone always expects the schism to be initiated by modernists, but we had better be careful it doesn't come from the traditionalist ranks. It can come from either extreme. There are already ultraconservatives who believe the only valid Mass is the Latin Mass and who describe John Paul II as a heretic for saying the *novus ordo*.

So we should be slow to judge and cautious about paranoia. Could we one day see a pope who is evil? Of course. A pope is always human. There have been popes who waged wars or were known for their partying. But that's very rare. We can only pray such prophecies are incorrect, while keeping obedience foremost in mind. Even when we disagree, we're called to be obedient to our spiritual superiors. There was once an archbishop who detested Padre Pio and disallowed him from hearing Confession or saying public Mass for ten years; but despite the grossly unfair treatment, Padre Pio remained obedient to him. Obedience is often a test, and my allegiance will always be with Rome.

But getting back to the question: Do you think there will be a formal schism?

I think the day is coming when all Christians will be forced to make certain decisions.

THIRTY-FOUR

~

THE FINAL OMENS

You've mentioned the scenario for potential wars, plagues, and just now, persecution. In Matthew 24, doesn't it also say the end of an age is marked by famine and quakes?

It does, and we should include these scenarios in our prayers. We should pray that mankind avoids such disasters, which have occurred alongside previous apparitions. They are additional harbingers. Events prophesied in Scripture happen in every age. Each generation gets a preview of great events in the future. Every period has its phenomena. Every period has its wars, rumors of wars, and tremors. Every age has its pestilence. And every age has its miniature tribulation. Sometimes it seems like every age builds on the previous ones, that with every proceeding age we come closer to what was described by Jesus as the final test, or Great Tribulation (see Matthew 24:15).

When I think of famine I think of La Salette. There Our Blessed Mother told Melanie and Maximin that *"if the harvest is spoiled, it is your own fault. I warned you last year by means of the potatoes. You paid no heed. Quite the reverse, when you discovered that the potatoes had rotted, you swore, you abused my Son's name. They will continue to rot, and by Christmas this year there will be none left."* She predicted that *"a great famine is coming."*

That same year, 1846, Ireland experienced a massive crop failure that led to the Great Irish Famine. As projected at La Salette, it involved the potato. It was caused by a fungus called *phytopthroa infestans*—or what Matthew 24 might call a pestilence. Over the next half a decade one million perished from fever, dysentery, and other effects of malnutrition. "In Ireland as elsewhere," wrote David Duckson, a fellow of Trinity College, "malign coincidence seems to be a necessary ingredient of truly calamitous famines, with extraneous factors—war, plague, or economic crash—being required to turn times of trial into trend-changing catastrophes."

In 1879 there was another famine in Ireland—and another apparition. This time it was the famous apparition at Knock on August 21. It occurred at St. John the Baptist Church as excessive rain threatened crops and the potato was again badly affected by blight. Hundreds of thousands went

> *When the Holy Spirit finds Mary in a soul—or in a nation— "He hastens there and enters fully into it," said St. Louis de Montfort. "He gives Himself generously to that soul according to the place it has given to His spouse."*

hungry. It was another trying time, and it seemed to call out to the world. An inscription on the west wall of the old stone church read, "My house shall be called the house of prayer to all nations."

Ireland always seems to be at the center of the storm. It has a history not only of food shortages but also of persecution. Yet along with the Philippines and Italy, Ireland remains among the most Catholic of nations. No land has more devout priests. No land has sent out more missionaries. And no land has exceeded Ireland in maintaining respect for Christianity. Until recently divorce was still illegal. Abortion still is. At the airport in Shannon there's a statue of Our Blessed Mother—right there in public. You see grottos dedicated to Mary, Queen of Ireland, in every hamlet, and towering spires atop classic churches.

That's why there are so many apparitions.

That's why Ireland is a benchmark.

The fact that there is now a chance for peace between the Catholics and Protestants in Northern Ireland should stand as a great sign of hope, a wonderful omen. If Ireland can find peace, so can the rest of the world. If Ireland can avoid chastisement, the same is true of us.

What it takes is something akin to the Irish respect of the Blessed Virgin, for when the Holy Spirit, her spouse, finds Mary in a soul—or in a nation— "He hastens there and enters fully into it," said St. Louis de Montfort. "He gives Himself generously to that soul according to the place it has given to His spouse."

She is the "safest, easiest, shortest, and most perfect way of approaching Jesus" and obtains great grace in those who surrender themselves to her in order to belong entirely to Jesus. "As all perfection consists in our being conformed, united, and consecrated to Jesus it naturally follows that the most perfect of all devotions is that which conforms, unites, and consecrates us most completely to Jesus," said St. Louis. "Now of all God's creatures Mary is the most conformed to Jesus. It therefore follows that, of all devotions, devotion to her makes for the most complete consecration and conformity to Him. The more one is consecrated to Mary, the more one is consecrated to Jesus."

And Ireland has long known that. The Irish are consecrated to Mary. And they've been rescued from many sufferings as a result.

But they face future challenges. Darkness creeps in. They struggle to maintain strict Christianity. On November 24, 1995, divorce was legalized during a bitter referendum that ended up with the closest vote in Ireland's history. Ireland stood as the last European nation where divorce was illegal, and there have been similar stirrings about its abortion laws. Though not to the same extent as elsewhere, when one opens up the *Irish Independent* one now sees some of the same things—news of scandal, infidelity, and crime— that plague the rest of Europe.

And the inference?

If, as a last bastion, Ireland falls, if it succumbs to worldliness, if it abandons its devotion, this will be another sign of the times. This will be one of the final omens.

THIRTY-FIVE

~

WHERE THE WIND BLOWS

What about earthquakes? What about other natural disasters?

God can use these too. When Israel sinned, God warned that He would cause the earth to tremble (see Joel 2:10). "The mountains quake at Him," says Nahum 1:5 (KJV). "The hills melt."

You really believe that? You really believe God manipulates things like earthquakes or the weather?

"In the hurricane and tempest is His path," prophesied the prophet Nahum (1:3), "When He utters His voice, there is a multitude of waters in the heavens: He causes the vapors to ascend from the ends of the earth; He makes lightnings for the rain; He brings the wind out of His treasuries" (51:16).

On Pentecost the Holy Spirit manifested like the sound of wind (see Acts 2:2), and at Medjugorje Our Blessed Mother said, *"The wind is my sign. I will come in the wind. When the wind blows, know that I am with you."*

And so whenever there's a strong wind we're supposed to believe it's heaven-sent?

No, but God has used the weather and storms to produce many of the signs of our time.

That implies that God sends hail and lightning to punish us. Isn't the concept of God's righteous anger a discredited concept?

Not if you believe in the Bible. God has always exercised His power. He does so to purify. He does so to save us for eternity. More than striking at us it's a matter of sending events to purge our evil. We're the ones who create the need for cleansing, and we suffer most when God leaves us to our own devices and doesn't correct what we're doing. We get in trouble when we turn away from God. We get in trouble when we forget Him and rely on ourselves. We get in danger when we cut ourselves off from His bonding force. Without God the world at all levels falls into decay and chaos.

You're implying a chastisement of our own making. Can you give us an example?

Pollution. While it's still a subject of debate, there are many studies indicating that pollution is altering weather patterns. All the carbon dioxide. It traps heat like a greenhouse and can raise the atmosphere's temperature, leading to drought in some regions and flooding in others.

A continued increase in temperature would eventually cause melting of the Antarctic ice sheets, and that in turn might cause oceans to rise in such a way as to gradually inundate coastal cities. That's an example of God lifting His protection and leaving us to our own arrogance.

When the Bible says God causes storms or quakes, how is that possible? How do natural events have an association with the supernatural?

God is the Creator. He's the organizing force of the cosmos. Forces like electricity and gravity are but manifestations of God's power. All forces are only subenergies of the Holy Spirit. Their job is to keep the sun and planets where they are, keep the earth sedate, keep the oceans from washing over the continents.

Keep our world in balance.

When we reject God, we're rejecting His forces. We're pushing our world towards its natural inclination for entropy. When God's Presence leaves, things begin to unravel—whether it's in the form of earthquakes, famines, or the weather. Without the force of God, nature descends into chaos. "If you hide Your face," says Psalms, "they are dismayed. If you take away their breath, they perish and return to their dust" (104:29).

So the sea and wind are at His command?

When He desires. One symbol is *El Niño*. That's the huge Pacific current that affects weather around the world. *El Niño* is a Spanish reference to the Christ Child.

What about societal disturbances?

These are also caused by imbalances. As a human population we're out of balance. We're out of balance when we exalt ourselves instead of God. It's the greatest insult. It's a sin on the order of idolatry. And God warns us by lifting His protection and allowing the forces of darkness to assault and undermine us.

This is very important. This is a major form of chastisement: Satan is allowed to act in proportion to our darkness.

It's evil that strikes in the way of bizarre murders and incredible crime rates. Across America there are more than a million men in prison at any given moment, and violent crime is quickly graduating to the rank of terrorism. We look at Oklahoma City and shudder at the explosion caused by extremists, or the doomsday cult in Japan that orchestrated a horrible gas attack and was trying to build its own nuclear bomb. The cult has a billion dollars in assets!

Nuclear terrorism is a foremost concern and seems all but inevitable without prayer to forestall it.

Chastisements will creep in without much notice. That's how prophecy unfolds, sometimes in fits and starts but most often in stages, gradually, so much so that we don't recognize chastisements except in retrospect.

They vary according to region. Hurricanes become larger storms and then mega-hurricanes. High water turns into floodwater, then inundation. Elsewhere dry spells become water shortages and then full-scale droughts. Plagues like the *Ebola* virus mutate and spread to humans through blood and then are transmissible through the air; or bacteria continues to change so that doctors have no more effective antibiotics, and illnesses begin to eat at various portions of the population like boring termites.

As we continue on the path of sin, there is more cancer, more infectious disease, more neurosis.

Riots break out, while the kind of civil strife seen in Rwanda spreads elsewhere.

There is continued disintegration of the family unit.

And as if to underscore the situation, earthquakes increasingly strike at large cities. There is overall imbalance.

Is that what seers think of as the greatest potential for natural disaster, earthquakes?

A tidal wave sent over several nations by a slippage of the tectonic plates would be among the most severe of chastisements but any such event can be averted by prayer. We are at the point right now where prayer can make a huge difference.

Is that a hint?
It's just a comment.

Are there prophecies to that effect?

There are more prophecies about earthquakes than about anything else. I get them constantly from locutionists who seem all but obsessed with California. There are predictions every week. Some of it wanders into the morbid: some have given specific dates for "the Big One," but naturally such predictions have proven inaccurate. I pay little attention to prophecies with times and dates.

New Agers are also in on the act, and such is the confusion that it's often hard to distinguish theirs from Christian prophecy. I remember the astrologer Jeane Dixon predicting things like a split in the Church, an attack on the pope, and an extraordinary natural event that would jar the world. It seemed like a locution. Recently I appeared on an NBC program about prophecy. I was there for a segment on the Virgin Mary. They did an excellent job on the Christian aspect, but the rest of the show delved into the New Age and Indian occultism, which makes me extremely nervous. Our networks tend to blend everything together, and it's another product of our confusing times. The most dramatic stuff comes from New Agers who see "earth changes" that will actually alter the map, turning Denver into a seaport and sending much of New Jersey and Florida to the bottom of the ocean.

I think my own area is supposed to get flooded by the Great Lakes and the Hudson. Or I hear people say the earth will tilt off its axis. I've heard a number of seers claim the earth is going to wobble and is out of balance. Now, that really would be frightening. Hopefully it is just a symbol for our spiritual imbalance! There are all kinds of scenarios. Among the third-level apparitions, they get especially apocalyptic, foreseeing every conceivable cataclysm. And there are those that go so far as to predict that the mainland U.S. will be invaded by enemy forces, and that they are already building concentration camps here in America.

This is where we venture into that dangerous territory of sensationalism, isn't it?

This is that territory.

How does it relate to Medjugorje?

It's as if other seers are trying to guess what's in those secrets and are coming up with every possibility.

But doesn't it sound like the Medjugorje secrets could include an earth-shaking calamity?

Of course that's possible. In Shaanxi, China, there was a quake in 1556 that killed 830,000 people. Today such a quake could disrupt a nation's entire infrastructure, leaving it without adequate food, water, or electricity for weeks. There have also been disasters like the influenza that spread across Eurasia earlier this century.

But when a locution strips us of hope and paints the future as only black, it's coming from the devil. It's his way of scaring us, discouraging us, and discrediting or confusing legitimate prophecy. He causes us to feel helpless and to want to simply sit around waiting for the Big One, when the main message from Our Holy Lady is that we can save the world. We can stem the tide of chastisement. For when we renounce sin and turn to God, we're immediately moving in that direction. There is an actual global improvement. Every soul counts. Every soul is equal. With each conversion there is suddenly that much less evil. The balance tips more toward God. He waits for our confessions. He waits for us to seek Him and rescue ourselves. It's a tall order, but with prayer, reading the Bible, and reciting the Rosary, it becomes a smaller order. It's manageable. The little army of God can do wonders. And repentance unleashes torrents of God's mercy.

God also waits for our prayer. We're called to intercede as Abraham interceded for Sodom. Remember, God was willing to let Sodom off the hook if He could find but ten righteous people. It's our responsibility to make sure that next time God looks for a few righteous, He finds them.

What about asteroids?

We get those prophecies too, though not from any major sites of apparition. They come mainly from scientists. They come from astronomers. In 1989, a good-sized asteroid missed earth by a mere six hours. It wasn't anticipated. You heard about it only afterward. It came from the blackness of space and crossed the earth's pattern of orbit. It wasn't much farther than the moon. Some have been yet closer. It startled NASA enough to order a study of the many other asteroids that cross our path, because had it hit earth, it would have caused what even the most conservative scientists describe as an unprecedented human disaster.

All it would take is a chunk of rock just over half a mile in diameter.

So far we've been lucky. Last time we were hit, it was a small one. It happened during June of 1908 in Siberia. It was known as the "Tunguska" fireball and it flattened two thousand square kilometers of forest. If such a projectile hit an urban area, it would cause hundreds of billions in damage. Larger asteroids slamming into earth at roughly sixteen miles a second could alter the very course of our civilization. Odds are one in five thousand that an asteroid will hit during the next hundred years, but the fear is that a large one could toss up enough dust to dim the sun, drop temperatures, and cause crops to fail, thus creating a worldwide famine—or untold other effects. Millions would perish. According to a report from NASA, objects large enough to cause widespread global mortality and threaten civilization occur from one to several times every million years.

And there are mystics predicting this?

It's always been a major subject of prophecy, and here again caution is in order because a comet hitting the earth has also been a favorite forecast of occultists like Nostradamus. I remember when the Shoemaker-Levy comet was ready to collide with Jupiter in 1994. Many scientists expected it to be only vaguely visible—a rather insignificant event—while New Agers blew it out of all proportion, expecting a truly immense happening. One New Ager prophesied on TV that Jupiter would explode into little fragments!

These were both extreme views: on the one hand, that nothing would happen, on the other that Jupiter would be in shambles.

The truth was in between. The truth was that when Shoemaker-Levy finally hit, the impact was surprisingly strong—more than most expected, detectable even through amateur telescopes. It released energy measuring in the millions of megatons of TNT and according to a NASA report "generated fireballs and dark clouds on Jupiter about as large as the earth."

Yet Jupiter survived. It remained intact. It never did explode as some predicted. But you want to hear something else? The day it began to hit was July 16, 1994. That's the feast day of Our Lady of Mount Carmel.

Mount Carmel is a mountain in Israel. It's famous as the place where the prophet Elijah worked a great miracle (see 1 Kings 18:38).

And?

It was in the attire of Our Lady of Mount Carmel—with brown scapular and holding *El Niño,* the Christ Child—that Mary appeared to the four children on a mountain in Garabandal.

That's the place in Spain. The apparition occurred during the 1960s and like Medjugorje involved prophecy of a coming warning, a great miracle, and a chastisement. One seer said the "warning" will be seen everywhere in the world and will be "like two stars... but they don't fall. It's not going to hurt us but we're going to see it and, in that moment, we're going to see our consciences."

Many wonder if "two stars" implies a close call with a comet.

Do you believe in Garabandal?

I spent a whole day praying there alone. It's a beautiful place, and from what I can tell the seers have conducted themselves with quiet dignity. They've never capitalized off the event. They've avoided publicity. But there are a number of questions and I hope they soon find a resolution. The Church has never ruled on it.

Questions about what?

Questions raised by theologians like Fr. René Laurentin about the unusual ecstasies, the strange way the seers fell into trance, or (as in Kibeho) contorted on the ground, or ran up a path backward. It's unsettling. There are also questions about what seemed like a riddle concerning the coming great "miracle." The seers gave hints that it would occur on such and such a day, between such and such months, at a specific time on a day that is a feast day of a mysterious martyr. They also said it will happen during a time when the Church is witnessing a significant event, perhaps proclamation of a new dogma.

It's a riddle and it's very interesting, but I haven't seen riddles like that at primary or even secondary apparitions—it's not Mary's normal way—and so I'm still trying to discern it.

There has also been a history of confusion among the seers, and though they said they were warned this would happen, when we see confusion we always raise our spiritual antennas. Satan is everywhere Our Blessed Mother is, and even a legitimate apparition can be infiltrated.

THIRTY-SIX

~

APPARITIONS IN AMERICA

What about visionaries in the U.S.? What about the seers we've seen on TV?

They're similar to Garabandal. They need love, and present us with a trial of discernment. Coast to coast. Off the top of my head I can think of fifteen states where apparitions are claimed, and I wouldn't be astounded if twice that number have at least one ongoing apparition. We counted at least seven visionaries—seers, not just locutionists—in Ohio and northern Kentucky.

It's a final stage in the episode. Rosaries turn gold and pilgrims experience conversion. And so, while on the one hand it all seems a bit much—and there are some prophecies that seem kind of far out—God grants grace to the faithful believers. Even when the apparitions themselves are not authentic, He inspires and heals, as long as they don't get ensnared in a demonic circumstance.

It's better to be positive than negative, but we must be very careful of deceptive spirits and recognize that there has never been an apparition in America that has been formally accepted by the Church. So far investigations in Texas, New Jersey, and Arizona have declared that there is no objective proof of supernaturality (*non constat de supernaturalitate*), meaning no evidence of a supernormal force suspending natural laws or of occurrences that clearly cannot be explained through natural causes.

How many American seers do you think are authentic?

There are several that are of interest, and soon we'll have a better idea of whether they're part of an authentic eruption of Marian apparitions or a wave of deception.

What happens if we've gone to an apparition and it turns out to be false?

God draws good out of any situation, and so people may be deeply blessed, even converted, as a result of an otherwise dubious situation. We receive graces because it's God we're praying to. The Blessed Virgin, when praised, immediately transfers those tributes to the Almighty (see Luke 1:46). We get into danger only when we ignore warning signals or go to a site out of curiosity and obsession, as if we're going to see a fortuneteller.

What's your final advice on discerning visionaries?

Remember that a revelation is only as pure as the vessel, and that the final rule is whether the fruits are permanent or superficial and temporary. Pray deeply, and see if you feel an uneasiness.

What about Maria Valtorta, the Italian mystic who received the famous revelations called Poem of the Man-God? *She's not an American, but her works are extremely popular among American Catholics.*

I've never read it, but everywhere I go I meet people who say they've benefitted from *Poem*, a five-volume set of books of what Valtorta considered to be supernatural revelations on the lives of Mary and Jesus.

Many tell me the books bring the Bible alive. There are positive testimonies. In 1959, *Poem* was condemned when it was placed on the Vatican's Index of Forbidden Books, but in 1966 the Sacred Congregation for the Doctrine of the Faith abolished the Index. And so, while the Vatican didn't actually change its negative position, the volumes are no longer officially forbidden because the index no longer exists.

The Congregation does ask that a notification be included with copies of the volumes stating that "the 'visions' and 'dictations' referred to in it are simply the literary forms used by the author to narrate in her own way the life of Jesus. They cannot be considered supernatural in origin." That's the Vatican's current position.

Didn't the Virgin herself recommend Poem of the Man-God *to a couple of the visionaries at Medjugorje?*

According to Sr. Emmanuel Maillard the matter involved only Marija and not Vicka, as widely reported. Sr. Emmanuel reports that in 1982 Marija was asked by a Franciscan friar to seek Our Blessed Mother's direction on *Poem*. The Virgin's response was simple and noncommittal. *"You can read it,"* she said.

What about "miraculous photos"? They seem to be all over the U.S.— photos that have images of Mary, Jesus, or angels hidden in them, or strange lights.

Many such photos can be readily explained as dust, light bleeds, or defects in a shutter, but once in a while I do see a highly striking image that doesn't seem to fit any logical explanation. Perhaps the most interesting I've encountered was taken by a woman from northern California. It shows a ray or spear of bright light, very defined, going through a prayer book held by Vicka. It's like a powerful ray from the sun—but even stronger and brighter, nearly like a lightning bolt. It was taken in broad daylight and enters from behind the book and comes out the front.

There is also a famous photo of an atomic blast over the French test site of Mururoa Island in the Pacific, and in the mushroom cloud are remarkable images of Mary and Jesus Crucified. It appeared in the July 12, 1989, issue of *Newsweek*. It was repeated in an issue commemorating Hiroshima in 1995.

I've seen the remarkable face of Jesus fill a photograph that was supposed to be of Mount Krizevac in Medjugorje. Instead of a mountain, there is Jesus' face, grave and sorrowful, as if on the way to crucifixion.

Most recently, on November 4, 1995, CNN was flooded with calls after showing a picture of stars being born in a six-trillion-mile-long cloud. The photo had been taken by the Hubble Space Telescope and when turned on its side, many viewers said they could see the face of Jesus in the astonishing space photograph.

You said no American apparition has been approved. Have any been condemned?

Local bishops have rejected several, most recently in New York and Colorado. I report this with a heavy heart: I knew and liked the seer in Denver. But there were significant doubts, and we must be obedient to the direction of local bishops.

There are other apparitions—still very active—that if not condemned have been set aside or restricted. This happens when a local bishop discourages pilgrimages or even bans liturgical services, as is the case at several American situations.

The strongest recent action was taken against a Swiss woman who for years has claimed that a heavenly force moves her hand to write prophecy. She was one of the biggest stars on the mystical circuit. But there were always questions about her technique of receiving messages. She seemed to let a force take over her hand and write the words for her, which bothered many people, including some at the Vatican. In an unusual announcement on October 6, 1995, it issued an official "notification" by the Congregation for the Doctrine of the Faith that was then published by its official newspaper, *L'Osservatore Romano*. It contained a strongly negative ruling on her (as strong as a previous bishop's ruling against the New York site known as Bayside). The ruling pointed out "basic elements that must be considered negative in the light of Catholic doctrine" and the "suspect nature of the way in which these alleged revelations have occurred."

I felt sorry for her, but the Vatican was troubled by messages about the Holy Trinity which appeared to confuse "the specific names and functions of the Divine Persons." The Congregation was likewise concerned with the nature of her prophecies. "These alleged revelations predict an imminent period when the Anti-Christ will prevail in the Church," it said. "In millenarian style, it is prophesied that God is going to make a final, glorious intervention which will initiate on earth, even before Christ's definitive coming, an era of peace and universal prosperity. Furthermore, the proximate arrival is foretold of a Church which would be a kind of pan-Christian community, contrary to Catholic doctrine."

Although a bit confusing, the Vatican reference was to the idea popular in certain Protestant circles that Christ will come and actually rule the earth for one thousand years—a millennium of peace—as opposed to a more definitive arrival and judgment at the end of time. Catholics do not believe in millenarianism. Nor do they accept the notion of secular messianism. They are taught that the Church will enter the glory of the kingdom only through a final Passover, when it will follow Christ in His death and Resurrection.

As *The Catechism of the Catholic Church* puts it, "The kingdom will be fulfilled, then, not by a historic triumph of the Church through a progressive ascendancy, but only by God's victory over the final unleashing of evil, which will cause His Bride to come down from heaven. God's triumph over the revolt of evil will take the form of the Last Judgment after the final cosmic upheaval of this passing world" (#677).

THIRTY-SEVEN

~

ARE WE IN THE END TIMES?

And so we approach the issue of the End Times, which you said you would address. We approach the issue of what all these apparitions have to say about the fate of the world. What's the bottom line? Are we in the End Times?

We've been in the End Times since the birth of Christ. He came to complete human history, and He will, when He returns. So it must be the "end times." We've been in the End Times for two thousand years now. The Beginning Times started with Adam; the Middle Times included Abraham and Moses; and the End Times commenced with Our Messiah.

It's the last hour. We get that not from mystics so much as official Church teaching. It's in our *Catechism:* "Since the Ascension God's plan has entered into its fulfillment. We are already at 'the last hour.' Already the final age of the world is with us, and the renewal of the world is irrevocably under way" (#670). We see the same in Scripture. "Children, it is the final hour. Just as you heard that the Anti-Christ was coming, so now many such antichrists have appeared. This makes us certain that it is the final hour" (1 Jn 2:18).

The question remains of how long the "last hour" will last. There are many periods within an age, and a number of ages in the End Times.

What we strive to determine is whether coming events will signal the end of a period, the end of a larger age, or the end of the End Times, which would be the Final Judgment.

But isn't there any way of guessing when the time will arrive? Isn't there a ballpark figure?

We know that "the day will come" because it's what Christ answered when He was asked the same question (see Luke 21:6). But no one can predict with more specificity. Heaven's time is different than ours, and God's actions are often flexible and evolving. They change with the human condition.

At the Vatican, Joseph Cardinal Ratzinger reportedly alluded to the End Times in an unedited portion of a transcript about the Third Secret, saying that the secret hadn't been released because it would add nothing to what we already know about "the seriousness of history, the dangers threatening the faith and life of the Christian, and therefore the world. *And also the importance of the last times* [emphasis mine]." If the second most powerful man at the Vatican can mention the End Times, it behooves us also to do so. Fatima leaned in the same direction. When asked about the End Times, Sr. Lucia saw a "diabolical wave invading the world" and explained that "the devil is in the mood for engaging in a decisive battle against the Virgin" but that "the Most Holy Virgin in these last times in which we live has given a new efficacy to the recitation of the Rosary to such an extent that there is no problem, no matter how difficult it is, whether temporal or above all spiritual, in the personal life of each one of us, of our families, of the families of the world, or of the religious communities, or even of the life of peoples and nations, that cannot be solved by the Rosary. There is no problem, I tell you, no matter how difficult it is, that we cannot resolve by the prayer of the Holy Rosary. With the Holy Rosary, we will save ourselves. We will sanctify ourselves. We will console Our Lord, and obtain the salvation of many souls."

Our Holy Mother stands as a rock on which to weather the coming change, for as St. Louis de Montfort said, "it is Mary, the singularly faithful Virgin, over whom Satan had never any power" and who leads us swiftly to the divine union, helping as we "pass through spiritual darkness, engage in struggles for which we are not prepared, endure bitter agonies, scale precipitous mountains, tread upon painful thorns, and cross frightening deserts."

She is always close to her faithful servants, always on hand, as St. Louis wrote in the 1700s, "to brighten their darkness, clear away their doubts, strengthen them in their fears, sustain them in their combats and trials."

When we become faithful servants, we are protected on all sides with no room for fear because this powerful Queen "would sooner dispatch millions of angels to help one of her servants than have it said that a single faithful and trusting servant of hers had fallen victim to the malice, number, and power of his enemies."

While the devil often leaves alone those who are finding their own way to hell, and even helps them accumulate wealth and thus worldly bondage, he attacks the people of God. He shoots his fiery darts. He seeks to diminish our faith. And yet he can never truly cause harm if we remain under the Virgin's mantle.

No matter how dark the night, no matter how anxious a trial, the clouds eventually clear. And when we invoke Our Holy Mother, the radiance of

Christ grows all the stronger.

We may rest assured that, as during the Chinese apparition, Mary has secured the blessing of Our Heavenly Father and union with Christ because she keeps us in Jesus and Jesus in us and watches her flock with a maternal love that's unceasing and indestructible.

These issues, the issues of evil, are what I believe are represented in the Third Secret of Fatima.

Sr. Lucia said the secret would become clearer after 1960, as it has.

It was during the sixties that the diabolical wave reached tidal force.

If you had to guess, based on mysticism, at what most realistically may happen, what would you guess?

Oh, I suppose that a couple of natural disasters would be followed by an economic gyration that really causes widespread anxiety. There would also be some sort of miracle in certain places, as there are currently miracles in Medjugorje, and perhaps there would be an unusual disaster in Europe, as well as chaos and civil strife in a highly populated nation. There may be involvement in some way of a nuclear device, perhaps in regional strife or as terrorism. If those warnings aren't recognized and heeded, then the great war would come. That's how I would render all the prophecies.

Do you think there's any significance to the year 2000?

There will be certain events before, during, and well after the year 2000. At Medjugorje there was never anything said about that particular year, but we head into a new and crucial millennium. If as Scripture says a "day" with the Lord is as a thousand years and a thousand years as one day (see 2 Peter 3:8), we've already been through two "days" since the time of Christ and now enter the third "day," which if you think about it makes matters all the more interesting.

Speaking of "days," there are many who say that one day soon the earth will go through a chastisement involving three days of darkness, that the world will be plunged into several days of indescribable night, in which the entire planet will come to a standstill. Still and dark. No electricity. No nothing. Do you believe that?

From what I can tell the "three days of darkness" gained currency at the beginning of our episode. Throughout the nineteenth century the terrifying, titillating notion of a planetary cataclysm picked up steam, mentioned by well-known mystics such as Gaspar del Bufalo and Blessed Anna Maria Taigi. "God will send two punishments," claimed Blessed Anna. "One will be in the form of wars, revolutions, and other evils. It shall originate on earth. The other will be sent from heaven. There shall come over the whole earth an intense darkness lasting three days and three nights. Nothing will be visible, and the air will be laden with pestilence, which will claim mainly, but not only, the enemies of religion."

It sounded like a description of the Final Judgment. Others such as Palma Maria d'Oria, who died in 1863, added that "the atmosphere will be infected by innumerable devils, who will cause the death of large multitudes of unbelievers and wicked men. Blessed candles alone shall be able to give light and preserve the faithful Catholics from this impending dreadful scourge."

Marie Julie Jahenny of LaFraudis, France, another prominent seer, further promoted the idea by adding that the surreal darkness will be "illuminated at times by streaks of lightning, flashes of fire, and flaming skies, along with firestorms or tempests." Many current locutionists, and also some visionaries, are predicting as much, especially a Franciscan monk from Texas. But where many seers see devastation after the darkness—some saying two-thirds of humanity will be wiped out—he sees the world renewed afterwards. So by his reckoning it's not the end of the world.

It's something that in a biblical sense would indicate a gargantuan change in human history. That's really all I can say. We know how major it would be from the precedents. In Exodus we see that "Moses stretched out his hand toward the sky, and there was dense darkness throughout the land of Egypt for three days. Men could not see one another, nor could they move from where they were, for three days." It also corresponds with Revelation 8:12, when a third of the stars will be "plunged into darkness."

If you want to take it literally and not as allegory, I suppose you could speculate that the earth may one day pass through cosmic clouds of unknown dark matter, or that an asteroid would kick up enough dust to blot out the sun. According to a 1992 report issued by NASA, "Meteoric phenomena associated with high-speed ejecta could subject plants and animals to scorching heat for about half an hour, and a continent-wide firestorm may then ensue. Dust thrown up from a very large crater would lead to daytime darkness over the whole earth." Blessed Faustina linked a similar darkness to the Final Judgment when, as quoted before, Jesus told her that before He comes as the just judge, there will be given to the people a sign in the heaven: *"All light in the heavens will be extinguished, and there will be great darkness over the whole earth. Then the sign of the cross will be seen in the sky, and from the openings where the hands and the feet of the Savior were nailed will come forth great lights which will light up the earth for a period of time. This will take place shortly before the last day."*

Didn't Padre Pio predict the three days of darkness?

No. He neither confirmed nor denied it. In 1977 the *Voice of Padre Pio* ran a special notice saying that he had never made such a prediction.

As for those who predict cosmic collisions or the earth tilting on its axis, which perhaps symbolizes the way we've turned everything upside-down, I would rather concentrate on the predictions of Christ's glory, and hear words of mercy such as those from Blessed Faustina to whom Jesus said, *"My daughter, tell the whole world about My inconceivable mercy.... I pour out a whole ocean of graces upon those souls who approach the fount of My mercy. The soul that will go to Confession and receive Holy Communion shall obtain complete forgiveness of sins and punishment.... Let no soul fear to draw near to Me, even though its sins be as scarlet. My mercy is so great that no mind, be it of man or angel, will be able to fathom it throughout all eternity."*

What about the Anti-Christ? Could our time be the time of the Beast?

Any time could witness the Beast. I believe he will come with stealth and, as the supreme deception, may be recognizable only in retrospect. But first there are the forerunners, which have materialized in various circumstances for two thousand years as the tyrants and mass murderers who John says are miniature antichrists. They foretell what will happen at the end of time when mankind faces the "final test" (see Matthew 24:8-15) that the *Catechism* says will "shake the faith of many believers" in a persecution which will unveil the "mystery of iniquity (see #675).

It will come in the form of a religious deception offering men a solution to their problems at the price of apostasy, or a falling away from the truth, which to at least some extent has already happened.

The *Catechism* explains that, according to Our Lord, the present time is "a time still marked by 'distress' and the trial of evil which does not spare the Church" (#672). The final Anti-Christ, in whatever era he comes, will be a man of influence and not necessarily raw political power. The Church describes him more as "a pseudo-messianism by which man glorifies himself in place of God...." (#675).

And the Church says his spirit will come when?
When there's enough evil and spiritual distress to precipitate it.

What would your description be?
A demon set loose upon the earth to express Satan's rage. He's furious because he can never ascend to God's Throne, and the reason he can never usurp Our Lord is that he can never attain knowledge of certain crucial mysteries. For one thing he will never be able to master the Mystery of Creation, although he does all he can to act like the arbiter of existence, as the master of life and death, by perpetrating abortion, euthanasia, and genetic experimentation.

In the design of God to bring the final defeat of Satan we're needed to live a life worthy of our calling. And especially we're called to love and humility, for it is humility that causes Satan and his antichrists to flee.

The devil thrives on pride, but chokes on humility. As long as someone has pride, the devil has a foothold. But where he sees someone who is humble, the devil does not tread. A demon on humble ground is like a fish out of water. He can't stand to be in the presence of a humble soul because it deprives him of his oxygen.

Have you yourself ever seen indications of the "mark of the beast"?
When I visited Turin, Italy, to see where the famous Shroud is kept, I saw young people right on the street with the mark of Satan painted on their foreheads. They advertised their membership in satanic cults. It's widely known that Turin is a center of witchcraft, which is openly advertised on radio and TV. The satanists have attacked the very church where the Shroud is kept, spraying it with their unsightly graffiti, and no doubt with their relentless curses, for they are trying to invoke the Anti-Christ.

But I'm more concerned about how the spirit of antichrist infects our entire society. I get reports from a northern suburb of New York City where school officials allow kids to play a magical "game" devised by "wizards" to invoke fallen angels; now they think it's cool to become "possessed," playing the game of incantation right there in the schoolyard. I'm also deeply concerned with our rates of divorce, theft, murder, and suicide.

Our job is to counteract that. Our job is to invoke Christ and the Holy Spirit. Our job is to dispel our current culture of death. That's what Pope John Paul II calls it. A culture of death.

Does the pope believe the Anti-Christ will appear?

In 1994, he spoke of "dark forces" threatening the family, and as *Newsweek* put it, he seems "driven by his foreboding that the world is heading toward a moral apocalypse."

Many don't know it, but John Paul II had a large role in the draft of the 1968 encyclical *Humanae vitae,* which declared the Church's stance against abortion and birth control. His fear is that as far as God is concerned, abortion may be the final straw. "Indeed," writes Cliff Kincaid, a contributor to *Human Events,* "there are signs indicating that the pope believes that humanity is entering a crisis stage in which divine intervention may occur."

What do you think of those who seek "one world government" and "one world religion" as part of a "new world order"? Couldn't this too be in the designs of an antichrist?

Satan always seeks to control global institutions and use whatever societies and organizations are available—especially organizations involved in finance, education, and media. He uses diplomats. He uses secret societies. He uses atheists and humanists and global pagans. He uses agencies that were formulated to do worldly good, and so I warn that any global infrastructure that is not founded on Christ or that tries to modernize Him is a potential danger. I'm especially watchful of organizations perpetrating "Mother Earth"-style religion as the spiritual answer to our environmental problems.

Mainly the devil wants to control and dehumanize us. He wants to break down our humanness through the overuse of technology. Already we've seen people treated as mere computer codes, flooded with such mechanization that it's now nearly impossible to get a real human voice on the telephone.

The devil steers us toward an impersonal, artificial, and overly automated society. I was startled while in the Bay Area to see an article in the *San Francisco Chronicle* describing how in a suburb called Novato the city council mandated on November 26, 1995, that cats in the area have identifying microchips implanted between their shoulder blades. While we're not at the point where humans could be injected by computer microchips on a massive scale, the insertion of a technological identification device into a living creature, even a cat, is wrong and Orwellian.

What about the actual personage of the Anti-Christ? Is that in current prophecy?

I hear many prophecies about the Anti-Christ. I get locutions that say he is coming or is already alive and even describe where he's from, where he's hiding, and what he looks like.

Of course, most of these prophecies are untrue, a smoke screen or the product of the subconscious. But true or not, they call us to pray that evil leave our world so there's not the soil for an antichrist to germinate.

Instead, we seek the atmosphere in which Jesus, whose Presence will break the evil, can most readily manifest. We are supposed to seek Jesus. We are supposed to call on Him. We're supposed to keep our eyes not on evil but on heaven.

THIRTY-EIGHT

~

THE FINAL QUESTIONS

L OVE DRAWS CHRIST AND DISARMS THE ENEMY. That's the final lesson. Patience and charity must exist toward all people. It's the highest reach of spirituality because as St. Thérèse of Lisieux said, with acts of love "our soul may be quickly consumed and arrive with short delay at the vision of God." When it comes to preventing destruction and war, which is what our prophets now tell us we face, nothing is more effective than love.

Every morning we should wake up praying for Christ to come and teach us detachment from our egos and how to put love in our hearts. We should always pray for more love, and we should practice love all day every day; for God to manifest in our world and live in our hearts, says Our Blessed Mother, we must first love. We must learn to send blessings on every person during the course of the day, even those whizzing by us in a car. We should send love to the mailman and to the people in the elevator. We should love our underlings and our bosses. We should love the annoying drivers in front of us on the way home and then show great love for our families the rest of the night.

You see, most of us have spent our lives focused on our own comfort and in so doing have found ourselves restless and unfulfilled because we're self-centered. We lack peace because we focus on ourselves. That causes us to become impatient with others.

And when we cast forth such aggravation, when we feel negatively towards a person—whether it's someone we know or someone who's standing in front of us at the supermarket—it's like a curse.

When we do that, when we curse, we send malice into the firmament. And with every bit of malevolence, every bit, the world tips closer to war.

It also brings us closer to eternal reckoning, for we're held accountable for every minor or major curse.

On the other hand, when we transmit affection, when we transmit caring, we take a step in the direction of heaven. Loving everyone—no matter how attractive or unattractive, no matter how strange or familiar, no matter how friendly or nettlesome—makes up for past curses. Every time we send out love we erase a past curse.

Love combines in a potent fashion with faith and humility. The more we pray, the more faith we have, because when we're praying with regularity, we can observe the little ways God answers prayers. Those observations, tnose answered prayers, build our faith so we pray more firmly.

The more we pray, the more faith we develop; the more faith, the more results.

Those who pray little, but expect much, are often disappointed—while those who pray often with firm faith will find themselves astonished.

That's not to say life becomes a bed of roses. On earth we all must experience both heaven and hell. Life is a grueling test, and once we accept that fact we transcend it. We conquer it. We conquer fear. We offer up suffering, and we are then open to true joy. Because existence really is joyful when we consider the afterlife and the fact that nothing on earth is significant—nothing is too hard—in the light of eternal reward.

Although everyone must go through trials in life, God answers those who are humble because they come to Him as children. When we're humble, Satan's arrows wing through thin air and find no target. They find no "self." In humility is perfect surrender to God. Surrender is the truest end of conversion. Unless we're converted and approach God as children, as faithful loving children, we don't gain heaven; instead we nurture evil in the world, which leads to chastisement.

Within the lifetimes of at least some of you reading this, our special time of grace will complete itself. God's mercy will turn into His merciful justice. However it fits with the End Times, it will be the denouement of our own era. Like denouements during the other episodes, especially during medieval times, it will purge our evil and resemble some prophecies in Scripture. The key word is "prepare." The message during the reported apparitions in Slovakia might sum it all up. Our Blessed Mother said, "God's visit is near. Search for love!"

Christ is coming, isn't He?

Many visionaries use the term Second Coming. The Church teaches that since the Ascension, the return of Christ has been imminent. But the precise times and seasons are not for us to know (see Acts 1:7 and Mark 13:32). I believe that we face some kind of manifestation that if we pray enough, Christ will reveal more of Himself and break the current hold of Satan. I believe that this revelation will be at a supernatural level, like the Virgin's manifestations. I believe Jesus is in wait behind the pulsing sun. He awaits our prayer. He awaits our calling out. That's why Our Blessed Mother uses the symbolism of solar miracles. She is *signum magnum*, the great sign, the dawn that discloses the Son. She is the crest of light over a morning horizon, but He is the Light itself. I believe if we ask, if we implore Jesus, He will be more present among us.

And maybe some day He will come not as a man of flesh but like His mother, who already nurses Him and holds Him in her arms, as a light and power. He will come in light. He will manifest in a way similar to her apparitions but more powerful. It will be exciting to many who hear, but initially it will not be heard by many others or will be disbelieved. It will be spiritual. I just don't see Christ coming back and riding a jet or appearing on TV. Let me never be so presumptuous as to act as if I know. But what mystics see is a series of first regional and then global events, interspersed with miraculous signs, that could be what used to be called a final judgment in miniature, or Minor Judgment. It would be a preview of Matthew 24. According to Matthew, on the Day of Judgment Christ will come on clouds of glory with light and angels. There may be a preview of that arrival, that appearance, in our own time. It could be in a sign or symbol. Our Blessed Mother told the Medjugorje seers, *"Do not think that Jesus is going to manifest Himself again in the manger; He is born again in your hearts."*

But when He comes, it will break the hold of Satan. It will be to save His Church.

I expect that Christ will manifest more of His presence through the Blessed Sacrament. He will radiate more light from heaven. He'll touch us more during prayer and adoration. Such is indicated by recent events in which the Host has bled or appeared miraculously on a seer's tongue. There are many such miracles. There are miracles in which the Host has levitated, surrounded by a sunburst of light. There are miracles in which the Host has been seen surrounded by flames and other lights similar to the lights in Moses' time and the lights reported at Medjugorje—taking us full circle and showing that the Age of Mary will be followed by the Age of the Sacred Heart.

There are miracles in which the Christ Child has been seen in the Host or whereby mysterious light has filled a Blessed Sacrament chapel.

These are all signals of the real power—the real presence—behind our sacraments, especially the Blessed Sacrament. Many souls will find refuge in the depth of Mary's soul, becoming what St. Louis called living copies of her, loving and glorifying Jesus. That day will arrive. That light will dawn. Blessed are those who bind themselves gratefully to her! Blessed are those who seek answers not so much in locutions as in praying before the Blessed Sacrament! This is where we not only gain special knowledge of Jesus and find our prayers gaining power—not only where we feel a special peace—but also where, in truth, we begin to form a union with Jesus. *"Adore the Blessed Sacrament continuously,"* says the Madonna; then we will understand. Then we will understand our lives and what God has in store for us without worrying about tribulations.

During these extraordinary days when there is so much evil, we need to know that prayer really does open the hearts of unbelievers and that God still seeks to shed His mercy; that during these days with so much darkness there is also much good. As Our Blessed Mother said to Estela Ruiz, an American seer, the times are coming when you will see the good overcome evil. *"Let us not look at these times as all bad,"* Mary told Estela. *"These are the days of God's great mercy and through prayer we will see many good things come about in the world. Sadly, my children, sometimes it is through world crisis that God's people begin to see His great power. It is through suffering that many of my children turn to their God and begin to see that they need Him in their lives. It saddens me that it is through hard times that Our Lord becomes needed and visible in the world. He has always wanted your love and devotion, but it has not been there for a long time. The technological age has hidden God's power as men have come to believe that it is men who control the world's destiny. But now the world begins to see that men have not been able to accomplish peace in the world, but through their own inventions have brought greed and hatred over the land. Through greed and hatred is bred turmoil and destruction. I have told you that the power of Our Lord is manifesting itself in the world. If we continue our prayers faithfully they will have an effect on how these events go. Our Lord sees the evil and corruption going on in the world— but He also sees your love and prayers and the commitment of all my little ones throughout the world who have opened their ears and their hearts to my call— to the call of your heavenly mother who is also His mother."*

She asks her Son to come. She calls for Him, as we should call for him, and she also calls us to look at our souls. In the end, says Holy Mary, our greatest concern should be with our eternity. Whatever else happens in the world, we're sure of one thing: at death we will all face a final hour or personal judgment and in the end, that's all that counts.

What about the afterlife? What do the visionaries have to say about hell, purgatory, and heaven?

They really do await us. There is an afterlife. The evidence is overwhelming. It's probably the main reason for the apparitions, to show us that the supernatural does exist. I'm always amazed at how closely the visions of seers such as those at Medjugorje fit with the reported experiences of those who come close to dying and have what are now known as near-death experiences.

I'm not endorsing all such experiences any more than I would endorse all apparitions. Misperception and deception exists here too. But despite their flaws, some near-death accounts seem to give us a real idea of what comes after life on earth, and they describe heaven as many visionaries do: a place of sheer peace and joy.

There, according to these descriptions, light seems to radiate from an object instead of reflecting off it; everything is alive, and even the flowers sway as if singing praises to God. "The grass was of a beauty I can't describe," Mirjana once told an interviewer about a vision she had. "The flowers were so beautiful I can't describe them."

According to the Medjugorje seers, Our Blessed Mother once said that *"we go to heaven in full conscience: that which we have now. At the moment of death, we are conscious of the separation of the body and the soul."* The spirit rises from its earthly exterior; in that moment, they say, God grants us the grace to see our lives as He saw them, and to review every single decision we made while on earth.

We see ourselves in the light of divine reality, and are made to feel exactly how we caused every person we ever encountered to feel with every word we ever spoke and every action we ever took. We're put in the shoes of everyone with whom we have ever had an interaction and we're asked, upon judgment, how much and how many we have loved.

We're accountable for everything, which is why each moment on earth is invaluable. Upon death we're made to feel the good and the bad. We are finally able to realize our true level of evil and goodness. That's precisely what we hear from many who were declared clinically dead in hospitals and felt themselves detach and hover above their own bodies before entering a "tunnel" that took them to a great and glorious light, which in a flash reviewed every moment of their lives.

We then decide for ourselves where we belong. We decide our own destinations. God doesn't send us to hell or purgatory, according to Our Blessed Mother; we send ourselves. We go where we fit in. We go where we belong. We choose our eternity by our words, actions, and thoughts. If we have much darkness and detest God, we choose hell.

If we believe in God but were indifferent, or if we have lust and pride, we choose purgatory because it would be excruciating to stand before the Light of our Creator while still in a state of impurity. We wouldn't be able to handle it. We'd be comfortable only in a place of corresponding shade or darkness. Our Blessed Mother says the great majority of people go to purgatory. Historical mystics say that the average stay in purgatory, if it could be compared to earth time, would be several decades.

Purgatory is God's mercy so that we can escape hell. There are many levels, and the time there can be greatly lessened by sacrifice and by love coupled with self-discipline here on earth. Purgatory is often described as a place of fogginess. When the seers from Medjugorje were shown it, everything seemed gray. They heard moanings and cries and pleas for prayer, for it is through our prayers that purgation is shortened. Our Blessed Mother told the seers that when we pray for souls in purgatory, they can see us while we're praying for them by name, and that's a beautiful thought. Even a quick Hail Mary can provide indescribable relief for a purgatorial soul—like a glass of cool water to someone in the furnace room.

Souls remain in purgatory to correct violations that have hindered God's loving plan for the universe. These souls are sometimes allowed to manifest in order to get our attention. *"There are in purgatory souls who pray ardently to God, but for whom no relative or friend prays on earth,"* said Our Blessed Mother, beseeching prayer for them. In her apparitions Mary has explained that most souls are released into heaven on Christmas Day.

The greatest torture in purgatory is the yearning to be with God. According to mystics, at the moment of death all souls are given a glimpse of paradise before heading off for purification. That's probably why many of those claiming near-death experiences speak only of heaven. They weren't yet designated their level of purgatory. But those who have glimpsed purgatory value each moment on earth. They now realize that a moment of suffering on earth is worth years of purgation afterwards.

The hardest life is easier, they say, than an hour in purgatory. While most souls need purgation, there are some who find themselves at a high level, known as the Threshold, that has far less suffering, and even elements of heaven, but with the excruciating inability to see God. Our Blessed Mother says some souls go to hell, most go to purgatory, and only a small number go directly to heaven.

What happens if we pray for a soul who is already in heaven?

It's said those prayers are applied to souls who need them. What a joy it would be to die and learn that our prayer helped others gain heaven. On several occasions Vicka described paradise as a huge endless tunnel with an unearthly light and countless people in robes or something like Roman tunics, walking and speaking with each other. "It's so beautiful your heart stands still when you look at it," she told an interviewer. She didn't see buildings. It was a huge area with a brilliant light unknown to earth. She and the others said people in heaven were dressed in gray, pink, and yellow robes. This reminds us of the description of Our Blessed Mother coming in a "gray" robe, but really not colors of the earth. The color of Our Blessed

Mother was divine, and the harmony of her clothing could not be described with human words.

The visionaries saw people in small groups speaking or singing or praying in a language they couldn't understand. They're happy and in a constant state of ecstasy because they now know the absolute fullness of a created being.

These are people whose sole concern on earth had been doing God's Will. Over and again we hear this formula: love, have faith, and do God's Will to get to heaven. Do His Will to find happiness. God's Will. God's Will. I can't repeat it enough. Our Lady once said, *"The people who are in heaven are thankful to the Lord for having allowed them in. They sought to live a good life. They sought to live according to the Will of God on this earth."*

If I had one sentence of advice, I'd say: If you want heaven, love everyone and do God's Will every day, every moment. Above all, love God.

According to Medjugorje, few make it directly to heaven. But when they do get there, they see the angels and hear the music and, more than anything, encounter an overwhelming feeling of tranquility. There is light, light, and more light—a supernatural light that is always present and that occasionally aims itself at earth. The veil is scrolled or lifted (see Isaiah 34:4 and Revelation 6:14) and gives us glimpses of God's real kingdom when earth is facing a turning point.

So while on earth we're in the dark except for a few apertures through which we see the Light?

Yes. Those apertures are the Lord's mercy. They include apparitions and miracles. And messages. The message is that with humility and faith as our shield, and with the sword of the Spirit—which is the Word of God—(see Ephesians 6:16-17), we move forward and destroy the evil around us. We take no part in vain deeds but instead expose and correct them, so that, brought into the light of day and set against humility, and thus in the presence of love, darkness is destroyed. There is no longer fertile ground for the mystery of iniquity (see Ephesians 5:13) nor for eternal loss.

No enemy can stand before love. It is stronger than any witch, any spell, any curse. It's stronger than the greatest strength of Satan because in casting forth light it takes away the cover of darkness.

Our Blessed Mother asks our prayers because Satan is trying to thwart her plan for our deliverance. As always the devil wants to disrupt God's plan for the universe. *"Satan is strong and wishes not only to destroy human life but also nature and the planet on which you live,"* says Our Lady of Medjugorje. *"I love you with my motherly love and I call upon you to open yourselves completely to me so that through each of you I may be enabled to convert and save the world. Listen and live what I tell you, because it is important for you, when I shall not be with you any longer. May every hatred and jealousy disappear from your life and your thoughts, and may there only dwell love for God and for your neighbor. Thus, only thus, shall you be able to discern the signs of this time. I invite you to open yourselves to God by means of prayer so the Holy Spirit may begin to work miracles in you and through you. I love you and want to lead you all with me to paradise. I invite you to pray for my intentions. I am looking for your prayers, that you accept me and accept my messages as in the first days of the apparitions. And only then, when you open your hearts and pray, will miracles happen. I invite you to become apostles of love and goodness. God has allowed me to stay this long with you, and therefore, little children, I invite you to live with love the messages I give and transmit them to the whole world, so that a river of love flows to people who are full of hatred and without peace. I invite you, little children, to become peace where there is no peace and light where there is darkness, so that each heart accepts the light and the way of salvation. I invite you now, in this time, like never before, to prepare for the coming of Jesus* [said on Christmas Day, 1993]. *The Holy Spirit will enlighten you to understand that you must convert. I invite you to fall in love with the Most Blessed Sacrament of the altar. Adore Him, little children, in your parishes and in this way you will be united with the entire world. Unity with Him will be a joy for you and you will become witnesses to the love of Jesus that He has for every creature. These times are special, and therefore I am with you to love and protect you, to protect your hearts from Satan, and to bring you closer to the Heart of my Son."*

It always comes back to Christ, doesn't it?

Yes, and I always can feel it—there's a palpable spirituality—when a church exposes His Blessed Sacrament. It's like a magnet. People can feel Christ there and at Mass, which Our Blessed Mother says is the most powerful prayer because at Mass we are reliving Christ's passion, the moment when He showed His power over all sin. We're sharing in His glory and sacrifice. We hear Scripture, we recite psalms, we pray for intentions, we ask for forgiveness, we beseech Christ's mercy, we thank Him for all of His gifts. We join, as He asked us, in the mysterious transformation of wine and bread into His flesh and blood, and in unison we pray the prayer He told us to pray, the Lord's Prayer (see Matthew 6:9-13) before we invoke the Lamb of God to feed us His bread and remove our transgressions.

I've heard mystics say they see incredible things during Mass, heavenly clouds like those same fogs I've mentioned at apparitions, angels in adoration, and the Face of Christ. I know I get a special lift at Mass, and a special protection against Satan, especially because at Mass we invoke His Blood.

Most of all we feel God's love. That love is His Spirit, and the Blessed Mother tells us to invoke the Holy Spirit constantly. She says when she prays it's to the Holy Spirit. She says the best prayer is prayer to the Holy Spirit. And we know when we have that Spirit because with Him comes love and peace. With Him is our only security. And we face calamity only if we continue to place a distance between us and His Spirit.

When we lack the Holy Spirit, we lack direction in life and we begin to prepare chastisements with our own hands. Jelena once said that "destruction is assured only if the world refuses to go back to God," while Fr. Vlasic's letter to the pope in 1983 mentioned that at least part of the chastisement "can be mitigated by prayers and penance." It was Vicka who added that the best preparation is "to pray every day, go to Mass, and read the Bible. With prayer and penance the chastisements can be substantially lessened."

So can Satan's influence. The devil's time is only supposed to last until the event in the first secret, reminding us of the message Mirjana received about our century being given to Satan as a special test of the Church and mankind.

We await a manifestation or unveiling in which the presence of Jesus, preceded or accompanied by tribulations, will break the power of evil (see 2 Thessalonians 2:8). Then the century of Satan, the modernistic heresy, will be over and Satan will be bound by the "angel come down from heaven" (Rv 20:1-2).

Soon, Satan will not exercise the same level of power. Every single person has a part in bringing him down. All that has happened in Bosnia-Hercegovina is but part of a larger plan. The Blessed Mother did not come primarily to speak about catastrophe; she came to show us the way to peace. When asked questions about the Apocalypse or End Times, the seers of Medjugorje have declined comment and said they don't speak of matters in such a way, and so we are left guessing. Asked if the future is long or short, Ivanka replied, "For some it is long; for some it is short." The priest who has served as a confidant, Fr. Vlasic, was quoted as saying that "life in the world will change. Afterwards men will believe like in ancient times."

What we can be certain of is that God exists and is trying to clean house here below so we have an easier way to eternity. Really, that's what it's all about. That's where we *know* we'll finally see Jesus. In the afterlife. We must help defeat the devil and bring into our world the presence of Jesus Who is on the way in some form. I believe that although the second coming of Jesus will be preceded by the conversion of Israel and the preaching of the Gospel to all nations (see Matthew 23:39, 24:14). I believe we face at least a Minor Judgment. And that reckoning will simplify us by breaking down our artificial reality. We will see a level of events comparable to those seen during the Middle Ages, or greater. If the period of evil ends with a manifestation of Christ, as opposed to the formal Second Coming, then obviously we are in a stage leading up to the End Times but not at its conclusion. The End Times might still have a way to go. It might go through the third millennium. For all we know, it may go beyond. Or it may conclude next month. "The Last Judgment will come when Christ returns in glory," says the *Catechism.* "Only the Father knows the day and the hour; only He determines the moment of its coming. Then through His Son Jesus Christ He will pronounce the final word on all history" (#1040).

But really He is always with us when we want Him to be with us, and He has no craving to make us fear, only to wake us up and dispel our wickedness in this day of mercy, this day of salvation. Oh holy day. Oh day of the Lord! He is near. He is as near as the nearest New Testament. This very moment, He sees us. He sees our sufferings, our problems, and our aspirations. They're dear to Him. They're in His Heart, which will come as Light in the dark, as that crest of dawn, as morning rays that touch the dew, that touch our tears, calling to us as we must call to Him: *Marana tha! Marana tha!* ("Our Lord, come!") We know Your day will come. But hasten it. Hasten Your return, dear Christ.

NOTES

Chapters 1 & 2: The main Bibles I use are the *New American* (published by Thomas Nelson Inc. in Camden, New Jersey) and the *King James* (also published by Nelson). I also employ as basic reference tools *Roget's Thesaurus of the Bible* by A. Colic Day (HarperCollins), the *Catechism of the Catholic Church* (Liberia Editrice Vaticana), and the *Reader's Digest Bible*. For other reference I use a computer Bible manufactured by Franklin Electronic Publishers (Mount Holly, New Jersey). The figure of 79 percent believing in miracles came from a Gallup poll conducted December 16 to 18, 1994, and faxed to me by Maura A. Strausberg, a research librarian at the Gallup Organization in Princeton, New Jersey. The woman in *Revelation* is in Chapter 12. The John Paul quote is from his book *Crossing the Threshold of Hope*, page 88 (Knopf in New York).

Chapters 3 & 4: I was delivering a lecture at the University of Arizona when I visited the bleeding Orthodox icon. Reports of the statue in Civitavecchia were widely disseminated on news wire services. The Fatima apparitions are described in many books, most especially *Our Lady of Fatima* by William Thomas Walsh, a classic in Mariology (Image Books, New York). For the prophecies of eighteenth and nineteenth century mystics, see *Catholic Prophecy* by Yves Dupont and *Prophecy for Today* by Edward Connor (both published by TAN Books and Publishers in Rockford, Illinois). Pope Leo XIII's vision is widespread tradition, but I could not verify it. It is well-known in devotional literature, including that dispensed by the Daughters of St. Paul, which mentioned it in a prayer book dedicated to the Archangel Michael. For Aristotle, see *A Concise History of the Catholic Church* by Thomas Bokenkotter (Image, New York). For St. Louis de Montfort, see his books *True Devotion to the Blessed Virgin* and *Preparation for Total Consecration*, available from Montfort Publications in Bay Shore, New York. I personally visited the site of the Miraculous Medal apparitions in Paris as well as La Salette, Lourdes, Fatima, Knock, Betania, Garabandal, Medjugorje, and many other sites of apparition. For further information on the Miraculous Medal, see *The Saint of Silence*, a booklet distributed at the shrine but with no official publisher or author. One of the lists of apparitions I use was compiled by the 101 Foundation in Asbury Park, New Jersey. The La Salette prophecy is taken from the pamphlet, "Apparition of the Blessed Virgin on the Mountain of La Salette the 19th of September, 1846" published with an imprimatur by the Bishop of Lecce. But the La Salette prophecy was very controversial—condemned by some bishops and cardinals, championed by others. The prophecy was recorded by Melanie Calvat and began circulating in a big way in 1879. There were bishops and cardinals who promoted her "secret," which she was inspired to release after what may have been another apparition; and there were bishops and cardinals who sought to dispel the secret, which in some ways seemed anti-clerical. While the apparition itself was approved by the Church in 1851, there was a Vatican rejection of certain pamphlets and commentaries associated with Melanie's longer and more apocalyptical prophecies. The only part of the prophecy that is widely accepted is a short message about the local potato crop, working on Sunday, and using the Lord's name in vain.

Chapters 5 & 6: The six seers at Pontmain were Joseph Barbedette, Eugene Barbedette, Eugene Friteau, Augustine Boitin, Jeanne Marie Lebosse, and Francoise Richer. My main reference for Pontmain was a booklet entitled "What Happened at Pontmain," by Abbe M. Pichard, printed in the U.S. by the Ave Maria Institute in Washington, New Jersey. Much of what I mentioned about apparitions earlier this century comes from *A Guide to Apparitions* by Peter Heintz (Gabriel Press, Sacramento). This is an excellent reference book, although one must be discerning about certain apparitions. For Josefa Menendez, see *Words of Love*, compiled by Fr. Bartholomew Gottemoller (TAN, Rockford, Illinois). I often use as a reference *A Woman Clothed with the Sun*, an excellent compilation of Marian apparitions edited by John J. Delaney (Image Books, New York), and *Encountering Mary*, an academic treatment of apparitions by Sandra L. Zimdars-Swartz. The estimate for 14 apparitions a year comes from W. A. Christian Jr., in his article "Religious Apparitions and the Cold War in Southern Europe," contained in *Religion, Power and Protest in Local Communities* (Published by Mouton in Berlin in 1984 and edited by E. Wolf). The exact years cited were 1947 to 1954. The article in *U.S. News and World Report* was March 25, 1993, which coincidentally is the feast of the Annunciation. The article on Mary was in *Time*, December 30, 1991. There were also cover stories about the supernatural in *Time* on December 27, 1993 ("Angels Among Us") and April 10, 1995 ("The Message of Miracles"). One of the articles in *The New York Times* was about miraculous reports in the Soviet Union and appeared on October 13, 1987, which ironically is the major Fatima feast day. It was at Fatima that Our Blessed Mother foresaw the advent of Communism and the spread of errors around the world. Wayne Weible's newspaper supplement was entitled, "Miracle at Medjugorje" and included columns printed over a period of six months starting in December of 1985. It included interviews with the visionaries and key messages. A friend of mine, Thomas Petrisko of Pittsburgh, publishes a newspaper called *Our Lady Queen of Peace*, and for his most recent issue had 1.25 million advance copies ordered. It is available by writing the Pittsburgh Center for Peace, 6111 Steubenville Pike, McKees Rock, Pennsylvania 15136. The seminal books on Medjugorje in the early phases were Fr. Svetozar Kraljevic's *The Apparitions of Our Lady at Medjugorje* (edited by Fr. Michael Scanlan and published by Franciscan Herald Press in Chicago) and *Is the Virgin Mary Appearing in Medjugorje?* by Ljudevit Rupcic and René Laurentin (The Word Among Us Press, Gaithersburg, Maryland). I also use *Queen of Peace in Medjugorje*, by Jacov Marin (The Riehle Foundation, Milford, Ohio). The account of Pope Pius XI and the cross is from *Spark From Heaven*, by Mary Craig, a historical treatment of Medjugorje and the religious milieu of Bosnia-Hercegovina (Ave Maria Press, Notre Dame, Indiana), and also from *Our Lady Visits Medjugorje, the Early Apparitions*, a pamphlet by Thomas E. Carberry. Some say the cross at Medjugorje is ten meters, others fourteen. The ten-meter figure comes from *The Hidden Side of Medjugorje* by Ivo Sivric, O.F.M., Volume One. When I contacted Croatian priests now stationed in Chicago, they remembered nothing about the pope's requesting a cross. The account of Saragossa comes from *The Irish Catholic*, November 7, 1968, and *Shrines to Our Lady Around the World*, by Zsolt Aradi (sent to me courtesy of the Marian Library at Dayton University). Some general background on Bosnia-Hercegovina and Croatia comes from M. Wesley Shoemaker in *Russia, Eurasian States, and Eastern Europe 1994*, which is part of the World Today Series, 25th edition, published by Stryker-Post Publications in Harpers Ferry, West Virginia. The parish of Medjugorje consists of the hamlets known as Bijakovici, Miletina, Vionica, and Surmanci, in addition to Medjugorje. The pious practices of peasants come from *The Visions of the Children* by Janice T. Connell (St. Martin's Press, New York) and from my own contact with the peasantry upon four trips to Medjugorje. I am familiar with Neanderthals because I once wrote a book on paleoanthropology, *The Search for Eve*, published in 1990 by Harper & Row (now HarperCollins). The book was dedicated to the "new Eve," the Virgin Mary. It had to do with use of mitochrondrial DNA to track back human ancestors. For the Neanderthals in Yugoslavia, see Bernard G. Campbell's *Humankind Emerging* (fifth edition, Scott, Foresman and Company) and the technical reports of Dr. Milford Wolpoff of the University of Michigan. Note that Israel too has Neanderthal-like remains and skulls that indicate some of the earliest modern characteristics.

Chapters 7 & 8: The account of Padre Pio is in *Spark From Heaven* by Mary Craig, a former BBC broadcaster. The quote from Sr. Briege McKenna comes from her book, *Miracles Do Happen* (Servant Books, Ann Arbor, Michigan 1987), p. 155. The account of Fr. Heribert Mühlen is from the Marin book, cited above. I also use this book for part of the account of Vicka and the mysterious rosaries. But my main source for the mysterious rosaries was *A Thousand Encounters with the Blessed Virgin Mary in Medjugorje* by Fr. Janko Bubalo (published by Friends of Medjugorje in Chicago). I first visited Medjugorje on May 16, 1989, and went to Fatima, La Salette, and Lourdes the following autumn. My subsequent visits to Medjugorje consisted of a pilgrimage there in 1990 and two visits in 1993. For the nature of the ecstasies see *Scientific and Medical Studies on the Apparitions at Medjugorje* by René Laurentin and Henri Joyeux (Veritas in Dublin). The accounts of Medjugorje come from many sources, including the books cited for the previous chapter, especially *The Apparitions of Our Lady at Medjugorje* and *Spark From Heaven*. I quote Vicka from Fr.

Svet's book. The Franic information comes from a publication named *Glas Mira*, but I do not have its publication date. The height of the Blessed Mother comes from Marin's *Queen of Peace in Medjugorje*. The quote on division comes from Laurentin and Joyeux's *Scientific and Medical Studies on the Apparitions at Medjugorje*, page 121. The Scanlan quote comes from *The Apparitions of Our Lady at Medjugorje*. The friend of mine who blurted "Medjugorje!" to the pope, and got an affirmative nod, was Ron Kyle, a former music promoter and now a radio station owner from New Jersey. For the pope, see "Medjugorje and the Church," an excellent booklet that details what various bishops, cardinals, and the pope have to say about Medjugorje. I use it as a key reference in this chapter, and it can be obtained through United for the Triumph of the Immaculate Heart, P.O. Box 1110, Notre Dame, Indiana 46556. It was published on March 1, 1995 and has the *nihil obstat* of retired Bishop Sylvester W. Treinen of Idaho. The authors are Sr. Emmanuel Maillard and Denis Nolan. This publication says that the visionary Mirjana Dragicevic met with John Paul II for twenty minutes in private and that this is when the pope said: "If I were not the pope, I would be in Medjugorje already." The description of "A great center of spirituality" was in the April 29, 1990, issue of the *National Catholic Register.* I interviewed Bishop Treinen about his visit with the Pontiff. Other details come from Medjugorje newsletters or flyers. The account about the archbishop of Paraguay came from *Medjugorje and the Church* as well as from the biweekly "Medjugorje Press Bulletin," issued from an information center in Medjugorje (robofax +387(0)88-642-709) March 1, 1995. The item on a delegation from Croatia was in the "Press Bulletin" April 26, 1995. It reported that the date for the meeting was April 7 instead of April 6. Again, it is often difficult to verify particular details. I took the date from "Medjugorje and the Church," which in turn is taking the information from a publication called *Nasa Ognjista*. The background on the pope and Marian Sodality, as well as Polish devotion to Mary, comes from *Pope John Paul II* by Tad Szulc (Scribner, New York). The pope's remark about St. Louis de Montfont is from *Crossing the Threshold of Hope*, which was published in America by Knopf in New York (with co-author Vittorio Messori). See page 215 for Marian devotion. For Archbishop Kim, see "Medjugorje and the Church," which quotes from *Korean Catholic* of November 11, 1990. The remark on the fulfillment of Fatima was reportedly to Bishop Paola Hnilica, titular bishop of Rusado. The letter from Vlasic to the pope comes from a number of previously cited books, including *Is the Virgin Mary Appearing at Medjugorje?* Lucia's description of the phenomena at Fatima is from *Our Lady of Fatima* by William Thomas Walsh, page 36, cited above. The Marinko Ivankovic quote and Fr. Luka Susac's testimony are both from Fr. Svetozar's book previously cited. The desire of Mother Teresa to visit Medjugorje came from a fax update issued by Sr. Emmanuel Maillard of Medjugorje on October 15, 1995. Ambassador Kingon's account came from a personal conversation with him.

Chapters 9 & 10: Mirjana's interview in 1985 was secured through a Croatian priest friend of mine and translated so capably for me by Zdenko "Jim" Singer of Burlington, Ontario. For Vicka's illness, see Father Bubalo's book, already cited, and Fr. Marin's *Queen of Peace in Medjugorje*. For the pope's attitude on Marian apparitions, and "a woman clothed with the sun," see, among other references, Malachi Martin's *The Keys of this Blood* (Touchstone/Simon & Schuster, New York), pages 48-54. The quote from the priest on the figure of Our Lady near the cross comes from Jacov Marin's previously cited book, page 34. The quotations from Mary are taken from *Words From Heaven*, published by St. James Publishing, Birmingham, and other sources. As indicated, the long quote from the Virgin at the end is a composite quote, the messages spanning 12 years. The messages of Medjugorje are published by dozens of newsletters and are issued each month from St. James Church. The quote on Jesus struggling for souls was from a 1981 message, for example, while the last couple of sentences come from the August 25, 1993 message. The composite is drawn from *Words From Heaven*, previously cited, and also from sources such as *Messages and Teachings of Mary at Medjugorje*, by René Laurentin and René Lejeune (Faith Publication, Milford, Ohio) and *The Visions of the Children* (cited in the Notes for chapters 2 and 3), as well as the monthly messages, which are faxed to my office. *Words From Heaven* is an excellent book that deserves more circulation. The dictionary I use is *Webster's New Twentieth Century Dictionary*

Unabridged, second edition (Prentice Hall, New York). The Virgin's messages about Satan as the destroyer and working hard in the world were given on February 14, 1982, and January 14, 1985. I use a number of sources for the messages, especially Words From Heaven, previously cited. For Fr. Vlasic's quote, see his pamphlet "Our Lady Queen of Peace," published by Peter Batty in East Sussex, England. It's this book that gave me the October 28, 1981 date for the fire on Mount Podbrdo (Apparition Hill). There was also at least one other similar occasion. The Virgin's quotes on the devil were given April 4, 1982, and July 30, 1987. The Mirjana quotes come from the private tape I obtained. My experience with Pentecostals and charismatics was in Manhattan with non-denominationalists in the East Village and also the Upper East Side. For David du Plessis, see David Manuel's foreword to Letters From Medjugorje (Paraclete Press, Orleans, Massachusetts). The Garabandal information comes from my book The Final Hour (Faith Publishing in Milford, Ohio). For more on atmospheric effects, see Light and Color on the Outdoors, by M. G. J. Minnaert (Springer-Verlag, New York), which details the many natural phenomena which occur. The sun naturally pulses every five minutes, but those pulsations are far different than what we saw. The normal pulsations cannot be detected by the naked eye. For the scientific tests I relied chiefly on Scientific and Medical Studies on the Apparitions at Medjugorje by Laurentin and Joyeux, as well as Spark From Heaven and an article reprinted from the February 1986 Reader's Digest. The device that placed a thread on the corneas is called an esthesiometer. As for the number of pilgrims and how such estimates are made, Sr. Emmanuel, who has served in the Community of the Beatitudes at Medjugorje since 1989 and keeps close track of such matters, says 18 million visited Medjugorje up to 1991, just before the Bosnian war erupted, and that the figure is based on the number of Communion hosts dispensed. I'm still not clear how this accounting is done, since pilgrims often receive Communion more than once a day during their trips there and many pilgrims have been to Medjugorje before. In January of 1992 the Associated Press ran an article about Medjugorje saying that one million were visiting there each year from around the world. It was also reported that there are 15,000 beds in town. The normal "cycle" of a pilgrim's stay is four or five days, so there are at least 73 cycles per year and thus at least 1.1 million visitors were going to Medjugorje each year before the war erupted in 1991, at least half of them American. The great influx started in 1987 and 1988. It's impossible to actually come up with a figure. I would estimate the likeliest range of Americans who have visited Medjugorje at two to four million. The anecdote on Janic and the pope comes from "The Church and Medjugorje." Scott O'Grady's book is Return with Honor (Doubleday, New York).

Chapters 11 & 12: For the views of popes on private revelation, see Adolphe Tanqueray's The Spiritual Life (The Newman Press, Westminister, Maryland or Desclee & Company, Tournai, Belgium). The decree of Urban is mentioned here. His quote on revelations is published by many Marian outlets, including a magazine called Signs of Our Times in Dulles, Virginia. The permission to publish private revelations without express Church permission came with a decree of the Congregation for the Propagation of the Faith (AAS 58, 1186), which was approved by Pope Paul VI in 1966 and is obvious in the many books by priests on Medjugorje or other reputed revelations published without an imprimatur. However, a good number of books on Medjugorje by priests do have formal ecclesiastical approval, most notably Fr. Svetozar Kraljevic's book, The Apparitions of Our Lady of Medjugorje, previously cited. The information on Split came from private interviews with two people, one a priest, who privately investigated the matter. The quote from Teresa of Avila comes from The Life of Teresa of Jesus, an autobiography (Image Books in New York). For the Medjugorje locutionists, see Messages and Teachings of Mary at Medjugorje and Words From Heaven. See also The Visions of the Children as well as Is the Virgin Mary Appearing in Medjugorje? and Queen of Peace in Medjugorje, all previously cited. I edit some of Jelena's messages and also use composites at certain times. The austerity of the messages is striking and directed at the special prayer group. I draw some about the Izbicno apparitions from this last book by the priest calling himself Jacov Marin (page 60) and also Messages and Teachings of Mary at Medjugorje. Further information came from correspondence with Archbishop Franic and Fr. Chris Coric in

Lackawanna, New York. For Mirjana on the last appearances, see *Scientific and Medical Studies on the Apparitions at Medjugorje,* page 124, and also Fr. Svetozar Kraljevic's *The Apparitions of Our Lady at Medjugorje.* I use a composite quote from these two sources. The accounts of mystics in the 1200s and 1300s is partly from Evelyn Underhill's book, *Mysticism* (Dutton, New York), as well as the treatise, *Graces of Interior Prayer,* by Fr. Augustin Poulain (Routledge and Kegan Paul in London). For Mariamante, see *The Apostolate of Holy Motherhood,* compiled by Mark I. Miravalle of Franciscan University in Steubenville, Ohio (Riehle Foundation, Milford, Ohio). I combine parts of messages given to Mariamante on February 13, 15, and 16, and also August 11, 1987.

Chapter 13 & 14: The dispatch on Kibeho comes from Fr. Gabriel Maindron (I also saw this spelled "Maindrone" and "Mendryon"), and I also use a dispatch by a French eyewitness, Raymond Halter, who was there on November 29, 1989. I also use a pamphlet called "The Apparitions of Our Lady of Kibeho," which basically reports a tape by Father Mendryon (published by the Marian Press in Galway, Ireland). Drew Mariani of Marian Communications in Aston, Pennsylvania, produced a video on Kibeho and has greatly helped promote the message, as he also did at Betania, Venezuela. Cardinal Ratzinger made his remarks on page 112 of the English edition of *The Ratzinger Report* (Ignatius Press, San Francisco). The *Time* report on Kibeho was May 8, 1995. For Ivanka's apparition see my book *Prayer of the Warrior* (Faith Publications) and also *Mary's Messenger,* one of the better Marian publications, issued from the Ave Maria Center in Toronto. From it also come the reports of the two deaths at Kibeho (Winter 1995 issue) and the consecration of Rwanda by the president, as well as the status of the apparitions. Some said a third seer had also died. I had poor luck trying to confirm any of that, despite trying to write and phone Archbishop Gahamanyi. I never directly confirmed the deaths. For one of Emmanuel's quotes from Jesus about the Second Coming, and also the approval of a devotional cult at Kibeho, see Fr. Laurentin's *The Apparitions of the Blessed Virgin Mary Today* (Veritas in Dublin). Among the spelling inconsistencies in various references, I also saw "Salima" spelled "Salina." St. Alphonsus is quoted from his "Six Discourses on Natural Calamities, Divine Threats, and the Four Gates of Hell" (Catholic Treasures). I got the figures on AIDS from *Facts on File.* They're through 1994. In addition, sub-Saharan Africa can boast 8 million of the world's 13 to 14 million HIV infections. The information on the Sese Islands and other background comes from *The Hot Zone* by Richard Preston (Random House, New York), who opens the book with a quote from the Book of Revelation.

Chapters 15 & 16: For the Fatima secrets, I use especially Fr. Joaquin Maria Alonso's *The Secret of Fatima: Fact and Legend* (The Ravengate Press, Cambridge). See also Frère Michel de la Sainte Trinité's *The Whole Truth About Fatima: The Third Secret,* (Immaculate Heart Publications, Buffalo, NY). William Thomas Walsh's quote was in his previously cited book, *Our Lady of Fatima.* For Dr. McNally, see his article "The Story Behind the Film" in *Soul* Magazine, January-February 1987, and also McNally's paper "The Nuclear Tornado Threat," presented as a handout at the 1986 Spring meeting of the American Physical Society. See also page C-5 of *The Oregonian,* November 19, 1986, which previews a film about McNally's observations. For chastisements that Blessed Faustina saw as threatening Poland, see her diary, *Divine Mercy in My Soul* (Marian Helpers in Stockbridge, Massachusetts). Fr. Gobbi's prophecies are in *To the Priests, Our Lady's Beloved Sons,* published by the Marian Movement of Priests, P.O. Box 8, St. Francis, Maine 04774-0008. I use the term "prayer session" in place of "cenacle" for simple clarity. The Medjugorje message to do with youth started in the early years and hit special points of relevance on May 16, 1985, and August 15, 1988, when Our Mother used phrases that are similar to what the pope used on August 15, 1993, in Denver at that youth conference (especially when he urged us to flee "the fruitless works of darkness").

Chapters 17 & 18: For Lourdes, and apparitions that followed Bernadette's, which I'll mention in a later chapter, see Laurentin in *Scientific and Medical Studies on the Apparitions at Medjugorje* and

348 / The Day Will Come

also Delaney's *A Woman Clothed with the Sun*, as well as *Encountering Mary* by Zimdars-Swartz. The first two to report seeing Mary after Bernadette were Marie Cazenave and Madline Cazaux. For the pope's Marian devotion, see Szulc's *Pope John Paul II*, previously noted, or *Crossing the Threshold of Hope*, also mentioned above. I use Szulc's book for the account of Padre Pio and the woman cured of cancer (page 141). The material on Esperanza is from *The Bridge to Heaven*, which I edited for Marian Communications in Lima, Pennsylvania. It's said that at least ten thousand people have seen Our Blessed Mother in Betania, according to Dr. Vinicio Arrieta, a medical doctor who has studied the situation. While all apparitions, especially the important ones, meet with initial controversy, such controversies usually fade after the first few years. When controversy lingers or is joined by new controversies, we become wary, and at least for now, classify it at a lower level. Often, seers will pray for the healing of someone with a serious ailment and then indicate that, with enough faith and prayer, the person will be healed. When the cure doesn't happen—and I've seen this take place from Betania to Medjugorje—the people become discouraged and disgruntled. It becomes a minor scandal. There is a direct line between La Salette in 1846, a reputed (and often contested) version of the Third Secret published in a German periodical called *Neues Europa*, and the dire Akita prophecies, as well as other recent second-tier apparitions. The Fulda incident is from Frère Michel de la Sainte Trinité's book on Fatima previously cited. For Akita, see *Akita, The Tears and Message of Mary*, by Teiji Yasuda, O.S.V., published in English by the 101 Foundation in Asbury, New Jersey, among other sources. For San Nicolas see *Messages of Our Lady at San Nicolas* (Faith Publications, Milford, Ohio). There was a statue of Mary held with special regard by the family of St. Thérèse of Lisieux and on May 13, 1883, while praying near it, she saw the statue come alive. Her vision lasted for four or five minutes and cured St. Thérèse of a horrible ailment. Thirty-three years later, the date of May 13 would become the day of the first Fatima apparition. The information on Hrushiw comes from my research trip to Ukraine and also from personal interviews with Josyp Terelya, a witness to the events.

Chapters 19 & 20: The information on Sr. Lucia comes from the fascinating booklet, "Two Hours with Sister Lucia," available through Carlos Evaristo, St. Anne's Oratory, P.O. Box 133, 2496 Fatima Codex, Portugal; and also conversations I've had with Ambassador Dee and his daughter, Angie. For the fire envisioned at Hrushiw see *Witness* (Faith Publications), pages 269-271. The statue that shed tears at Akita, the wood statue ruled an authentic miracle by both bishops, was fashioned after an apparition in Amsterdam, Holland, in which Mary appeared as "Our Lady of All Nations" with a globe and cross behind her. There was much controversy over this series of apparitions, during which Mary warned of a "disaster upon disaster," a "flood of punishments." She also mentioned the conversion of Japan, which is interesting because it was later in Japan that the statue representing Our Lady of All Nations was positioned in the chapel of a convent in which the nun, Sr. Sasagawa, received her apocalyptic messages. For further background see Howard Q. Dee's *Mankind's Final Destiny*, published by Assisi Development Foundation in Manila. That the Third Secret was kept in a small safe was reported in *Paris Match*. It was in the safe in 1957, anyway. For Hippolytus see the *Dictionary of Mary* (Catholic Publishing Company, New York). The vision from Dubovystsya came from *Witness* (previously cited). Cardinal Ratzinger's quote comes from *The Ratzinger Report* by Joseph Cardinal Ratzinger with Vittorio Messori (previously cited).

Chapters 21 & 22: Once more I'm using that unpublished 1985 interview with Mirjana, as well as my interviews with certain of the seers, and books like *Queen of Peace in Medjugorje; A Thousand Encounters with the Blessed Virgin Mary in Medjugorje; Words From Heaven; The Visions of the Children;* and *The Apparitions of Our Lady at Medjugorje*, all previously cited. For St. Margaret Mary, see *The Autobiography of Saint Margaret Mary* published by TAN Books and Publishers in Rockford, Illinois. It was translated by the Sisters of the Visitation. For Blessed Faustina, see her diary published by the Marian Helpers in Stockbridge, Massachusetts. For the Ecstatic of Tours, see Thomas Petrisko's *Call of the Ages* (Queenship Publishing, Santa Barbara, California) and also the books by TAN referenced above for 19th century mystics. For Christina Gallagher, I use *The*

Sorrow, The Sacrifice, and The Triumph, by Thomas Petrisko (Simon & Schuster, New York); *The Final Hour* (Faith Publications); and a publication in Ireland called *Ireland's Eye,* which ran some very interesting articles about Christina in 1991. For more on Cuapa and Marienfried, see *A Guide to Apparitions* by Heintz (previously referenced for chapter 5). As for disasters, some of the estimates come from *Facts on File* while other estimates come from sources such as a January 20, 1994, chart in *USA Today.*

Chapters 23 & 24: Once again, I often rely upon the 1985 interview with Mirjana and the sources referenced for Medjugorje above. It has been reported that Our Blessed Mother approved of Fr. Ljubicic as Mirjana's choice, so one would assume he will live to see the first secrets. But we still aren't sure if Mirjana's secrets will be the first to happen. At times the seers have said the Great Sign will be preceded by two warnings, at other times it has been reported that there will be three warnings. Perhaps the sign itself is counted as a warning, or perhaps a third warning piggybacks with the sign in the third secret. The date of the *Wall Street Journal* article was November 9, 1992 (front page). The pope's comment to which I alluded, comes directly from *Crossing the Threshold of Hope,* page 221. My question to Vicka was posed during my fourth visit to Medjugorje, arriving on November 2, 1995. Vicka's remark on the apparition before the sign is taken from Fr. Laurentin's *Medjugorje 13 Years Later* (published by Faith in Milford). Jakov's comment was taken from Jan Connell's book, as were some of Ivanka's, Vicka's, and Mirjana's. Ivanka's quote on our roles, as well as a couple of comments from Vicka and Marija, are from Jan Connell's *Queen of the Cosmos* and *The Visions of the Children,* two excellent collections of the interviews. Jelena's quote is from Fr. Laurentin's *Messages and Teachings of Mary of Medjugorje,* done with René Lejeune. Mirjana's quote on how she maintains silence about the secrets is from the Ljubicic interview I obtained in 1991. The best compilation of apparitions and their secrets is *A Guide to Apparitions* (Gabriel Press, Sacramento, California).

Chapters 25 & 26: The information on Betania comes from personal interviews and my book *The Bridge to Heaven* (Marian Communications). For Underhill and the three waves of mysticism, see her book *Mysticism,* previously cited. For mystics such as Canori-Mora and the vision of Pius IX, see *Catholic Prophecy* by Yves Dupont, previously cited. The information on *Signum Magnum* came from *Call of the Ages,* previously noted. Mirjana's remarks in Modesto were at a conference where she, Fr. Jozo, and I were speakers. For St. Margaret Mary, again see *The Autobiography of Saint Margaret Mary* published by TAN. And for Blessed Faustina, her diary previously cited.

Chapters 27 & 28: The information on apocalyptical literature from the episode of Christ comes from *Mysteries of the Bible,* compiled by the Reader's Digest Association in Pleasantville, New York. The date for Domitian comes from the New American Bible. The mention of the burning bush is from an article in the February 1995 *Harper's,* cynically entitled "Souvenir Miracles." The survey for *Time* and CNN was conducted by Yankelovich Partners Inc. and appeared in the December 27, 1993 issue of *Time.* See Poulain's *Graces of Interior Prayer* for mistakes made by saints. See also Fr. Benedict Groeschel's *A Still, Small Voice* (Ignatius Press, San Francisco). See *Encounters with Mary* for more on Lourdes, previously noted. For St. Ignatius, I use his classic, *The Spiritual Exercises.* For one quote I use a translation from the Catholic Book Publishing Company. The quotes from St. John of the Cross were taken from *John of the Cross: Selected Writings,* edited by Kieran Kavanaugh, O.C.D. (Paulist Press in New York), while St. Teresa of Avila's quotes come from *The Life of Teresa of Jesus,* translated and edited by E. Allison Peers (Image Books, New York), or from her book *Interior Castle.* The quotes from St. Thérèse, the Little Flower, are from her autobiography, *Story of a Soul* (Institute of Carmelite Studies, Washington). I also use a book called *Complete Spiritual Doctrine of St. Thérèse of Lisieux,* by Rev. Francois Jamart (Alba House, New York).

Chapters 29 & 30: The information on Gala came from private research, mostly communication with Archbishop Franic and also Fr. Bavcevic. For Mirna, see *The Miracle of Damascus* by "The

Publican" (The Messengers of Unity, Glendale, California). I also use Fr. Laurentin's *The Apparitions of the Blessed Virgin Mary Today*, previously cited. The quote from St. Francis de Sales comes from *Introduction to the Devout Life*, abridged by Madame Yvonne Stephan (TAN in Rockford, Illinois). Mary described the dispensation of graces at Medjugorje on August 31, 1982. For the de Montfort quote, see again his wonderful book *True Devotion To the Blessed Virgin* (Montfort Publications, Bay Shore, New York). There was consternation in Medjugorje at one time because it was said that Our Blessed Mother announced that a Muslim woman in the village who prayed very much was a "saint." I visited Ireland for research, and also Oliveto Citra in Italy. Obviously, I was also in Ukraine. The shrine of Zarvanystya there is one of my favorites anywhere. At Hrushiw there was a painting that seemed to foretell a nuclear holocaust. I visited Ecuador in 1991. For St. Dominic and St. Simon Stock, see *Cause of Our Joy*, by Sr. Mary Francis LeBlanc (published by the Daughters of St. Paul, Boston). The experience of the knight at Fatima is contained in Carlos Evaristo's pamphlet "Saint Michael and the Fatima Connection," available by writing the author at Apartado 133, 2496 Fatima Codex, Portugal. The account of the thornbush on fire comes from Joan Carroll Cruz's *Miraculous Images of Our Lady* (TAN Books and Publishers, Rockford, Illinois).

Chapters 31 & 32: The information on Mozul, Iraq, comes from "The World Report," a periodic newsletter issued by the Pittsburgh Center for Peace in McKees Rocks, Pennsylvania, as well as a video I was provided on the alleged phenomena. For Babylon's reconstruction, see *The Rise of Babylon* by Charles Dyer (Tyndale House in Wheaton, Illinois). For the prophecy about Israel and the seven-year covenant, see *Major Bible Prophecies* by John F. Walvoord (Zondervan, Grand Rapids, Michigan). The information on India came in private correspondence from two priests stationed there. June Keithley-Castro graciously faxed me the Filipino information. For Slovakia, see *A Guide to Apparitions* by Heintz, previously noted. The figure on abortion in China comes from Human Life International in Gaithersburg, Maryland (see "HLI Reports," volume 13, number 10).

Chapters 33 & 34: The Chinese phenomena were reported in "The 101 Times," a newsletter out of Asbury, New Jersey. I received further information about the Chinese phenomena from Joseph Kung of Stamford, Connecticut. The statistics on Catholic beliefs come from the October 9, 1995 *U.S. News and World Report* and also a *USA Today*/CNN/Gallup Poll. The gender-inclusive version I cite is entitled *The New Testament and Psalms* and was written about in an editorial in the *New York Daily News*. I spoke to Fr. David Johnston of St. Peter's Episcopal Church in Salem about the infiltration of witches into an interfaith clergy group. I was checking on a tabloid report that said a witch had in fact been invited to join the Salem Religious Leaders Association, but Fr. Johnston said he neither heard of that group nor that particular situation. Meanwhile at Harvard, which was founded by Puritans to train clergy, the school newspaper now lists events for the Harvard Theosophical Union. Theosophy is occultic. For more see the article "Annihilation of the Soul" on page 23 of the April 7, 1994, *New York Post*. The prophecy by St. Anthony of the Desert is in Yves Dupont's *Catholic Prophecy* (TAN Books and Publishers in Rockford, Illinois). The Gallup figure on belief in the devil is reported in a book by Jeffrey Victor entitled *Satanic Panic: The Creation of a Contemporary Legend* and was originally taken from an article by George Gallup and Frank Newport in *The Skeptical Enquirer* (winter 1991). For the Irish famine, see *The Great Irish Famine*, edited by Michael Littleton in the Thomas Davis Lecture Series (Mercier Press, Dublin).

Chapters 35 & 36: The quote on Medjugorje and the wind came from *Words From Heaven*, cited several previous times. The message was given on February 15, 1984. For *El Niño*, see *The New York Times* science section, April 25, 1995. For asteroids, I used two NASA reports, "Report of the Near-Earth Objects Survey Working Group," June 1995, issued to me from the Washington office, and "The Spaceguard Survey, Report of the NASA International Near-Earth-Object Detection

Workshop," chaired by David Morrison, January 25, 1992. See also "Odds are, the Earth is on a calamitous collision course," in the February 8, 1994, *USA Today*, page 5D, as well as "Asteroids, a Menace to Early Life, Could Still Destroy Earth," *The New York Times*, June 18, 1991, page C1, and "Asteroid Defense: 'Risk is Real,' Planners say," *The New York Times*, April 7, 1992, page C1. For Garabandal see *The Final Hour*, or Joseph A. Pelletier's *Our Lady Comes to Garabandal* (identified as "An Assumption Publication," Worcester, Massachusetts). On apparitions: There is one list, provided by the 101 Foundation, that showed 185 apparitions or noteworthy visual manifestations of Mary between this century up to 1990. That was before the height of the current eruption. Compare that to fifty-two for the 1800s, eighteen in the 1600s, and twelve in the 1500s. Due to fax and other technology, word now spreads faster and it's hard to compare with other historical periods because we now have so much more information. I would say there are currently more ongoing claims of apparitions than in the entire 19th century. The seer at Bayside, New York, died of heart failure after a long illness in August of 1995. The information on *Poem of the Man-God* came from a newsletter faxed by Sr. Emmanuel of Medjugorje on October 1, 1995, and also a letter sent to Medjugorje centers by Fr. Philip Pavich on February 2, 1992. The comment by the Vatican on *Poem* and how it should be viewed is from a letter written by Bishop Raymond J. Boland of Birmingham, Alabama, to Terry Colafrancesco of Varita of Birmingham on May 11, 1993. The remarks from the Vatican about Vassula Ryden were in *L'Osservatore Romano*, October 25, 1995, back page, as mentioned. The information on bishops' declarations elsewhere comes from the various chanceries that faxed them or sent them to me. Likewise, the more recent messages from Medjugorje are those directly sent by the parish each month via fax to Medjugorje centers. For standards of Church discernment see the 1993 Proceedings of the Mariological Society of America (Marian Studies), especially an article by Fr. Fred Jelly, "Discerning the Miraculous: Norms for Judging Apparitions and Private Revelations."

Chapters 37 & 38: Cardinal Ratzinger's remark in which the "last times" were alluded to can be found in Frère Michel de la Sainte Trinité's *The Whole Truth About Fatima: The Third Secret*, previously cited. The same is true of Sr. Lucia's remarks. The remarks of St. Louis are again from *True Devotion*, cited above. For three days of darkness, see the book by that title, *The Three Days' Darkness*, by Albert Hebert, which has the history and prophecies. The brother from Texas was quoted in a newsletter called "Weible Columns" in 1992 (Myrtle Beach, South Carolina). The NASA report was the 1995 study cited above. There were news articles in 1960 saying Padre Pio denied making prophecies about the end of the world, and in *Voice of Padre Pio* there was an item in 1977, as I mention (Volume VII, Number 2). It said that when Padre Pio was asked about the three days of darkness, "He himself denied this with a resounding 'No' to a spiritual daughter a few years before his death." I visited Turin, Italy, in 1989. See also an article about Satanism in Turin in the July 1, 1990, *Atlanta Journal and Constitution*. The *Newsweek* quote was used in an ad by Roman Catholic Books. The pope is said to have spoken about "dark forces" on April 24, 1994, in St. Peter's Square, according to *The Medjugorje Star*, May 1994. The Novato microchips were written about in the April 27, 1995, *San Francisco Chronicle*. For St. Thérèse, see above mentioned books. For miracles with the Host, see Joan Carroll Cruz's *Eucharistic Miracles* (TAN). For the quote of Mary on adoration, see *The Antidote*, by Heather Parsons (Paraclete, Orleans, Massachusetts). For Estela Ruiz, see *Our Lady of the Americas*, published by the Pittsburgh Center for Peace, 6111 Steubenville Pike, McKees Rock, Pennsylvania 15136. These are excellent messages. Fr. Vlasic's letter as previously noted was in the Laurentin book *Is the Virgin Mary Appearing in Medjugorje?* For other quotes from Medjugorje, see *The Visions of the Children, Medjugorje—13 Years Later*, and *The Apparitions of Our Lady at Medjugorje*. The Jelena quote is from *Spark From Heaven*. Fr. Vlasic's comment on "ancient times" was printed in Fr. Joseph A. Pelletier's *The Queen of Peace Visits Medjugorje* (Assumption Publications, Worcester, Massachusetts), which took it from an August 15, 1983, talk by Fr. Vlasic. Vicka's quote is from *Queen of the Cosmos*, as is Ivanka's. See also *Messages and Teachings of Mary at Medjugorje*, where Mirjana described the secrets as mostly containing "grave" events, things that will be "catastrophic" (page 51). The information on heaven, hell, and purgatory comes from many Medjugorje sources, and also from a phenomenal mystical book, *An Unpublished Manuscript on Purgatory,* printed by the Reparation Society of the Immaculate Heart of Mary in Baltimore and also available through Fatima organizations such as the Blue Army. For Kincaid, see his book *Global Bondage* (Huntington House).

INDEX OF APPARITIONS AND VISIONARIES